PRAIRIE REPUBLIC

PRAIRIE REPUBLIC

The Political Culture of Dakota Territory,

1879–1889

JON K. LAUCK

UNIVERSITY OF OKLAHOMA PRESS : NORMAN

Also by Jon K. Lauck

American Agriculture and the Problem of Monopoly: The Political Economy of Grain Belt Farming, 1953–1980 (Lincoln, Nebr., 2000)

Daschle vs. Thune: Anatomy of a High-Plains Senate Race (Norman, Okla., 2007)

This book is published with the generous assistance of
The Kerr Foundation, Inc.

Library of Congress Cataloging-in-Publication Data

Lauck, Jon, 1971–
    Prairie republic : the political culture of Dakota Territory, 1879–1889 / Jon K. Lauck.
        p. cm.
    Includes bibliographical references and index.
    ISBN 978-0-8061-4110-7 (hardcover : alk. paper)
    1. Dakota Territory—History.   2. Dakota Territory—Politics and government.   3. Political culture—Dakota Territory.   4. Republicanism—Dakota Territory.   5. Land settlement—Dakota Territory.   6. Dakota Territory—Religious life and customs.   7. Christianity—Dakota Territory.
I. Title.
    F655.L38 2010
    978'.01—dc22

                                                    2009041236

The paper in this book meets the guidelines for permanence and durability of the Committee on Production Guidelines for Book Longevity of the Council on Library Resources, Inc. ∞

1 2 3 4 5 6 7 8 9 10

For John E. Miller,

scholar, friend, civic republican

[The pioneers] had faith in themselves and their destiny. . . . They felt both their religion and their democracy, and were ready to fight for it. . . . This enlarged neighborhood democracy was determined not by a reluctant admission that under the law one man is as good as another; it was based upon 'good fellowship,' sympathy and understanding. . . . Counties in the newer states rose from a few hundred to ten to fifteen thousand people in the space of less than five years. Suddenly, with astonishing rapidity and volume, a new people was forming with varied elements, ideals and institutions drawn from all over this nation and from Europe. . . . They were idealists themselves, sacrificing the ease of the immediate future for the welfare of their children, and convinced of the possibility of helping to bring about a better social order and a freer life. They were social idealists. But they based their ideals on trust in the common man and the readiness to make adjustments, not on the rule of a benevolent despot or a controlling class. . . . Challenging the spaces of the West, struck by the rapidity with which a new society was unfolding under their gaze, it is not strange that the pioneers dealt in the superlative and saw their destiny with optimistic eyes.

Frederick Jackson Turner,
"Middle Western Pioneer Democracy" (1918)

Contents

ILLUSTRATIONS

FIGURES

MAP

Except for those as noted in their captions, all illustrations are courtesy of the South Dakota State Historical Society, Pierre.

PREFACE

The journalist I. F. Stone once pronounced: "No book can be fully understood unless the writer discloses the motivation that led him to embark on his onerous task."[1] Stone's disposition in favor of authorial disclosure has merit, and, for the benefit of readers who appreciate such background, it will be honored here. Part of my motivation is uniquely personal—a truism for most historical inquiries. As a native South Dakotan born to a farm family near the small town of Madison, and as someone who is curious about the historical roots of present social and political configurations, I was naturally inclined toward the story of Dakota's origins. This inclination took root in grade school, where South Dakotans take mandatory courses in South Dakota history. In college at South Dakota State University, I took a course South Dakota history from John E. Miller, a master historian of the Midwest and small-town America. For one summer in college, I received a National Endowment for the Humanities grant to write a history of the early decades of Lake County, South Dakota, my home county. As a graduate student at the University of Iowa, I wrote a dissertation about agrarian antimonopoly sentiments in the Midwest and the late-twentieth-century struggles of midwestern family farmers. The story of Dakota Territory, then, is connected to my own background and historical interests, and my decision to further explore Dakota's formative years is by no measure random.

Another motivation relates to the paucity of research on the territorial history of Dakota. When I began practicing law in South Dakota, some early legal research projects led me to delve into the origins of various provisions in South Dakota's constitution and the historical context of its ratification. My exploration revealed the scarcity of research about the crucial decade of South Dakota's development and the even greater shortage of material about the framing of its fundamental law. I recall noting that my set of South Dakota's codified laws began with a reprinting of the Magna Carta—a clear signal that a broader political and constitutional heritage had not been uncovered but deserved to be. With several boxes of materials on the early history of South Dakota already in hand, I went to work as an assistant professor of history at South Dakota State University, where I was tasked with teaching the South Dakota history course of the then-retired John E. Miller. At SDSU, I compiled more research files and outlined and wrote some journal articles on Dakota's early history and made plans for a future book on the subject.

Why, in an age when studies of the trans-Mississippi West are thriving, do the Dakotas suffer from relative historiographical poverty? One reason is that the eastern region of Dakota Territory under review in this book is closely linked to the Midwest, the history of which has been understudied and undervalued until the past few years. Also, graduate students in the history programs of large research universities located near the coasts have probably considered research efforts far out in the Dakotas less than appealing, if they have considered such forays at all, and unlikely to spark enthusiasm among hiring committees. South Dakota also lacks a Ph.D. program in history; in other states such programs often generate the basic monographs on state and local history that become books and the building blocks of later synthetic treatments. A more fundamental reason may stem from the relative normality and calm of the eastern Dakotas' early history, which pales in comparison to the violent culture clashes of other pioneer immigrations and settlement efforts.[2] Nathaniel Hawthorne once remarked on the "difficulty of writing a romance about a country where there is no shadow, no antiquity, no mystery, no picturesque and gloomy wrong."[3] Whatever the explanation for the limited academic attention paid in the past to Dakota history, I hope this book stirs interest among scholars and students in the nation's active centers of historical research.

A third motivation for this book is the need for an alternative to the long-standing account of the history of Dakota Territory. The only professional history of the region published to date is Howard Lamar's *Dakota Territory,* written a half century ago and reflecting the currents of that age. With a great deal of assistance from Howard, surely one of the most generous historians in the history of the profession, I reviewed much of the material relating to the history of Dakota Territory and analyzed the intellectual origins of Howard's early work on the territory. With a fellowship from Yale University's Beinecke Library, home to a rich collection on western Americana, and more advice from Howard, I completed the bulk of the research for this book. Although I reach different conclusions than Howard did in *Dakota Territory,* I cannot stress enough the debt I owe him for his assistance with this project, and I thank him for his great warmth and humanity. In the interest of recognizing and understanding scholarly precedents and of explaining how historical interpretations can change, I have analyzed in detail the intellectual environment that shaped Howard's earlier work and that led us in different directions. Howard put Dakota Territory on the broader historical map during the 1950s, but much historiographical water has passed under the bridge since then, much of it flowing from reservoirs developed by Howard and his many pathbreaking and productive students. In keeping with Howard's discovery of the important history to be examined in the Dakotas, his openness to new perspectives on the past, and his and his students' work in chronicling the West, it is time for a new look at the history of Dakota Territory.

A fourth reason for undertaking this project is to underscore an existing alternative to at least one recent interpretative trend in the history of the American West. During the past few decades, a growing body of historical scholarship has cast a critical eye on the American West and has revealed a darker side to its history. Much of this scholarship deserves the great praise it has received, but to provide balance and complexity to the western story, it is also important to recognize the genuinely democratic moments in the history of the trans-Mississippi West. The story of Dakota provides a glimpse at one of those moments.

The interpretative alternative I see is not unrelated to my own political proclivities. Some of the elements of life in Dakota that I identify are also characteristic of contemporary political conservatism, an outlook I tend to support. The image of a conservative writing a history of political and social life during a particular time and place in the American past might jolt some in the academy, where conservatives are few. Peter Novick cites the discerning observation that "thoroughgoingly conservative social historians were about as numerous as Republican folk singers."[4] But a perspective such as the one I put forth here may help one to see elements of the past that now hover in the shadows or to recover emphases that have now faded or remain formless and unarticulated. It may bring distant objects back into the historians' range of view and mitigate the dangers of one point of view crowding out alternative angles of vision.[5] Some of the historians who have been most critical of older histories of the American West, to their great credit, have encouraged such perspectives, the clear expression of historical arguments, and open debate among historians who offer differing interpretations of the past.[6]

The final reason for writing this book stems from our collective need to take American democratic institutions more seriously. In its third century, the American republic is home to alarming levels of doubt and discord. At such a time, it is valuable to ponder the moments of the republic's history that can become sources of hope. Along with the obvious human faults of Dakota settlers, there is much to be admired in their arduous work and democratic spirit. Rescuing them from historical obscurity can only deepen our understanding of the American democratic tradition, whatever its past flaws.

In his recent study of the evolution of democratic practices in nineteenth-century America, Sean Wilentz reminds his readers that democratic progress is not foreordained, cautions them about the great risk of democratic reversals, and consistently highlights the many perils and crises that American democracy has endured.[7] Wilentz's reminders help illuminate the generally reassuring features of political life in Dakota Territory: respect for democratic victories that preceded settlement, for Anglo-American republicanism and constitutionalism, for the rule of law, and for the honor and virtue of those who toil, Dakota's reapers and stackers and threshers of wheat; the absence of feudalism, royal charters, state-sponsored churches, ecclesiastical monopolies, military governors, aristocratic clans, landed estates, land barons, serfdom, slaves, whipping posts, urban ghettos, squalid tenements, oppressed coolies, dark and greasy factories, Satanic mills, and debtors' prisons; no Committee of

Public Safety, no guillotine, no Commune, no iron chancellor, no czarist militarism, no mafia, no pogroms, no bloody strikes, no race riots, no anarchist bombings, no political assassinations, no coups, no gang warfare, no state-induced famines. In an age of democratic doubt, we would do well to remember the Dakota settlers who built a workable little republic along the fluid border of the Midwest and Great Plains.

This book focuses on the political culture of what is currently the eastern half of South Dakota during the 1880s, when a settlement boom populated Dakota Territory. Many of the settlers of Dakota were midwesterners who brought with them a deeply held devotion to democratic practices that Frederick Jackson Turner famously celebrated. In recent decades, some historians have properly categorized this devotion as a variation of the civic republicanism ascendant during the early years of the American republic, a set of beliefs that evolved over time but remained a powerful force throughout the nineteenth century. The salience of republicanism in Dakota Territory forms the thematic thrust of this book. Chapter 1 explores the particular time and place under consideration and explains the book's methodological grounding. Chapter 2 describes the various elements of the republican political culture of Dakota Territory, and chapter 3 reviews an important component of American republicanism, Christianity. Chapter 4 analyzes how the people and political culture of Dakota Territory shaped the framing of the constitution that became fundamental law upon statehood. Chapter 5 reviews the intellectual origins of Howard Lamar's book *Dakota Territory* and argues that the story of its construction can help highlight the overlooked aspects of the history of Dakota Territory.

In this analysis of the political culture of Dakota Territory, one common element of life on the prairie is not discussed in detail but should be noted at the outset. The material lives of many Dakota settlers, it should not be forgotten, often involved many hardships and personal tragedies. During the winter, settlers had to bring their cows into their sod homes to shield them from fierce storms, and they had to burn buffalo chips to stay warm. During the summer they battled prairie fires, grasshopper infestations, tornadoes, hail, and drought.[8] A few anecdotes make the point. In the spring of 1887, one pioneer woman in Lake County left her housework to help her husband plant the corn. After one row had been planted, the woman turned to see her house in flames. Her two little boys, Jacob and Francis, were burning alive inside. Due to the extent of the injuries and in order to save money, at the boys' funeral their charred remains were placed in a single casket.[9] Another settler went outside to fix his well during a blizzard in 1888, and when conditions worsened, he took shelter in a haystack. First his wife and then his son came searching for him. When he left the haystack after the storm had passed, the farmer first found his wife and then his son dead. They had frozen to death trying to locate and help him.[10] One afternoon in 1889, a man near Highmore saw his entire farm, all his livestock, and his wife and oldest son engulfed by a prairie fire. He was left a widower, caring for the four surviving children, including a baby girl of fourteen months.[11] Such tragedies, memories of which may be found in the records of the pioneers, should be remembered when envisioning life on the Dakota prairie. Although these hardships could often provide the most vivid memories to pioneers in their later years, the reader is forewarned that this aspect of life in Dakota is not a focus of this study. The fortitude and toughness of Dakota pioneers, however, deserve a place in the readers' imagination and the attention of future scholars.

Finally, for readers unfamiliar with the history of political republicanism, a preliminary word of explanation is in order. The republicanism I find to be a powerful current in Dakota Territory relates to a political ideology with roots in ancient Greece and Rome and early modern Italy and England. This republicanism was influential during the American founding and throughout the nineteenth century, including, in my view, in Dakota Territory. Readers unfamiliar with the term should consult chapter 2 and should remember when they encounter references to republicanism to think of the general political principles of Thomas Jefferson, not of the specific platform of Ronald Reagan. Although republicanism and Reaganism are not unrelated, the two should not be used interchangeably here. In order to avoid confusion, a capital *R* has been added to certain quotations that refer to the Republican Party and not to civic republicanism.

There is no shortage of people to be thanked for their assistance on this long-running project. Especially helpful were George Miles and Natalia Sciarini at Yale University's Beinecke Library; Harry Thompson at the

Center for Western Studies, Augustana College; Ken Stewart, Matthew Reitzel, Marvene Riis, Chelle Somsen, and Jay Vogt at the South Dakota State Historical Society; Jim Davis at the North Dakota State Historical Society; Robert Kvasnicka at the National Archives; Bill Hoskins, Adam Nyhaug, and April Woodside of Siouxland Heritage Museums; and Nancy Koupal and Jeanne Ode of the journal *South Dakota History*. Without the encouragement and support of Charles E. Rankin at University of Oklahoma Press, this project would not have been possible. I also want to thank scholars Allan Bogue, Dave Danbom, Phil Deloria, Jason Duncan, Glen Ely, Gene Gressley, Howard Lamar, John Mack Faragher, Gilbert Fite, Herbert Hoover, Karl Jacoby, Joel Johnson, Deirdre McCloskey, John McGreevy, David McMahon, John E. Miller, Clyde Milner, Mark Milosch, Gary Olson, Colleen O'Neill, Jeffrey Ostler, Lynwood Oyos, Ron Parsons, Dorothy Schwieder, Don Simmons, Ona Siporin, Cathy Stock, Sam Truett, Jami Van Huss, Louis Warren, and David J. Weber for their willingness to discuss at least some of the matters related to this book over, lo, these many years. John E. Miller, whose dedication to the study of South Dakota and the rural Midwest and whose vision, understanding, and genuine respect for small-town culture have few equals, is owed special recognition and thanks for his unceasing aid and support. Miller has done more than any other scholar to map the contours of South Dakota history for three decades, and this book is dedicated to his yeoman pursuit of Dakota's heritage. Chief Justice David Gilbertson of the South Dakota Supreme Court also deserves thanks for his thoughts on the constitutional history of South Dakota and for his devotion to advancing this field of study. My mom and dad, pillars of the republic, have also been constant sources of support and encouragement for this project. As the product of farm families, as farmers themselves, and as proponents of community life and faithful participants in the public sphere, they are the direct heirs of the political culture described in this book. Finally, I want to thank Amy, Brendtly, Jack, and Harry, who never doubted the need for research trips to Pierre and Bismarck in the dead of winter nor questioned the exponential growth of books, maps, and research files about Dakota Territory that continuously narrowed the confines of our basement.

Earlier versions of sections of this book have been previously published as "'You Can't Mix Wheat and Potatoes in the Same Bin': Anti-Catholicism in Early Dakota," *South Dakota History* 38, no. 1 (Spring 2008), 1–46; "'The Organic Law of a Great Commonwealth': The Framing of the South Dakota Constitution," *South Dakota Law Review* 53, no. 2 (2008), 203–59; and "The Old Roots of the New West: Howard Lamar and the Intellectual Origins of *Dakota Territory*," *Western Historical Quarterly* 39, no. 3 (Autumn 2008), 261–81. I thank the editors of these publications for their many pieces of advice and their permission to publish these works.

Sioux Falls
January 2009

PRAIRIE REPUBLIC

CHAPTER 1

TIME, PLACE, METHOD

Have seen the wild flowers on the broad expanse of virgin prairie nodding to the breezes one week and on the next have seen the same sod dotted with homesteader's cabins, and church-spires and school-houses looming up in the new settlements.

Dakota pioneer Dan Scott, 1885

During the summer of 1802, a French army mustered in Holland along the river Scheldt, awaiting the conclusion of ongoing diplomatic negotiations between France and Spain. Napoleon's diplomats had reacquired Louisiana from the Spanish as part of the French emperor's plan to rebuild his empire in North America, most of which had been lost to the English during the 1760s. The final negotiations with the Spanish for the reacquisition of Louisiana took too long, however. By the time the final order for its departure was issued, the French army in Holland was icebound. By the spring thaw, when the French commander was again making final preparations to depart for Louisiana, word arrived from Paris that the territory had been sold to the Americans. Napoleon had lost interest in reviving his New World empire. "Thanks to the ice that had formed across the waters of a remote Dutch harbor," historian Oscar Handlin once observed, "the advancing host of American settlers moving westward towards the Pacific at a turning point in our history now found the way open before them."[1] The Americans were relieved that French imperial ambitions in North America had waned, that the port of New Orleans was secure for the United States, and that the path was now clear for the expansion of the American "empire of republicanism."[2] President Thomas Jefferson, an icon of American republican thought and practice, sent Meriwether Lewis and William Clark to explore the territory the new American republic had purchased. Accord-ing to Jefferson's vision, these new American lands would anchor the republican commonwealth.[3]

After Lewis and Clark completed their exploration and surveys, American Louisiana was divided into territories. In 1861, after South-ern secession ended sectional bartering and bickering over the status of states and territories by leaving Congress in the hands of Northerners, Congress passed and Abraham Lincoln signed the bill creating Dakota Territory. The real estate that became Dakota Territory had earlier been a formal part of New France, Spanish Louisiana, French Louisiana again, the American Louisiana purchase, and the American territories of Mis-souri, Michigan, Wisconsin, Iowa, Minnesota, and Nebraska.[4] When Dakotans ultimately made their case for statehood, in a sign of their attentiveness to historical and legal precedent, they cited as a justification for their cause the provisions of the treaty transferring Louisiana from France to the United States.[5] The machinations of the American founders and European diplomats and the exchange of titles between midwestern territories prefigured the heritage that would be planted in Dakota Ter-ritory by its settlers, a heritage derived from the late-eighteenth-century political conflict between England and its colonies and from the cultural patterns of New England and of the states of the American Midwest.

Since the creation of Dakota Territory coincided with the eruption of the U.S. Civil War, the development of the territory stalled. The rather prosaic early years of the territory featured the construction of military forts, steamboating on the Missouri River (which divided the territory), the organization of trading posts where traders bought Indian furs and pelts, the creation of Indian agencies run by the federal government, and halfhearted attempts at governance by various federal appointees. This typical territorial experience came to an end by the late 1870s. There-after, the Great Dakota Boom transformed the structure of social life in Dakota Territory as settlers poured in by the hundreds of thousands and, in 1879, spawned a statehood movement that ultimately brought the Dakotas into the Union in 1889. This book explores the elements of the political culture planted by the settlers of the Great Dakota Boom during the final decade of territorial status for Dakota.

The Dakota boom provides a unique view of the American settlement process, a view that diverges from a prominent interpretive emphasis in contemporary historiography. The American historical imagination in recent decades has been given to focusing on episodes of terror and destruction and images of conquest and savagery in the American West. New Western historians such as Donald Worster have emphasized the "radical defects of society" in the American West.[6] In contrast to the more positive narrative spun by historians such as Frederick Jackson Turner, some of the New Western historians, as Gene Gressley has noted, view westward expansion as a story of "greed, debasement, and exploitation."[7]

In the past decade or so, the battles over the New Western History have abated, and historians have offered more complex depictions of western history in the place of narratives crafted from various bleak subplots. The settlement of Dakota helps to justify this embrace of multiple and complex views of the American West. In contrast to some of the dark interpretations of the West rendered in the past few decades, this study emphasizes that the settlers of one major expanse of Dakota Territory vigorously embraced American democratic practices and a centuries-old republican tradition. Dakotans were active participants in the democratic process and embraced the essential goals of republicanism—inculcating personal virtue, promoting the interests of the commonwealth over personal gain, fighting corruption, and celebrating the agrarian tradition. Although often associated with the American Revolution, a powerful republican tradition, as Jackson Lears has noted, lived on into the 1880s.[8] The republican tradition, in tandem with the settler's devotion to Christianity, shaped the construction of a stable social and constitutional order in Dakota Territory. Although far from perfect, the political culture of Dakota Territory deserves to be remembered for its many democratic qualities. This political culture is less a part of a legacy of conquest than it is a legacy of democratic enlargement.

TIME

After the U.S. victory in the war with Mexico in 1848, most of the American West was opened to settlement. In the 1840s and 1850s, many

Americans traversed the Overland Trails to California and Oregon, but largely bypassed what they considered the barren plains of the north-central United States. The phobia about the northern plains persisted until the Civil War. Into the 1870s, the flow of settlers into Dakota remained but a trickle. Unlike many settlement booms in the West, the Great Dakota Boom was a decidedly post–Civil War affair. As a result, Dakota statehood was never tangled up in the issue of slavery as were the antebellum admissions of Kansas and other states.[9] Many of the settlers of Dakota were Union veterans of the Civil War, however, and they carried with them its memories, Northern ideals, and traumas, along with a fierce loyalty to the North.

The settlement of Dakota also occurred at a moment when political reform was ascendant. The postwar experience of "Grantism," corruption, and excessive devotion to patronage left many observers soured on the political system. When the reformer Carl Schurz became Secretary of the Interior in 1877, he compared his duties to "wallow[ing] in spoils like a rhinoceros in an African pool."[10] By the 1880s, however, an intense reform sentiment had gained traction and its influence was felt in Dakota. The assassination of President James Garfield by a political office seeker in 1881, at the beginning of the Dakota boom, placed political reform squarely on the national agenda.[11] In Dakota a dedication to self-rule and anti-corruption efforts by the boomers fueled a passionate antipathy toward the territorial system and its spoils-based appointees. The anger at territorial hacks in Dakota Territory galvanized support for statehood, which the settlers thought would deliver them from federal control.

The 1880s were the formative years for Dakota. During this decade, the territorial population boomed by almost 350 percent, expanding from 135,000 in 1880 to 600,000 in 1890. The bulk of the new Dakota settlers became farmers. Dakota wheat production increased from 2.8 million bushels in 1880 to 38 million bushels in 1890, and the value of all farm produce increased ten-fold.[12] Railroads that brought in settlers and hauled out Dakota grain also boomed. Railroad mileage in Dakota Territory increased from 1,200 in 1880 to 4,500 in 1890.[13] One settler in Aurora County wrote in 1883 that "we are on the boom" and that in his area the "land is about all taken up, and there are houses all around."[14]

Another settler in Edmunds County counseled his brother to "strike a country when it is on the boom if you do not want to wait a hundred years to realize. It will do no good to wait five or ten years and then come out here."[15] One newspaper warned, "To dally is dangerous, to delay is death. Dangerous to your fortunes, and death to these opportunities that now lie open before you."[16] Many Americans took this advice and seized the moment. More federal land was distributed in Dakota Territory in the early 1880s than in any other state or territory.[17]

The migration of a half million people to Dakota Territory in the 1880s deserves the familiar western moniker "boom." One railroad official called the migration to Dakota a "marvel in the history of human colonization."[18] The Great Dakota Boom was twice as large as the California Gold Rush, which increased the population of California from 15,000 in 1848 to 260,000 by 1852.[19] It was also larger than the much more famous overland migration, which, from 1841 to 1867, brought 350,000 people to Oregon and California.[20] Population statistics for the formative period of the American republic also provide perspective on the size of the Dakota boom. In 1760, only 500,000 people inhabited all of New England.[21] During the fifteen years prior to the American Revolution, only 220,000 people emigrated to the thirteen colonies that later became the United States.[22] The total English, Irish, and Scottish immigration to the Atlantic colonies prior to the American Revolution totaled 700,000.[23] By the standard of population movements in early American history, the Great Dakota Boom was impressively large. But the migration of the half million Dakota boomers is perhaps best placed in context for modern readers by using more recent comparisons. The Dakota boom was larger than the number of Americans killed in World War II (408,000) and far larger than the number of New Orleanians displaced by Hurricane Katrina (estimated at 200,000).

The Great Dakota Boom was an important component of a much grander burst of settlement in the West. From 1870 to 1890, more land was settled in the United States than during any other twenty-year period in North American history, an "epic" migration that historian Ray Allen Billington deemed the "greatest movement of peoples that the world had known to that day."[24] Between 1880 and1889 alone, 41 million acres of

American land were settled, and much of it was in Dakota. During the heart of the Dakota boom (1883–85), the federal government distributed a portion of the public domain equivalent to the size of Ireland.[25] Forty percent of the land disposed of by the federal government in 1884 was in Dakota Territory.[26] Within a year of the Huron land office opening in the territory in 1883, it was conducting more business than any other land office in the nation.[27] In one six-hour period, settlers at the office filed on 100,400 acres.[28] As the expanding railroads deposited settlers at depots in places such as Watertown, Huron, Mitchell, Aberdeen, White Lake, and Kimball, the lands in between quickly filled with homesteads.[29] In 1880 the number of farms in the territory totaled only 17,435; by 1885 they totaled 82,017. Within a few years, entire counties would fill with people. From 1880 to 1885, the population of Brown County grew from 353 people to 12,241, Spink County from 477 to 10,446, and Beadle County from 1,290 to 10,318.[30]

Many observers at the time noted the settlers streaming into Dakota. In 1882 the *Chicago Tribune* reported that five hundred trains carrying 9,000 European and Canadian immigrants had rolled into the windy city and that 7,200 of these immigrants were bound for Dakota.[31] The *St. Paul Globe* reported in 1883 that in one week a thousand railroad cars loaded with immigrants and their stock had headed for central Dakota.[32] The "wonderful country known as Dakota Territory," one minister wrote in the early 1880s, "seems to be the country that is attracting more emigration than any place on this continent."[33]

Events in Europe and the Atlantic world helped shape the Dakota boom. The mid-nineteenth-century political conflicts in Europe, for example, ultimately spilled onto the Dakota plain. The revolutions of 1848 fired democratic enthusiasms in Europe, created democratic heroes, and spurred the demand for written constitutions considered and ratified by popular means. Debate over constitutions in the wake of the democratic ferment of the 1840s could be heard in Dakota Territory during the 1880s, where settlers debated an organic law in three different constitutional conventions.[34] The influence of the refugees of the 1848 revolutions was felt on the Great Plains, especially from German immigrants. The unification of Germany and the centralization of the German state alienated many Germans and sparked thoughts of migrating to America. Otto von Bismarck's Kulturkampf caused many German Catholics to flee. In Russia, Germans who had earlier accepted the czar's offer to farm the Volga River valley and the Black Sea region in exchange for exemption from military service also departed for the United States when the czar revoked the deal in the 1870s.[35] Reflecting the heavy German population in Dakota, a town on the Missouri River, which would become the territorial capital, was named Bismarck.[36]

Land scarcity in Europe also prompted emigration. German emigration reached its peak in the 1880s as land shortages worsened in southwestern Germany and "peasant land hunger" intensified in the northeast.[37] Many of these emigrants from Germany proper joined the "German-Russians" in the United States.[38] Due to crop failures and land shortages in Norway during the 1880s, more than 1 percent of the Norwegian population emigrated each year, as did three-fourths of 1 percent of the Swedish population. The Scandinavian outflow was comparable to the "sudden depopulation of Ireland in the 1840s and 1850s" during the potato famine.[39] By 1890, 32 percent of the people in southern Dakota were foreign born, and immigrant Germans and Norwegians constituted the bulk of this population.[40]

Although the influx of foreign immigrants was large, the direct source of most Dakota settlers was the American Midwest.[41] Some of these migrants were second-generation German and Norwegian immigrants whose families had settled earlier in the Midwest. Most of the Dakota settlers, however, were "old stock" Americans who left their parents' farms in New England or, more commonly, the states of the Midwest. These midwesterners brought with them service records from the Civil War, a devotion to the Union, a common commitment to the Republican Party (born in the Midwest), a deeply entrenched patriotism, an attachment to midwestern agrarianism, support for late-nineteenth-century midwestern reform efforts, and long experience with the American political tradition. The republican faith of these midwestern immigrants formed the bedrock of Dakota Territory's political culture.

National politics during the age of the Dakota boom was intense and bore directly on politics in Dakota. From the mid-1870s to the mid-1890s, the jousting between the major American political parties resulted in a rough balance of power. Robert Cherny has described party politics during these years as seeming "to freeze into deadlock."[42] The fate of Dakota Territory was caught in this stalemate. In an age of divided government, the GOP "pressed harder than ever for the admission of Western states with trusty Republican majorities," and the Democrats resisted just as intensely.[43] The continued blockade on Dakota statehood catalyzed a political ferment in Dakota Territory and fierce denunciations of the territory's "colonial status," a condition that persisted much longer than it did for other states. These protests were frequently voiced in the language of republicanism and often referenced the ideals of the American Revolution. Finally, in 1888, GOP electoral victories disrupted the balance of power. The "fourteen-year partisan deadlock" was broken, and in 1889 Dakota Territory became the states of North and South Dakota.[44]

One prominent political current of the 1880s was a fear of the end of the American frontier. Some commentators thought that the sturdy republican yeomen trekking to Dakota Territory could soon be relics of a bygone era. At the time of the Dakota boom, political leaders and intellectuals began to worry openly about the general weakening of American character brought on by urbanization and consumption and to fret about the "closing" of the western frontier, which was seen as a great source of national strength.[45] Josiah Strong's book *Our Country*, published in 1885, described the West as "the heart of the Republic and the repository of its peculiar civilization" and interpreted its final settlement as a fearful development for the republic.[46] Observers increasingly feared that American men, in the absence of a Western frontier, would lose the "toughness and strength necessary to keep civilization evolving upward."[47] For some, Dakota provided one last chance at the true American experience, which at least partly explains Teddy Roosevelt's cattle-ranching adventure in Dakota. The year that the Dakotas achieved statehood, Roosevelt published his book *The Winning of the West*, which further heightened the allure of the region and did so, as Christopher Lasch once noted, by using the Dakotas as its point of reference.[48] In 1890, a year after the Dakotas entered the Union, federal officials announced that the frontier was officially "closed" (although statehood still eluded a few territories), and Frederick Jackson Turner found the inspiration for his frontier thesis.

PLACE

This study examines the eastern half of what is now South Dakota during the territorial years of the 1880s. Several qualities of this geographic space during this period are important, including its natural dimensions. Dakota had a unique environment. It was not, for example, the Kentucky frontier, where timber, water, and game were once plentiful.[49] Whereas Kentucky was wooded and green, Dakota had once been panned as part of the "Great American Desert." The 100th Meridian, a line of demarcation that Wallace Stegner made famous, bisected Dakota Territory. Beyond that meridian, a reliable supply of water proved to be a consistent problem for settlers and hindered agricultural development, which is one of the reasons that this study does not extend beyond the Missouri River.[50] The area east of the Missouri River, however, is by no means secure from moisture shortfalls. An East River drought stalled the momentum of the boom in the late 1880s. Another reason to focus on the East River area is the construction of railroads, which stopped at the Missouri River in the 1880s and did not resume building westward from that point until the early twentieth century. The area's position on the edge of the humid Midwest and its railroad network makes Eastern Dakota a unique geographic space that ends rather abruptly at the Missouri River.

Beyond geography, another reason for focusing on events east of the Missouri is the history of the Sioux Indians. After the 1858 Yankton Treaty and the 1862 Great Sioux Uprising in southern Minnesota, most of the Sioux bands ceased to be a significant presence in Eastern Dakota.[51] The largest Sioux bands lived in Wyoming until 1877, when the Great Sioux Reservation was created, comprising all of present-day South Dakota west of the Missouri River. A large corpus of historical work exists on the Sioux, in contrast to Eastern Dakota, which few historians have examined. Although there were few Indians in Eastern Dakota in the 1880s, anti-Indian views remained strong, and some Dakotans certainly supported the "opening" of the Sioux reservation in Western

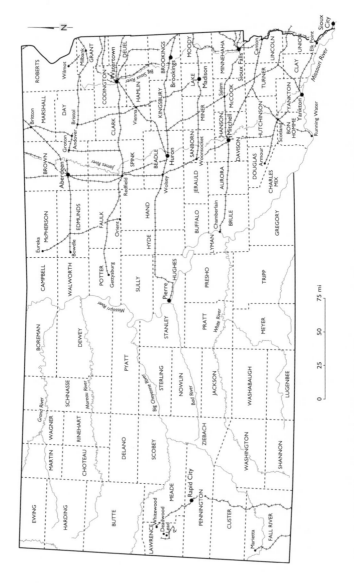

The railroad network in Dakota Territory at the end of the territorial period, in 1889. Based on a map created by the South Dakota Department of Transportation.

Dakota to white settlement. They tended to view the 23,000 Sioux on the reservation as "utterly idle and shiftless" and undeserving of the lands they held.[52] One unsentimental superintendent of education in Dakota had little sympathy for the Sioux because, he said, they had driven out and "exterminated" earlier Indian tribes in the area. He argued that humanitarians should understand that the "Indian had just done the same for those who went before him and his predecessors had repeatedly done the same; and if moral title to land must rest on first occupancy, no race on earth has such title to its territory, as none can now be found that did not drive out some previous race."[53] While such sentiments suggest the unfavorable attitudes most Dakota boomers held toward the Sioux, most of the critical episodes in the history of the Sioux occurred either before the 1880s or west of the Missouri River and so are not closely examined here.[54] While many of the settlers of Eastern Dakota may have feared and loathed Indians, there were few in their midst.

This study also focuses on the southern half of Dakota Territory east of the Missouri River. This is done, in part, to make the source material manageable and in part because the northern area had its own peculiar characteristics. The economy of the north was defined to a greater extent by large transcontinental railroads such as the Northern Pacific and Great Northern. Southern Dakota did not have a transcontinental railroad or lose a large amount of land to public railroad land grants. The Northern Pacific obtained 20 percent of the land in North Dakota and thus created its own set of public issues, such as large- versus small-scale farming, and the NP was supported by a group of territorial officials loyal to its interests. Intraterritorial differences can also be detected in regional politics, in which the northern bloc often allied itself with a Black Hills contingent in the West River country (i.e., west of the Missouri River) against southern Dakota.[55]

Although often considered part of the American West, Dakota Territory was distinct from the Far West, the focus of many contemporary western historians. Eastern South Dakota is in the orbit of the Midwest, which explains why some of the insights of Frederick Jackson Turner apply to its history and development.[56] The first seminar that Turner offered at the University of Wisconsin was titled "The Old Northwest," designating the area that remained the source of his insights that relate to Dakota Territory.[57] As Ray Allen Billington noted, Turner's critics said that "he based his examples on the Old Northwest, and that his theory collapsed if applied to other sections of the country."[58] Wallace Stegner, for one, argued that Turner's theory of the frontier "fails" when it crosses the 100th meridian.[59] The extent to which Turnerian characteristics defined places in the Far West is debatable, but there is certainly evidence of their existence and influence east of the Missouri River in Dakota Territory. The Midwest that Turner studied was the central font of Dakota settlers, and its political culture shaped Dakota Territory. Many late-nineteenth-century Americans viewed the midwestern states as successful republican experiments, rich in farmsteads, literacy, schools, colleges, churches, nationalism, and civic pride. A newspaper editor in Cincinnati opined that the Old Northwest was home to "an Experiment in Humanity higher in its character and sublimer in its results" than could be found in any other physical space and that it enjoyed the "freest forms of social development and [a] higher order of human civilization."[60] Midwesterners carried this culture to Dakota Territory during the 1880s.

The midwestern influence on Dakota is perhaps best emphasized by noting what it did not include. Dakota Territory was not, for example, shaped by the South, where, as C. Vann Woodward argued, the "manners, customs, standards, ideas, and ideals of society were fixed by the cotton farmer," whose "ideas and interests were reflected in pulpit, press, courtroom, legislative halls, classroom—even the cities took their tone from the farm. Never did a class more completely dominate a society than then."[61] Dakota Territory was unlike Georgia, for example, which grappled with the consequences of war and slavery and which maintained institutions such as a convict lease system in the 1880s that Woodward deemed a "mudsill of human misery and degradation."[62] The "distinctive heritage" of the South, Woodward noted, had created a culture obsessed with its own faults and defeats.[63] The midwestern cultural heritage carried into Dakota Territory was decidedly more hopeful and confident in its republican traditions.

Dakota Territory was also not shaped by the institutions and culture of the Spanish borderlands of the Far West, where a heritage of "Spanish absolutism," according to Herbert Eugene Bolton, "stifled initiative, individual liberty, and self-government."[64] In the Spanish Southwest, unlike the area of Dakota Territory under examination here, Howard Lamar found that "every generation of settlers knew the fear, or the harassment, of savage Indian warfare."[65] The settlers and their influence in the Southwest were also decidedly different. In contrast to the rapid influx of midwesterners, New Englanders, Germans, and Norwegians into Dakota, in places such as New Mexico, Anglo-Americans remained a minority until as late as 1928.[66] In contrast to the dominance of Protestantism in Dakota, in New Mexico, Spanish priests "controlled the spiritual lives of the Spanish residents," medieval customs persisted, and battles between the Catholic Church and civil authorities led many Americans to denounce the territory as a "priest-ridden country."[67] A confusing jumble of Spanish land grants, the absence of a common-law tradition, a history of political violence, ferocious Indian conflict, and periods of military rule also made New Mexico quite distinct.[68] A Chicago newspaper during the 1880s rejected a comparison between Dakota and the Far West, where life was shaped by a "different order of things" and had created a "civilization peculiar to that section." The more appropriate comparison for Dakota, the newspaper argued, was the midwestern state of Iowa.[69]

The eastern areas of Dakota Territory, in short, were not Woodward's Deep South nor Lamar's Far West, were not defined by the "strange career" of southern institutions and culture nor the "wild" aspects of the Far West, and were not the planter-dominated South with its legacy of aristocracy and slavery nor the peculiar Spanish borderlands with their legacy of monarchy and Catholicism. Andrew Cayton has explained why the more dramatic histories of other sections of the United States draw attention away from the Midwest: "While the South is indelibly linked with racial slavery and the West with conquest, the Midwest's reputation has to do with empty normalcy."[70] It is easy to lose sight of the importance of the influence of the Midwest, Cayton notes, because it "lacks the kind of geographic coherence, historical issues, and cultural touchstones that have informed regional identity in the American South, West, and New England."[71] Susan Gray believes that the "Midwest itself is perhaps the most understudied portion of the United States."[72] These neglected social structures of the Midwest made their way to Dakota. As John D. Hicks once noted, there was "indeed little about the civilization that has grown up at the forks of the Ohio that has not been reproduced on a greater or lesser scale along the bend in the Missouri."[73]

Recognizing the role of the Midwest in the development of Dakota, and not being immediately diverted to the more exotic history of the Far West, enables one to take Turner and the history of the Midwest more seriously. The Midwest, Marilynne Robinson emphasizes, is a "highly distinctive and crucial region which," regrettably, "is very generally assumed to have neither culture nor history."[74] But Turner understood the importance of the Midwest, and this history of Dakota Territory gives Turner his due. A leader of the New Western History, Patricia Limerick, criticized Turner for his focus on whites, the Midwest, the influence of the frontier on American history, and his neglect of nonwhites, government aid, class conflict, the aridity of the West, and the environmental consequences of western settlement.[75] Although Limerick is dismissive of Turner's focus on the "agrarian settlement and folk democracy in the comparatively well-watered Midwest," this region had the most influence on the development of Dakota Territory.[76] Turner and his recent critics talk past one another when it comes to Dakota Territory and other places along the midwestern-western seam; thus, these places risk being lost in the newest history of settlement of the trans-Mississippi West. Howard Lamar once reminded historians that Turner always meant to apply his work and findings not to the Far West but to the Midwest.[77] Some historians, in keeping with Lamar's admonition, recognize that Turner was often correct in his conclusions about the Midwest.[78] By extension, his conclusions are valuable to the study of Dakota Territory.

Turner's appreciation of the democratic qualities of midwestern political culture certainly applies to Dakota Territory, but critics also correctly note deficiencies in his vision. Turner overemphasized the uniqueness of frontier democracy, for example. In his efforts to debunk Herbert Baxter Adams's emphasis on the European origins of American democracy, Turner went too far. Links to Old Europe, especially English institutions, were clearly present in the West and were even revived in places such as Dakota Territory, which attracted a large number of European emigrants. Turner's notion of an "atomized" frontier society also does not square with the extensive evidence of social capital, community, and republicanism in places such as Dakota. In a related oversight, Turner overlooked the influence of religion, whereas in Dakota Territory, Christianity proved to be an important social force. The cleavages between Christian denominations in Dakota Territory, especially Protestant doubts about the influence of Catholicism, had an Old World flavor that Turner generally sought to purge from frontier history. Still, Turner was amenable to the notion that no single factor determines the ultimate shape of a particular time and place. His emphasis on the inherited ideals of pioneer democracy subordinating mere economic calculation and on a "common historical inheritance, a common set of institutions, a common law, and a common language" fits the experience of Dakota Territory during the 1880s.[79] Some historians criticize Turner for neglecting class conflict, but on the critical economic issue of the 1880s in Dakota Territory—the railroads—there was a great deal of consensus on adopting regulatory reforms.

Recognition of Turner's insights on the Midwest and thus on the development of Dakota Territory necessarily entails recognition of the influence of republicanism in Dakota Territory. Reflecting on the great surge of interest in republicanism in studies of early American history in the 1970s and 1980s, Donald Pickens concluded that the characteristics of republicanism fit Turner's description of frontier life.[80] David Allen Johnson, after studying eighteenth-century republicanism, was reminded of the writings and speeches he had encountered when studying the settlement of Oregon. Instead of discounting what he heard in the sources as "rhetorical flourishes," Johnson found settlers in Oregon "thinking in a republican 'idiom'" that some historians believed had already been exhausted. Oregonians' criticism of corruption and promotion of agriculture and their fears about rampant self-interest suddenly had a new meaning.[81] Unlike California, whose formative moment involved a gold rush in the context of a strong Hispanic heritage, and Nevada, which was shaped by silver mining, Oregon was defined by yeoman agriculture.[82] Farmers from the Midwest who traveled the Overland Trails populated Oregon. Johnson concluded that these farmers gave Oregon a "homogeneity that contrasted starkly with the individualist and cos-mopolitan cast of gold rush California."[83] With these Oregonian farmers, republicanism persisted. The same republican political culture that Mid-western farmers took to Oregon in the 1840s also shaped the political outlook of the settlers of Dakota Territory. They drank from the same well.

The influence of the Midwest on Dakota Territory and the particu-lar characteristics of Dakota Territory are highlighted, if only by their absence, in the most recent work of western historians. These historians, in keeping with Turner's affection for things "significant," have found and explained other peoples and other dynamics that, though critical to the history of the West, Turner failed to address.[84] David G. Gutiérrez, for example, has explained how older histories of the West neglected or trivialized the role of Mexican Americans, who suffered a subordinate status in the West and thus became known as the nation's "forgotten peo-ple."[85] Gail Nomura has also passionately explained how, until the past decade, the story of Asian Americans in the West went "unrecognized."[86] Quintard Taylor has similarly noted the "paucity" of research on African Americans in the West and the "dearth of black western scholarship."[87] Scholarship on Mexican Americans, Asian Americans, and African Americans in the West has greatly expanded in recent years, but the ben-efits of this great leap forward in research for the study of Dakota Ter-ritory is limited by the particularities of place. In the region of Dakota Territory under investigation here, these groups were not numerically significant.[88]

While it is important to acknowledge the impressive quality of recent work in western history, this research also serves as a reminder that the immigrant groups that older histories once emphasized, especially the midwesterners that Turner examined, constituted the bulk of the popula-tion in places such as Dakota Territory. It is a reminder, in other words, of what Elliott West calls "the particularity of the past."[89] It is critical, other scholars have emphasized, to understand unique regional characteristics and variations in western history and "how different regions and local communities precipitated out from the general tide of Euro-African-Asian settlement."[90] Robert Johnston has also warned of the tendency of "The West" writ large to undermine our understanding of "smaller, analytically contingent geographic spaces" in the West.[91] Historians who have embraced the study of specific regions and have recognized the importance of focusing on the particulars of times and places in the trans-Mississippi West have paved the way for a close look at the portion of Dakota Territory envisioned by this study.

Although there is much to be said about Dakota, a territory in its time surpassed in geographic size only by California and Texas, its history has been sorely neglected in comparison to other regions of the West.[92] The boom in western history in recent decades has largely bypassed the region of Dakota under examination here, much as the Overland Trails once largely bypassed the northern plains. Historians, to be sure, have studied mining in the Black Hills, the colorful history of Deadwood, and the history of the Sioux quite thoroughly, but except for Howard Lamar's *Dakota Territory,* published more than a half century ago, the area of Dakota east of the Missouri River has received little scholarly attention. The present study is intended to spur interest in the history of Dakota by analyzing one component of life in Eastern Dakota—the political sphere. Such a study involves some overlap with studies of class and gender in the West, but also contends that class friction in Dakota during the boom was minimal and recognizes that the political world was largely inhabited by men. While my focus remains on the political culture of Dakota, this is not to argue that other angles of vision on the Dakota past are not important. To the contrary, if successful, this book will help to justify further inquiries into the lives of territorial Dakotans.

METHOD

Frederick Jackson Turner once commented that it "would be sad if historians became obsessed with methodology and especially borrowed methodology, to the exclusion of intuition and unfettered perusal of evidence."[93] This project began with such a perusal of the source materials, prompted by an obligation to teach a course on the history of South Dakota. Much as with David Allen Johnson's experience with his history of Oregon, I recognized that the voices the sources contain would take me in a direction that did not match the reigning research categories of contemporary western historians. In contrast to western historians who now emphasize the importance of including the experience of ethnic minorities, a project that has added enormous diversity and complexity to the narrative, this study, in recognition of the particular characteristics of Dakota, focuses on the settlement of Anglo-Americans and, to a lesser extent, the arrival of immigrants from Northern Europe. In keeping with the findings of David Allen Johnson and the one-time interest of Turner in pioneer democracy, I focus on these Dakotans' political practices and seek to promote interest in the older focus on democratic life on the frontier. Although recent western histories have certainly addressed the question of which people and groups were included and excluded from the political sphere, this study more specifically focuses on the elements of the dominant political culture and the legal products of that culture.[94]

The path of my research deserves explanation. David Hackett Fischer once denounced historians for the "conceptual poverty" of their books and called on them to specify the beliefs and assumptions that ground their research.[95] In keeping with Fischer's admonition, I should say at the outset that I have been impressed with the work of historians who have examined political republicanism in the United States. Beginning with the pioneering works of Bernard Bailyn, Gordon S. Wood, and J. G. A. Pocock in the 1960s and 1970s, historians have increasingly taken note of the influence of republican beliefs in American history.[96] Subsequent to these pathbreaking works, historians began to recognize the continued invocation of republican ideals throughout the nineteenth century.[97] The importance of republicanism can be also found in the work of Turner, although he did not use such a moniker. A respect for the findings of historians of republicanism necessarily entails recognition of the important social role of ideas, symbols, rhetoric, and the invocation of history and precedent, or, generally, the study of political culture.

Historians of republicanism reacted, in part, to earlier historians' thoroughgoing concern with material motivations.[98] Progressive historians, whose research was in full flower by the 1930s, focused on evidence of economic interestedness and class conflict in the American past rather than on political culture and the influence of ideas. Many of these historians were particularly concerned with challenging Turner's rosier portrait of the workings of American democracy. The burst of scholarship focusing on the persistence of republicanism conflicted with the progressive historians' emphasis on economic conflict and thus breathed new life into the writings of Turner.

Some historians of republicanism have also noted the prominence of Christianity in the American past, which complements their focus on the role of ideas and political culture.[99] A "perusal" of the sources relating to Dakota Territory, to use Turner's word, quickly reveals the ubiquity of Christian symbols, structures, practice, and belief. Early-twentieth-century progressive historians, in contrast, did not take religion as a social force very seriously. Henry F. May commented that the ideology of progressive history included the "assumption that religion was and must be declining."[100] Research on the history of religion in the United States in recent years has helped to emphasize its importance to earlier generations of Americans, as has a raft of books arguing that religious and ethnic factors were more important influences on the behavior of voters in the late nineteenth century than were economic concerns.

The historiography of republicanism and recent insights from religious history have yet to make major impressions on the field of western history.[101] In the past several years the New Western historians, in much the same way that progressive historians focused on economic conflict and social class, have focused on race, gender, and environmental concerns.[102] While western historians have made great strides in advancing our understanding of these dynamics, they should be more careful not to place certain social factors in "high relief," in the words of Peter Burke, to the exclusion or subordination of other important factors that operated in and influenced the lives of most people.[103] Race, gender, and class, Carl Degler once noted, "are not the only or even necessarily the most important source of personal or group identities."[104] In Dakota Territory, being a farmer, a midwesterner, a pioneer, a Union veteran, a Christian, a Norwegian, German, or Yankee, or a patriot devoted to the American republic were stronger sources of identity.

In the interest of satisfying Fischer's demand that historians explain their assumptions, it should be said that this book does not embrace the progressive historians' interpretative focus on class conflict or the somewhat broader interpretative focus of the New Western historians on class, race, gender, and environmental issues. It also does not endorse the rejection of Turner, a cause of the progressive historians taken up by the New Western historians. Instead of beginning an examination of Dakota Territory with these categories of analysis in mind, I started with perusing the historical sources and organized the book based on my reaction to what I found. Specifically, I was struck by the republican ardor of Dakota settlers in both language and action and by the prevalence of Christianity in their lives. The forces of republicanism and Christianity deserve a prominent place in the history of Dakota Territory because they were central to the lives of Dakota settlers. These influences, moreover, were important to Dakota settlers' efforts to build a stable polity that fostered community involvement and political participation.

The principles and teachings of republicanism and Christianity were far more pervasive and heartfelt, in my view, than the other social forces and conflicts that historians have focused on in recent years. This is not to argue that there were no other social dynamics or that these other dynamics should not be studied, but simply to maintain that Dakotans tended to focus on building a republican social order and living Christian lives. In the universe of influences that informed their actions and beliefs, these two forces seem to have been the most fundamental. Richard Hofstadter once noted that a "very large part of what historians differ about boils down to *questions of emphasis*, to arguments about how much stress we want to put on this factor rather than that, when we all admit that both were at work."[105] The factors emphasized by western historians of late were surely at work in the West, but I have concluded that other social forces were more critical to the lived experience of settlers in Dakota Territory.

This book's focus on the persistence of republicanism in Dakota Territory and on the political realm more generally is not the lonely endeavor of a few historians that it once was. After the pioneering work of a few scholars won acclaim, the study of republicanism was taken up by a number of historians, and now some histories aimed at a general audience are highlighting the expanding parameters of American democracy in the decades preceding the settlement of Dakota Territory.[106] This new focus helps explain the democratic enthusiasms of Dakota settlers during the 1880s. Lord Bryce, who visited Dakota during the great land boom, published his popular study of American democracy in 1888 and found much to recommend in Tocqueville's earlier findings about the American commitment to democratic practices.[107] Despite republican critiques of corruption and periodic scandals and failures to meet republican standards, as George Wilson Pierson noted in his biography of Tocqueville, in the nineteenth century "most Americans were proud of their political institutions."[108] The settlers of Dakota shared this pride.

CHAPTER 2

A MACHIAVELLIAN MOMENT ON THE MIDDLE BORDER

The settlers are a most excellent class of people, many being educated, devoted to religious enterprises and generally interested in
the moral and social welfare of the communities where they live.

W. H. Ware, *Aberdeen Daily News,* 1885

The pioneers who settled Dakota Territory during the great land boom
of the 1880s tapped a deep well of republican social thought and practice and built a republican social order. They drew, in particular, upon
the political culture of New England and the Midwest; the existing
institutions, language, and symbols of American democracy that dated
to the Revolution; and Old World antecedents such as the English anti-
monarchical tradition. The intense and immediate memories and political battles of the Civil War served as another wellspring of republican
ideology. Dakota boomers embraced the fundamental tenets of republicanism, including patriotism, agrarian sympathies, civic virtue, a vision
of independent and educated citizens wrestling with political questions
in the public square, an intense desire to detect and circumscribe political corruption, promotion of community and civic participation and the
rule of law, and a general hope of building a workable social order and of
marginalizing destabilizing influences.

The forerunners of the republicanism present in Dakota Territory in
the 1880s have been intensely studied by historians. In a classic treatment, J. G. A. Pocock described the revival of classical republican ideas

24

in early modern Europe, an episode he described as a "Machiavellian moment," thus highlighting the role of the Florentine Niccolo Machiavelli.[1] After this revival, republicanism was embraced by reformers in England who sought to limit the power of the king, and later by English colonists in America who sought political independence from the crown.[2] Although the definition of republicanism is not always precise in these studies, certain elements are well established and are discernible in Dakota Territory. Generally, republicans sought to promote the moral virtues necessary to produce citizens who could preserve and wisely govern a republic. True republican citizens would overcome simple self-interest and an attraction to extravagance and luxury and instead promote the "common good" and the interests of the "commonwealth." By securing personal virtue, dedication to the public interest, and the maintenance of a stable social order, early modern European republicans would avoid the corruption and civil wars that had enveloped earlier republican experiments. Although republicanism became more intertwined with the workings of the market after the American Revolution, and thus distinct from its classical forms, it remained a powerful influence in American political culture throughout the late eighteenth and nineteenth centuries.[3]

The civic spirit of the settlers of the Great Dakota Boom drew upon the republican sentiments of the American Revolution and their subsequent nineteenth-century manifestations. The Civil War further deepened republican convictions, especially among Northerners who fought the divisive sectionalism of the aristocratic South in order to preserve the American commonwealth. By the 1880s, public frustration with political corruption and concerns about the disruptions wrought by industrialization heightened public consciousness of the need to pursue republican ideals. Aggravation at the absence of local control inherent in the territorial system and the corruption of territorial officials gave republican principles a sharper edge in Dakota Territory. The principles and precedents of republicanism prevailed in the thoughts and actions of Dakotans as they assembled and built the political and social infrastructure of their new republic on the prairie. As Donald Pickens and John Patrick Diggins have noted of the nineteenth-century American West in general, the settlers' political "activities did vaguely resemble the formulation of the polis," and they confirmed "a kind of Machiavellian moment with the opening of each new territory."[4]

The republicanism extant during the American Revolution evolved through the nineteenth century to become the republicanism prominent during the settlement of Dakota Territory. Even if classical republican references were not as common in nineteenth-century rhetoric as they had been during the Revolutionary period, Jean Baker has noted, "there were other ways to preserve beliefs." In particular, "republican behavior" was promoted through schools and political parties. "White male Americans who never gave speeches, framed resolutions or wrote pamphlets," Baker finds, "daily practiced and, through their public behavior, observed its tenets." Republicanism survived "through various institutions and forces that conveyed the importance of an organic community larger than its discrete parts, along with the conviction that the moral basis of American politics rested in civic obligations, mutually undertaken."[5]

The political culture of republicanism, in other words, persisted as an "underlying popular mentality" long after the American Revolution.[6] Unlike its classical formulation, which championed individual land ownership as essential to the preservation of republican institutions, in the nineteenth century, republicanism came to include landless merchants and workers as worthy republicans. "Jefferson's classical doubts about the civic virtue of merchants were being forgotten," Rowland Berthoff has explained, and market-oriented Americans now claimed the "old-fashioned, fixed virtues of civic attachment and personal independence." Although some observers were concerned about the absence of republican virtue among the growing number of industrial workers, the act of voting, which was increasingly venerated and celebrated, and the education of the young in the common school system could ensure that workers became good republican citizens.[7] Physical labor, moreover, could by itself instill the "manly virtues of the republican citizen" and was increasingly "touted as the best means for individual success and for the economic progress of the country."[8] Vice and idleness became signs of "unrepublican behavior," and free enterprise and entrepreneurship, long after the Revolution, became the "heart of the republican ethic that dated from the Declaration of Independence."[9] In addition to embracing the work ethic, nineteenth-century republicans maintained their opposition to political corruption. To counter the manipulations of machine bosses and politicians, reformers would periodically rise to "stamp out corruption" in traditional republican fashion.[10] Hardworking Dakota settlers who despised the undemocratic territorial system embodied this republican spirit. The settlers of places such as Dakota Territory, according to Donald Pickens, "were republicans in cultural values long before being labeled so by historians."[11] Many of the attributes of the American frontier that Frederick Jackson Turner identified in his famous speech in 1893, Pickens notes, were basic elements of the republican tradition.[12]

REPUBLICANISM IN DAKOTA TERRITORY AND ITS SOURCES

As settlers in Dakota Territory pushed for statehood, they consistently invoked the republican tradition. Congregational minister Joseph Ward, a prominent civic leader in Dakota Territory, called for an end to federally controlled territories and for Congress to promote self-governing states that were "truly republican, and in entire harmony with the spirit that created the present Union."[13] When the pastor of the First Congregational Church of Sioux Falls gave a prayer at the 1883 constitutional convention, organized to bring an end to federal control of the territory, he said that the convention's work would "redound to the glory of the commonwealth."[14] At the 1885 constitutional convention, Chief Justice Alonzo Edgerton, who served as convention president, said he was honored to "be a member of a convention called to form the organic law of a great commonwealth" and to write a "republican" constitution. He had faith in the "patriotism" of national leaders to act on Dakota's statehood request.[15]

The frequent invocation of the term "commonwealth" and the emphasis on the maturity of the Dakota citizenry reflected the continuing strength of republicanism in the 1880s. General William Beadle insisted that Dakota settlers "were intelligent, self-respecting citizens, used to governing themselves, trained to hold meetings, to organize movements and direct events" and were creating "a commonwealth of high purpose," following the unruly era of early territorial politics.[16] Doane Robinson, a territorial lawyer, editor, and later historian of Dakota, argued that the "intelligence, education and morality" of the citizenry generated a "genuine pride in the commonwealth and its accomplishments."[17] The statehood advocates' petition to Congress also pointed to the components of republican citizenship in Dakota by highlighting the high rates of literacy, numerous schools, thriving newspapers, and many churches, all of which demonstrated the "intelligence and morality of the people" of Dakota Territory.[18]

The origins of republicanism in Dakota Territory can be traced to New England and the Midwest, the two regions that supplied most of the pioneers who settled in the territory. Citations to English history and the tradition of "Anglo-Saxon liberty" were not uncommon among Dakotans, who recognized the migratory chain of democratic ideas and institutions that preceded settlement. The English folkways of New Englanders made their way to the Midwest, where, as Louis B. Wright put it, they "exerted their genius in the perpetuation of orderly towns with schools, churches, and colleges as nearly like those of New England as they could achieve."[19] The Yankees who migrated to the Midwest, according to Susan Gray, imposed "New England values and institutions as the template of all American culture" and sought to promote and preserve social order through a Yankee institutional framework composed of community churches, common schools, and local government.[20] The Yankees in the Midwest maintained their "older sectional loyalties," and their Yankee-midwestern identity intensified during the Civil War and further shaped the consciousness of many of the settlers who migrated to Dakota in the postwar years.[21]

The influence of English history, institutions, and traditions, which traveled by way of New England and the Midwest, were readily identifiable in Dakota Territory. Dakota town names, for example, captured this cultural migration. Settlers often attached English or New England–related monikers to their new towns, including Aberdeen, Alcester, Amherst, Andover, Avon, Bangor, Bath, Beresford, Brandon, Brentford, Bristol, Canning, Castlewood, Chelsea, Chester, Columbia, Ethan, Georgetown, Groton, Hartford, Hudson, Ipswich, Kennebec, Manchester,

Montrose, Oldham, Onida, Putney, Rutland, Salem, Scotland, Scranton, Sheffield, Springfield, Stamford, Stratford, Turton, Utica, Vermont City, Watertown, Wentworth, Wolsey, Woonsocket, and Yale.[22] The operative law in Dakota Territory remained the precedents of the English common law, and Dakota jurisprudence relied heavily on eastern and midwestern judges and case law.[23] English literary culture also persisted. Hamlin Garland, who coined the term "middle border" to refer to the late nineteenth century's moving line of settlement, remembered that his boyhood education in Dakota spurred his affection for Scott, Byron, Wordsworth, Shakespeare, and a "long line of English masters" with the help of the McGuffey Readers.[24] Sir Walter Scott, who published *Ivanhoe* in 1819 and whose works were consumed widely in the Midwest, was honored by Dakota settlers who named their towns Ivanhoe and Rowena.[25] The county named after General Beadle, known for repeating the lines of the English classics and promoting common schools modeled on those in New England, even included townships such as Lake Byron and Carlyle.[26] The first schoolteacher in Dakota was a descendent of Puritan founder William Bradford, and one Dakotan noted the presence of a strong contingent of Yankee teachers: "We have got a real nice teacher. she is a full bludded Yankey from Maine. I like her first rate. there are nine schollars in all they are most all Yankeys. we have a regular Yankey time of it."[27] Another pioneer woman in Alexandria wrote fondly of her study of English history: "Am trying at odd moments to wade through the early hist of England, am so anxious to read the later hist, that the first I take more from as sense of necessity than choice."[28]

Reflecting on the statehood process years later, General Beadle believed that the "great freedom loving race of Teutonic people occupying Northwestern Europe" inherited Greek and Roman culture and that in "England all these elements best united." Of England, Beadle wrote that the "whole body of her people's high desires, or her Magna Charta, and, later of her revolution, was transplanted to America," where self-government flowered and produced the Declaration of Independence, the U.S. Constitution, and the Northwest Ordinance. The ultimate state of South Dakota, Beadle declared, was "a growth originating in the principles of English institutions planted in the several colonies and in the race instinct for local self government."[29] Beadle's praise for the English tradition of republicanism and its manifestations in American democracy was frequently echoed by the other civic leaders in Dakota Territory.

The cultural cohesiveness of the Midwest, according to Louis B. Wright, can be traced to the "Anglo-Saxon tradition, the tradition of English law, the English language, English literature, and British religion and customs."[30] English tradition and culture were filtered through New England and then through the Midwest, the two regions that were the greatest source of immigrants to Dakota Territory. In southern Dakota at the time of statehood, 83 percent of native-born Dakotans hailed from the Midwest, and 14 percent came from the North Atlantic states. With only 1.5 percent having come from the South, that region's heritage of aristocracy and slavery, its high degree of racial consciousness and conflict, and its pattern of inequitable landholdings had little impact on Dakota.[31] The majority of Dakota settlers came from midwestern states, especially Wisconsin, Iowa, Illinois, Minnesota, Ohio, Michigan, and Indiana.[32] A contemporary account noted that southern Dakota's population was "homogenous" and that its people were "mainly of American birth, natives of New York, Ohio, Michigan and the States of the Mississippi Valley."[33] Herbert Schell's history of Clay County found that the settlers of the formative period hailed from Michigan, Wisconsin, Ohio, Indiana, Illinois, and Iowa.[34] John Hudson found that settlers in Sanborn County held Iowa, Michigan, and New York picnics so they could socialize with others from their states of origin.[35] Thirty-five thousand people came to Dakota Territory from Wisconsin alone.[36] During the boom, one newspaper reported that nearly every train leaving Mason City, Iowa, included "five to a dozen cars loaded with emigrants bound for South Dakota."[37] The movement of Wisconsinites and Iowans into Dakota Territory comports with Frederick Jackson Turner's conclusion that most of the "men who built up the West beyond the Mississippi" originally "came as pioneers from the old Northwest, in the days when it was just passing from the stage of a frontier section."[38]

The Midwest bore the direct imprint of the American revolutionaries. While the delegates to the American Constitutional Convention were meeting in 1787, the Confederation Congress was enacting the

Northwest Ordinance, which shaped the political and economic structure of the Midwest.[39] Congress sought to create new republican states in the Ohio Valley and to preserve the area for "orderly and industrious settlers."[40] The Northwest Ordinance sculpted the contours of the Midwest by prohibiting slavery and primogeniture, promoting public education, preserving religious freedom and the common law tradition, ensuring jury trials and the right of habeas corpus, and fostering stable governments. This statute, written specifically by the American revolutionaries to provide the fundamental law for the future Midwest, "proved decisive in shaping the region's political and social orders."[41] The brainchild of Thomas Jefferson, the Northwest Ordinance advanced his goal of "exporting republicanism" to the new territories of the Northwest, which were required by the new law to adopt republican constitutions.[42] The political debates within the new states of the Northwest Territory took place within the parameters set by the republican currents of the American Revolution and focused on the republican themes of ensuring liberty, instilling virtue, and combating corruption.[43] "The political leaders of the Old Northwest in the early nineteenth century," according to one study, "remained wrapped in the mantle of republicanism."[44]

Whereas the region south of the Ohio River was influenced by southern states, which "favored the expansion of the planter civilization" and the maintenance of aristocracy and landed estates, the area north of the Ohio River was governed by the republican mandates of the Northwest Ordinance.[45] The institutions and political culture of the Midwest, shaped by the Northwest Ordinance, a product of the American founders, in turn laid the foundation for political and social life in Dakota Territory. The midwesterners who set out for Dakota Territory brought a deeply ingrained tradition of American republicanism with them.[46] Advocates of statehood in Dakota Territory who grounded their claims directly in the rationales cited and precedents created by the American founders, both in the form of the federal Constitution and the Northwest Ordinance, were not guilty of grandiosity, but were speaking an essential truth.

The influence of the Midwest is readily apparent in Dakota Territory in the form of settlers, laws, cultural institutions, and a commitment to republicanism. General Beadle noted the "similarity of experience" among the midwestern settlers of Dakota and their "familiarity with certain systems of institutions, customs and laws" that shaped the "character of the Commonwealth, laws and institutions" of Dakota.[47] Malcolm Rohrbaugh has noted the "structural continuities" between the settlement of the Midwest and that in lands farther west. The same culture and institutions, according to Rohrbaugh, thus "stretched across time and place from the first to the second American West."[48] Most of the midwestern settlers of Dakota Territory, according to H. Wayne Morgan, "wished to reproduce the settled communities they left behind."[49] The region of Dakota under examination here is politically and socially derived from the American Midwest.

In addition to the derivative influence of English folkways on Dakota Territory via New England and midwestern settlers, the territory also included a more direct European influence in the form of Old World immigrants. Promoters of settlement in Dakota Territory encouraged the migration of not only New Englanders and midwesterners but also Northern Europeans.[50] A large majority of these immigrants were from Norway or Germany (either from Germany proper or from German settlements in Russia). General Beadle noted that the Americans in the territory from Wisconsin, New York, Iowa, Minnesota, and Michigan were joined by a "large and excellent" German and Scandinavian population.[51] A future governor of South Dakota boasted of the large number of Dakota pioneers who could "trace their lineage to these liberty-loving, God-fearing countries."[52] The critical cultural touchstones for Dakota were thus the Midwest, New England, and Northern Europe, especially Germany and Norway. These three sources of culture are demonstrated by the first three governors of South Dakota, who were born in Indiana, Vermont, and Norway.

POLITICAL CULTURE

The settlers of Dakota consistently embraced the symbols and revered personages of the American republican heritage in their choice of historical allusions and political imagery. The American founders, for example, received constant adulation. The Reverend Joseph Ward frequently

32

appealed to "the principles so strenuously observed in the founding of our nation" and trumpeted the tradition of ordered liberty established by the American revolutionaries.[53] General Beadle said that no Americans exceeded the Dakota settlers "in loving reverence for the Fathers of the Republic."[54] Statehood proponent and future governor Arthur Mellette linked himself to the cause of the Founders when he criticized federal officials for "denying the right of self-government to a half million American citizens" in Dakota.[55] Judge Gideon Moody similarly denounced Dakota Territory's treatment as a "colony" with the same oppressiveness as American colonials had once been treated by the British crown. He added that this treatment had finally triggered the Declaration of Independence, a precedent embraced by some of the more strident advocates of statehood, who sought to break free of Washington-based territorial governance.[56] A resolution adopted by the 1888 GOP convention in Dakota declared that the federal government "exercised a tyranny over this territory" contrary to the "principles of the founders of the republic."[57] The body also claimed one of the causes of the American Revolution as its own: "We are taxed without representation."[58] South Dakota towns such as Jefferson, Madison, Franklin, and Mt. Vernon likewise carried on the legacy of the founders. In 1889, in a typical demonstration of reverence for the founders, the city of Yankton sponsored a major celebration of the hundredth anniversary of Washington's inauguration replete with patriotic speeches, sermons, and a parade featuring the National Guard, the local firemen, the Grand Army of the Republic, the Modern Woodmen, and many other civic groups.[59] The political discourse of the territory was firmly grounded in the language, ideals, symbols, and history of the American Revolution.

Allusions to the American founders were coupled with praise and admiration for the federal Constitution. Ray Allen Billington noted that the typical late-nineteenth-century American considered the Constitution "his Holy Grail."[60] At the time Dakotans were framing their constitution during the 1880s, the historian George Bancroft completed his famous multivolume history of the United States. Bancroft's magnum opus included two volumes entitled *The History of the Formation of the Constitution of the United States*. Bancroft's celebration of the U.S. Constitution bolstered its reputation even more, and his historical writings in general helped foster and promote the American democratic tradition after Civil War.[61] Faith in the Constitution and American democracy "pervaded the intellectual climate" in which Bancroft crafted his famous history of the United States, and this confidence was shared by Dakotans.[62] In the three full-scale conventions organized in the 1880s to draft a state constitution, Dakota statehood leaders consistently praised the wisdom of the federal organic law. Members of the Dakota State League signed a petition stating, "I pledge my sacred honor"—a reference to the devotion of the American founders—to the adoption of the Sioux Falls constitution written in 1883.[63]

While the American founders and the Constitution provided powerful images and precedents for many Dakota settlers, the more immediate and personal cultural reference point was the Civil War. One U.S. Senate report noted of Dakota that it was "safe to assert that in no State or Territory can there be found so large a proportion of the people who fought the battles of the Union."[64] A large percentage of Dakota settlers, a pioneer fondly recorded in his memoirs, "carried the musket to the front in the darkest days of the rebellion."[65] Arthur Mellette said that many Dakota settlers had been "scarred and maimed in defense of the Union which they helped to preserve."[66] Service to the Union in the Civil War could be the measure of a man in Dakota Territory. When candidates for political office were evaluated, their attractiveness grew if they had been a "good soldier" in the war, had "enlisted as private at first call for troops," or had been "severely wounded and taken prisoner at 1st Bull Run."[67] The Union war veterans' memories of battles and wartime camaraderie was strong. One "old soldier" who had emigrated to Dakota from Ohio would frequent the Grand Army of the Republic (GAR) meetings in Huron with another veteran. A young man who witnessed their interaction remarked on the "strong bond of friendship between those men that time could not erase."[68] Oliver Wendell Holmes, Jr., a Civil War veteran, similarly recalled the distinctiveness and power of this bond forged in war. Of the Civil War generation, Holmes wrote, "in our youth, our hearts were touched with fire."[69] The continuing resonance of the Civil War was reflected in the "bloody shirt" politics of the late nineteenth century. From 1865 to 1900, five of the six men elected president were

Union veterans, and in 1890 there were still a million living Union war veterans, many of whom were active in civic and social affairs.[70] Dakotans shared the national veneration of Civil War service.

Adoption of Civil War monikers and imagery and respect for the Northern cause and its leaders were ubiquitous in Dakota Territory. In and around Potter County, towns took the names Union, Appomattox, Gettysburg, and Shiloh, and one of the county newspapers was the *Potter County Union*.[71] In addition to the naming of lakes and towns for Civil War generals such as Lake Sheridan and the town of Sherman, Union County was named for the Civil War cause, Lincoln County was named for the assassinated president, and McPherson and Meade counties were named for Union generals.[72] When the memorial for Ulysses S Grant was unveiled in Woonsocket in 1885, businessmen were asked to "drape their places of business and cooperate in rendering the occasion as impressive as may be" and to close their shops for the day.[73] Civil War veteran Melvin Grigsby, when running for territorial delegate in 1888, made dramatic use of a Civil War analogy when he addressed the prevailing economic concerns in the nation. He declared that the problem of monopoly was a "danger greater than the danger of African slavery" and recalled that "African slavery once deluged the land in blood."[74]

Allusions to the Civil War were especially common in the debate over statehood since both conflicts were entangled in disputes over popular sovereignty. While hoping for a reasonable compromise in a standoff during Dakota's battle to join the Union, Arthur Mellette offered the dark reminder that "Kansas struggled to statehood through blood."[75] Judge Gideon Moody similarly noted that the unjust treatment of Dakota paralleled the earlier era when the "plains of Kansas were made to bleed with the blood of our martyrs."[76] When calling for an end to territorial status, Major J. K. P. McCallum called on Dakotans to "throw off political thralldom" so that "we will no longer be slaves."[77] Territorial governor Gilbert Pierce, in criticizing those who advocated declaring statehood despite the absence of congressional approval, invoked the name of the "thousands of [men who] fought and shed their blood" for the Union during the Civil War.[78] In Congress, supporters of Dakota statehood openly waved the bloody shirt when protesting efforts to stall its admission to the Union. One Republican asked whether "20,000 scarred veterans now residing in Dakota, who marched through the burning sands and miasmatic swamps of the South to put down a wicked rebellion, [should] stand with bared heads and beg long of their old opponents in arms to be admitted to the Union they helped save? We say again, ten thousand times no! Men of '61 to 8, stand upon your own rights as freemen . . . even if Dakota must remain out of the Union until an uprising of the free men of the states drives the rebel yell from the halls of Congress."[79]

Amidst the pervasive memories of the Civil War the cult of Abraham Lincoln lived on in Dakota Territory. Lewis Bloodgood, for one, kept the flame alive. Bloodgood hailed from Iowa and, while serving in the Union Army, was wounded in an attack on Mobile. Like so many other midwesterners, he moved from Iowa to Dakota Territory in 1880 and homesteaded near Huron. During the war, Bloodgood and his comrades told fellow soldiers in their regiment they were traitors for voting for George McClellan in 1864, and he proudly reported that Lincoln won the regimental balloting soundly: "Old Abe received 432 votes, Little Mc 32."[80] After Lincoln's assassination, Bloodgood wrote, "I heartily wish our honest old President could have lived to have fully recognized the great end for which he had so long toiled, but he has long gone to his home."[81] Bloodgood's son, recalling his father's discussions of his war service, noted that "when the news of Lincoln's assassination came through, the soldiers cried like babies. They all loved this man whose great, tender heart bore the sufferings of the soldiers. Father said no one except Jesus was ever loved by so many people and he hoped that his children and their children would love their country and revere Abraham Lincoln just as their Grandfather Bloodgood did."[82] During the 1870s, there was even a proposal to split off the Black Hills from the territory and call it Lincoln, as well as a proposal to divide the territory in two, with the southern half becoming "Dakota" and the northern half becoming "Chippewa" or "Lincoln."[83] In 1889, the Union Veteran Club of Chicago reminded Dakotans that the "men of 1861–65 made statehood possible for Dakota" and requested that one of the Dakotas be named "Lincoln."[84]

The deference paid to Union veterans of the Civil War affected politics and policy in Dakota. In 1887 the territorial assembly authorized the burying at public expense of "Soldiers, Sailors or Marines, who Served in the Union Army During the War of the Rebellion" when their relatives could not afford a proper burial.[85] The assembly also passed a law giving a preference in public works projects to "honorably discharged Union soldiers and sailors of the late war."[86] Under amendments to the national Homestead Act adopted in 1870 and 1872, old soldiers and their families were afforded generous advantages over other settlers, privileges that "unquestionably were responsible for a large influx of settlement into the West" and "were widely heralded by the railways" that promoted settlement of veterans in the West.[87]

The influence of Civil War veterans was also directly felt through Grand Army of the Republic lodges, which grew dramatically during the years of the boom and included many territorial leaders. In 1884 alone, the number of GAR posts in the territory increased from thirteen to sixty-two, and they grew to one hundred by the time of statehood.[88] The GAR reunion in Aberdeen in September 1885 typified the grandiosity and patriotic spirit of such occasions and featured reveille, a grand parade, music, prayers, speeches by the governor and other officials, the reading of a long paper entitled "The Life, Service and Character of General Grant," and the singing of "Marching through Georgia."[89] In 1889 the territorial legislature created a Dakota Soldiers' Home not long after an encampment of the Dakota department of the GAR requested it.[90] Dakota political leaders, in keeping with their support of Civil War veterans and reflecting the influence of the GAR, were also quick to denounce President Cleveland's veto of a Union soldier relief bill passed by Congress.[91]

The political identities of many of the midwesterners who moved to Dakota Territory was molded by the Civil War and served as another stimulant for republican ideology. The election of Lincoln in 1860 was viewed as a "regional triumph" for midwesterners and marked the "moment in which the Midwest emerged as the preeminent region of the nation."[92] In going to war against a different region with distinct cultural practices, "large numbers of Midwesterners" came to realize all that they had in common and were thus able "to imagine themselves as citizens of a regional community defined largely by the middle-class residents of small towns from Ohio to Iowa and beyond."[93] The Civil War helped to focus the energies of midwesterners on larger republican ideals and to transcend petty intrasectional squabbles.[94] The war, David Noble concluded, "marked the triumph of midwestern democracy."[95] This triumphant midwestern culture of republicanism migrated with the settlers to their new Dakota homesteads.

THE ELEMENTS OF REPUBLICANISM

The traditions of England, New England, and the Midwest and the symbolism and language of the American democratic tradition, especially those of the Revolution and the Civil War, defined the politics of Dakota Territory, where the traditional principles of republicanism were readily evident. The republican focus on liberty and local control, for example, can be detected in Dakotans' persistent attacks on colonialism and the strictures of the territorial system. Dakotans constantly complained of their subservient status as dependent provincials who lacked the rights of independent men.[96] The Vermillion newspaper asked pleadingly, "When shall we slough off this chrysalis or bondage and be free, independent, and self-governing?"[97] The *Mitchell Sun* criticized Democratic president Grover Cleveland in 1888 for treating Dakota Territory as a "dumping ground" for political hacks and "kneelers" and reported that most Dakotans thought the devil should take Cleveland and "shake him over hell."[98] When criticizing the territorial system, the Reverend Joseph Ward of Yankton relied on ample precedent, including the historic freedoms of the Saxon people, the ideals of Thomas Jefferson and William Penn, the bravery of the original American colonists, the Founding Fathers in general, the Northwest Ordinance of 1787, the 1803 treaty with France, and the movement for statehood in Michigan, which went forward in the absence of congressional approval.[99] Local government, Ward declared in the language of republicanism, was necessary "for the sake of the common weal."[100] Much of the animus that Dakotans directed toward the territorial system was based on the traditional republican fear of corruption. Local control, the election of locally known officials, and accountability for such officials would create a "more representative commonwealth" in which the "tendency and temptation to corruption and graft in government should not be so possible."[101]

The goal of improving the commonwealth by ending the territorial system and electing local officials to run the government instead of federal appointees depended on the character of the elected officials. Thus did the traditional republican concern with virtue manifest itself. Although republican virtue had once been considered the province of an elite few, by the middle of the nineteenth century it had been claimed by hardworking, property-owning farmers and mechanics.[102] No longer limited to aristocratic "glory," virtue had become a "synonym for the independence conferred by property ownership and an honest calling."[103] Dakotans often commented on the "virtue and intelligence" and the "enterprise and sturdy vigor" of the territorial residents and contrasted these qualities with the venality of appointed territorial spoilsmen.[104] Conscious of the popular appeal of republican virtue, those who campaigned for candidates for governor billed them as "upright, temperate, wise, trustworthy" and as having "high integrity," a "good, hard, practical, every day sense," and the "character, integrity and sound political faith fit for any political office."[105] Those preoccupied with personal self-interest or solely with making money were viewed as "shirking" their duties to the polity.[106]

A fundamental measure of an individual's republican virtue in Dakota was his capacity for work, which could determine success or failure on the Dakota frontier. One government commission said that Dakota Territory was a "place for a man to rebuild his fortune again; here there need be no destitute, for all that will work there is abundance."[107] Arthur Mellette spoke for many when he pronounced that "God's first law" was "that man should live to labor." Mellette condemned any government policies that would "foster idleness" or "destroy ambition."[108] A pioneer song in Dakota captured this spirit:

Far away in the West lies the land of the free,
Where the mighty Missouri flows down to the sea;
Where a man is a man if he's willing to toil
And reap his reward from the fruits of the soil.[109]

For nineteenth-century republicans, hard work, productivity, self-denial, diligence, and thrift defined virtue.[110] The hardworking self-made man was a popular figure in nineteenth-century America, who succeeded through his "industrious work habits, extraordinary moral discipline, and above all an indomitable will."[111] In Dakota, success would likely come to those who worked "plainly and economically," and scorn awaited those "negligent" in regard to labor.[112] The sternest derision was reserved for idlers and slackers. Norwegian farmers in "Dakoty" proudly compared their hard "vorkin" to that of the "Yankee faller," who set the standard for industriousness.[113]

Work in Dakota Territory primarily meant farming, the occupation most favored by republicans. One account predicted that the Dakotas "were destined to be great commonwealths of farmers."[114] Southern Dakota east of the Missouri River approximated the agrarian ideal of a polity dominated by small farms operated by independent proprietors. Of the more than 50,000 farms in this area at the time of statehood, 92 percent ranged between 100 and 500 acres, and 86 percent of them were farmed by their owners.[115] In 1890, South Dakota's 50,158 farms averaged 227 acres in size.[116] Such an egalitarian distribution of land contrasted sharply with the landed estates of Europe and the plantations of the American South, where peasant agriculture and widespread tenancy were common. Because of the resulting land ownership pattern, Gilbert Fite concluded that the "democratic objective" of the Homestead Act was realized in Dakota.[117]

Dakota settler Frederick A. Fleischman was typical. The son of a German immigrant to Wisconsin, he homesteaded near Oldham in Kingsbury County in 1880. With very little capital he "achieved that elusive Jeffersonian ideal of owning a family farm." According to Fite, Fleischman "represents the thousands who achieved modest success" as farmers in Dakota Territory and who, through consistent hard work, endured many sacrifices and times of economic stress but made "a good home for himself and his large family."[118] Fleischman's success underscored the pioneers' belief in the equality of opportunity for those willing to work.[119] One observer said of Dakota that the "great charm of life here is that every man stands on his own individual merits. If he has no merits, he has no standing."[120] Privilege was subverted by a rigorous meritocratic competition. For Dakota settlers, their "station in society [would] simply depend on their character, deportment and capability, and little or not at all on their ancestry, wealth or occupation."[121]

In Dakota, where the agrarian tradition thrived and industriousness was a broadly shared social ideal, farmers' arduous work was consistently praised. One minister who witnessed hundreds of hardworking settlers migrating to Dakota homesteads said they would "make that desert region bud and blossom like the rose, because they are the salt of the earth."[122] A unique respect was afforded to those whose "roots were deep in the soil" and to "those who make things grow, those who are the producers."[123] The celebration of the agrarian order in Dakota Territory gained additional intensity from growing national fears that the farming frontier was near exhaustion and that cities, which Jackson Lears has called the "republicans' bete noire," would increasingly overshadow rural culture.[124] Irish immigrants who hoped to lure more of their countrymen to Dakota Territory stoked these fears by urging their brethren to escape the "contaminating influences of city life."[125] The growth of cities and the filling of the Dakota prairie, the last farming frontier, signaled a future in which the strength of agrarian culture—farmers who owned their own land and enjoyed an independence denied to industrial workers, who maintained a work ethic essential to virtue, and who held an aversion to corruption and urban vice—would inevitably be diluted.[126]

The celebration of work and the labors of farm life underscore the market orientation of Dakota farmers. Dakotans worked hard to make a profit and willingly participated in market transactions.[127] They respected private property and bought and sold land, equipment, livestock, and household items; Dakota newspapers were filled with advertisements and notices that promoted the buying and selling of goods.[128] Many farmers, Gilbert Fite noted, were "small-time speculators" in land and broadly respected the "sanctity of property ownership."[129] Many of the Dakota pioneers were, after all, from the Midwest, "a veritable bastion of liberal capitalism."[130] One historian of the Midwest traced the market orientation back to England and found in the Midwest "an inheritance of practicality from a nation of shop-keepers who taught us that commerce is honorable and that fair play in business is part of the code of decent men."[131]

Pioneer farmers were not motivated solely by material gain, however.[132] The settlers' market orientation was circumscribed by their attachment to republican notions of virtue, their obligations to their neighbors, their sense of civic duty, their vision of a decentralized agrarian economy, and their religious commitments.[133] While these social forces created limits to the operation of the market economy that varied by person and place, there is scant evidence of socialistic attitudes or of a hostility to market capitalism in general.[134] What support there was for government economic regulation focused on promoting competition and a decentralized economy and combating monopolies.[135] Dakotans also strongly supported the adoption of anti-corruption laws aimed at preventing monopolists from unduly influencing the political system.

While the labor-intensive and market-oriented agrarian order was conducive to republicanism, schools in Dakota Territory also worked to directly inculcate the work ethic, civic virtue, and republican patriotism. Throughout the 1880s, Dakotans strongly supported the organization of schools and attempted to protect school lands from speculators. By the time of statehood in 1889, 647 school districts had been organized with an enrollment of 72,406 students, who were taught by 4,372 teachers.[136] County superintendents of education found among Dakotans an intense interest in education.[137] The *New York Independent* reported in 1888 that there was "less illiteracy in Dakota than in any New England state" and that the territory spent more on education than Connecticut.[138] Dakota Territory led twenty-two states in school appropriations, and by 1885 there was one schoolhouse for every 132 people in what would become the state of South Dakota.[139] Eighty-nine percent of the total school-age population was enrolled in school, yet concern that children's duties on the farm would keep them out of school spurred passage of a compulsory school attendance law in 1883.[140]

Dakota schools expressly promoted republican virtue. According to historian John Unruh, "character building stood out as the primary objective of all educational effort." "In our social life today," one superintendent asserted, "the tendencies toward evil are so strong that the moral training of the youth in our schools is one of the most important questions that now confronts educators; for, if crime is increasing and immorality threatens to undermine our social institutions, the fault, in a great degree, may be charged to our system of public education."[141] To ensure the instillation of virtue in pupils, the territory also made a strong effort to ascertain the "moral character" of teachers.[142] The promotion of education was central to nineteenth-century political culture since "republicanism, more than any other form of government, rested on the virtue, intelligence and integrity of its people."[143] As Jean Baker has explained, "Schooling emerged as the taproot of a uniform republican culture, and the felt need for civic instruction sparked an enduring national commitment to education, not for its liberating benefits or as economic training within a modernizing economy, but as a political tool for training Americans in the eighteenth-century understanding of civic virtue."[144] The constitutions drafted by Dakotans during the 1880s openly pronounced that the "stability of a republican form of government" depended on education.[145]

Schoolbooks in nineteenth-century America celebrated the triumphs of the U.S. republic and emphasized the biographies of the American founders, the history of the Revolution, the nation's military victories, and the virtues of sacrifice and honor.[146] The curriculum in Dakota Territory, too, emphasized civic education and included classes focused on American history, American literature, geography, the Constitution, civil government, and the workings of the "American commonwealth."[147] The McGuffey Readers, use of which was mandated by statute in Dakota Territory, also instilled republican virtue by praising "perseverance, truth, honesty, and hard work while denouncing laziness, gambling, purposeless frivolity, and drinking." Through these readers, students also "learned to revere the family and the church and to believe in the desirability of material progress and self-improvement: character was the key to success."[148]

In addition to promoting civic education, personal virtue, and the work ethic, the Dakota curriculum also recognized the broader English and classical heritage that had shaped American institutions. The first report of the Territorial Board of Education in 1888 noted that high school classes in Dakota included Latin, which was taught through the study of Caesar and Virgil. The courses offered by the high school in Yankton, for example, included Caesar, Cicero, Virgil, and English history.[149] The general curriculum later included English, Greek, and Roman history in addition to the courses on Caesar, Cicero, and Virgil.[150] The Greek and Roman classics had also played an important role in "shaping the outlook of the founders of cultural institutions in the old Northwest," the place of origin of many Dakota settlers.[151] The founders of towns in Dakota, not coincidentally, adopted names such as Seneca, Carthage, and Virgil.[152]

Teacher training in the territory also emphasized these traditions. The test for territorial teaching certificates required translation of Latin texts and required teachers to answer questions about republican governance and the English and classical heritage: "Describe in brief the three forms of government of the Romans." "What races at different times have been dominant in England?" "What literary traits are most conspicuous in the writings of Macaulay, Irving, Emerson, Swift, Tennyson, Holmes, Pope?" "Name the five leading poets, three historians and three novelists of America and their masterpieces." "What works have you read of Shakespeare, Milton, Bunyan, Macaulay, Tennyson, Fielding, Dickens, Thackeray, Scott, Byron, Emerson, Irving, Howells, Cable, Lowell, Whittier?" "What difference can you see in the people who settled Virginia and those who settled New England? Can you trace those differences in the history of the two sections?" "How was the constitution of the United States made and adopted?" "What causes led to the framing of the Constitution?" "How are territories governed? How may a territory become a state?"[153] The teachers of territorial Dakota were expected to impart to the young the classical and English heritage and the basics of civil and constitutional government.

Another component of republicanism emphasized by the Dakota schools was simple patriotism, what Maurizio Viroli calls a "charitable love of the republic (caritas reipublicae) and of one's fellow citizens (caritas civium)."[154] During the 1880s in Dakota Territory, patriotic celebrations, speeches, decorations, and rituals were an integral component of civic life and often involved invocations of past American glories. In her study of Dakota in the 1930s, Catherine McNicol Stock noted that "Dakotans were ardently patriotic," a reflection of the patriotic pride planted deep during the territorial period.[155] Patriotic celebrations captured this passion. During a ceremony in Vermillion in 1889, for example, while singing "America" and waving flags, girls "arrayed in flowers and sashes bearing the names of the States of the Union, were arranged in a semi-circle around a monument erected in memory of the fallen heroes." Each girl in turn made a patriotic statement and then approached the monument and "laid her offering in the shape of a lovely garland."[156] Patriotic speeches often accompanied such celebrations. Jefferson Kidder, a product of Braintree, Vermont, gave a typical speech on July 4, 1880, in which he praised the "heroes who took a hand in giving us the gorgeous inheritance of human liberty," which "shook the Island Empress of the sea [Great Britain] with terror and scattered the brightest jewels from her crown." Kidder added that because of American independence the world could "hear the deep oath muttered to the winds by the free sons of the Pilgrims," who said "they would 'die or live freemen.'"[157] In the hierarchy of civic festivities, few occasions bested Independence Day. One settler recalled the importance of Fourth of July celebrations to Dakotans: "It rated higher than birthdays, Valentine's Day, or last day of school, in importance."[158] The patriotic impulse was passed on to the young. In Dakota Territory, schoolchildren marched with the GAR, learned to decorate the graves of the Union dead, and flew flags over their schoolhouses.[159] The McGuffey Readers were also known for their "uncompromising nationalism."[160] The West in general, according to John Hicks, promoted civic pride and national unity and came to be a "stronghold of nationalism."[161] In the nation at large, public celebrations involving the flag blossomed throughout the 1880s. The American Flag Association was organized, flag statutes were passed, legal sanctions against flag misuse were adopted, public singing of "The Star Spangled Banner" became more common, and in 1890, North Dakota mandated the flying of flags at schoolhouses.[162]

Patriotism was not reduced to flag flying, however. It was also linked to the duties of republican citizenship. To be patriotic required pursuing the best interests of the commonwealth and serving the public good, not simply following one's personal ambition. Patriotism and attentiveness to civic responsibilities were considered signs of a manly sense of duty. Manhood also involved the building of "character" and the development of the "self-mastery" and "restraint" necessary to control one's passions and to meet the social obligations of citizenship.[163] Statehood advocates Robert Dollard and Bartlett Tripp serve as examples. Dollard was born in Fall River, Massachusetts; signed up for the Union cause as a private and ended the Civil War as a major; moved to Dakota Territory; served in both houses of the territorial legislature and in two constitutional conventions; and was a GAR commander and state attorney general.[164] For all his civic commitments, Dollard was remembered for his "patriotic life" and his "higher conception of true manhood."[165] Tripp was born in Maine, attended Colby College, studied law, served as a territorial judge, attended the territorial constitutional conventions, and earned "unsullied honor in the public service." He was remembered for possessing the "highest-qualities of our common manhood."[166]

For the settlers of Dakota Territory, manhood was defined by the elements of republicanism, including hard work, personal virtue, patriotism, service to the commonwealth, and pursuit of the agrarian ideal. General Beadle saw the qualities of true manhood in the pioneers who sought "to redeem a wilderness, to plant the institutions of American liberty upon a new soil."[167] The natural environment of Dakota, it was said, helped "to breed the sturdy man, the rugged, vigorous citizen, who, triumphant in his struggle with nature, is fitted to build a perfect state."[168] The contrast with yeoman pioneers was visible in the corrupt machinations of territorial appointees, who lacked the pioneers' "vigorous manhood."[169] In the 1890s, by which time the prairies of Dakota had been populated, intellectuals increasingly worried that the "closing" of the frontier meant the loss of sustenance for American manhood. Teddy Roosevelt, who had lived in the Dakotas during the 1880s, famously championed "the strenuous life" in 1899, openly fearing that "vigor, manliness, and audacity" had "given way to effete overcivilization among the once-hearty Anglo-Saxon race."[170] The contrast to the manliness of the farmer in places such as Dakota could be found in the idleness, luxury, and effeminacy of the nation's expanding urban centers.[171] The republican manhood on display during the Dakota boom was but fleeting, some feared, destined to be submerged in an urbanizing America.

Attentiveness to the survival of republican manhood underscores the fact that civic affairs in Dakota Territory were largely a world of men. Dakota women, as Deborah Fink noted of the women of frontier Nebraska, were "identified with the separate moral world of the home."[172] This "female frontier," according to Glenda Riley, was based primarily in the private household but also included work on the farm.[173] Although this study does not delve deeply into the interior life of the Dakota home and instead focuses on the public world of politics, that public world was made possible in part through the sacrifices of pioneer women, who managed the household and farm while men were politicking.[174] Women also shaped the public sphere through child-rearing, which would "transform sons into republicans"; women were charged with the "maternal inculcation of that compendium of inexact but critical behaviors based on industry, honesty, frugality, and public responsibility."[175]

Recognizing the contribution of women to the social order in Dakota, some men promoted breeching the wall that kept politics primarily a male world and openly supported women's suffrage. General Beadle remembered that "many" men in Dakota Territory favored granting women "all political rights" and others insisted on recognizing the "honor" and "virtue" of the women in Dakota by extending them the right to vote.[176] Prohibitionists also allied themselves with the advocates of women's suffrage in the hope that women would provide a strong base of political support for banning alcohol.[177] Some suffrage advocates, in keeping with the republican tradition, thought female voters would have a "purifying influence" on politics by undermining the corrupting power of such interests as the liquor trade, by bolstering American culture and civilization, and by diluting the influence of European immigrants.[178]

Understanding the power of republicanism in Dakota Territory, advocates promoted suffrage through music that portrayed female voting as a blow against tyranny, the spoils system, and bossism and that invoked the flag, the Civil War, and the heritage of American freedom:

Dakota, Land of Liberty

A tyrant does thee oppress, Dakota, land of liberty; Lift up thine hand in thy distress and smit him for humanity. Thy daughters fair demand of thee before the law, equality; Deny them not—'tis tyranny—Dakota, land of liberty. Thy yeoman true will thee defend,

Dakota, land of liberty; For equal rights they'll e'er contend, to guide thee on in purity. No more will spoilsmen law defy, no sycophants on pelf rely, For woman's vote will purify Dakota, land of liberty.

The Big Boss Politician (to tune of "Brewer's Big Horse")
The big boss politician comin' down do road / A drivin' of de bandwagon, hol'rin "all abode"; / He crack his whip dis way, doan' you see; / But dat politician das'nt run ober me.

Give the Ballot to the Mothers
(to tune of "Marching through Georgia")
Bring the dear old banner, boys, and fling it to the wind; / Mother, wife and daughter, let it shelter and defend. / "Equal Rights" our motto is, we're loyal to the end— / Giving the ballot to the mothers.

New America (to tune of "America")
Women in every age, / For this great heritage / Tribute have paid. / Our birthright claim we now, / Longer refuse to bow; / On freedom's altar now / Our hand is laid.[179]

Advocates of women's suffrage struck republican chords during the 1880s and did win some support for their cause. Suffrage legislation was passed by the territorial legislature, but the federally appointed governor vetoed the measure. Although many were supportive of suffrage, pragmatists in the statehood movement sought to postpone women's suffrage and thus decouple the issue from statehood to avoid generating additional opposition to it from the liquor interests, supporters of drink, traditionalists, immigrants, and Democrats in Congress.[180] The republican urgency to achieve self-rule through statehood trumped republican sympathy for the suffrage claims of women.

THE PUBLIC SPHERE

Despite the near-exclusion of women, the public world of Dakota Territory was active and intense. Political debates could prompt partisan exchanges that by the mid-nineteenth century were viewed as signs of republican spiritedness.[181] In the 1800s, according to Jean Baker, "party affairs were the measure of public life."[182] Partisan sparring was at its height during the late nineteenth century, when the national parties were deadlocked in rough parity.[183] In the presidential elections between 1876 and 1892, neither party's candidate received a majority of the popular vote. The federal government remained divided between the parties—a precarious balance of power that helped drive party loyalty to an all-time high. Robert Cherny notes that during this period voters were "engaged and committed to the democratic process" and that the "common voter understood that his ballot really mattered."[184] During the election cycles preceding statehood, as many as 80 percent of eligible Dakota voters went to the polls during the fall elections.[185]

In Dakota Territory, the Republican Party—the party of Lincoln. the Midwest, and the Homestead Act—was the majority party. In 1880, 80 percent of the territory was Republican.[186] At the time of statehood in 1889, Republicans would outnumber the Democrats in the state House by 108–8 and in the state senate 37–3.[187] Because of Republican dominance in the territory and the even division of the federal government, Democrats in Congress opposed Dakota statehood, a fact observers in the territory consistently pointed out. The *New York Times* reported that Democrats in Congress would block statehood for southern Dakota because the new state would send "two Republicans to the Senate."[188] The *Utica Gazette* of New York opined in 1884 that Republican-leaning "Dakota will be kept knocking at the gate as long as the House remains Democratic."[189] The intransigence of congressional Democrats spurred partisan passions in the territory and fueled the cause of statehooders, who condemned those who stifled republican self-rule in Dakota.

Due to the level of political partisanship and the frequent exchange of arguments and counterarguments, one pioneer woman in Alexandria confessed confusion over the debates she observed in the newspapers: "Just as my indignation was roused at Garfield's swindling operations, another paper tells one he is almost a saint." "If women vote in my time," she wrote, "what a serious time I shall have."[190] This settler's confusion over conflicting newspaper reports provides another glimpse at the liveliness of the Dakota political scene. Another clear indicator of the health of the public sphere in Dakota Territory was the large number of newspapers that sparred with one another.[191] By 1889, more than 400 newspapers were published in Dakota Territory, more than double the number in states such as Maine, Connecticut, Maryland, West Virginia, Florida, Louisiana, Colorado, Nebraska, Arkansas, Alabama, and Mississippi; five times the number of newspapers published in Vermont; and ten times the number in Delaware. The Dakota newspapers included 25 dailies, 392 weeklies, and 4 published in Norwegian, 3 in German, and 1 in Dutch.[192] The *New York Independent* noted that in 1888 there were "as many newspapers in Dakota as in Maine, Connecticut and Rhode Island combined."[193] The residents of Yankton could even read the newspapers published in St. Paul on the same day they were printed if they waited up for the 10 P.M. train.[194] Augustine Davis, president of the Dakota Press Association, actively encouraged editors and reporters to participate in and report on legislative activities, constitutional conventions, and public life in general.[195] The enormous newspaper output was actively consumed by Dakotans, who were highly literate. One pioneer remembered long evenings when his family members would read such newspapers as the *Weekly Inter Ocean* of Chicago, the *Toledo Blade*, and the *Northwestern Christian Advocate*.[196]

Dakotans also attended numerous public lectures, organized study groups, and supported public libraries. One woman recalled of a chautauqua she attended, "I remember thinking that one lecture in particular was the finest, wittiest, most polished address I had ever heard, and probably it was."[197] In keeping with the influence of English culture in Dakota, the Ladies History Club of Sioux Falls was organized in 1879 to study English history, and in 1889 the Women's Club of Watertown took up the study of English and American history.[198] The territorial legislature also passed a law to promote the organization of "free libraries" for settlers.[199] The New England and midwestern emigrants to Dakota brought with them a keen interest in free public education, public lectures, lyceums, and library associations.[200] One study noted that midwesterners were "obsessively interested in communicating with each other" and that "residents of the Old Northwest wrote and spoke at great length; they kept diaries, gave lectures, read books and newspapers, listened to sermons, and filled their days with discussions of the place in which they lived."[201] The 627 post offices in Dakota similarly fostered the exchange of letters, often with friends and family members back east, and the territory's four hundred newspapers kept Dakotans apprised of public events.[202] A number of historians have recognized the "western appetite for books and newspapers," the high level of literacy, the prominence on the frontier of newspapers and their editors, and the ubiquity of literary societies, study groups, women's clubs, farmers associations, debating societies, lectures, lyceums, libraries, and public readings.[203]

The public square in Dakota Territory, enlivened as it was by elections, patriotic celebrations, public lectures and speeches, and other civic events, indicates the depth of civic engagement and the strength of community ties.[204] The territory also featured, however, less formal forms of community activity such as socializing and "visiting" at church services, church suppers, farmers' picnics, community dances, strawberry socials, ice cream socials, basket socials, theatricals, musicals, roller and ice skating, sleigh rides, toboggan sliding, teas, circuses, weddings, fairs, sporting events, game hunts, shooting events, and bob-sled races, along with the day-to-day interaction among neighbors.[205] One settler noted that many of his Dakota neighbors had been his neighbors back in Iowa, indicating a pattern of chain migration to Dakota that promoted social and community interaction. "Neighbors in those days were neighbors indeed," this settler recalled. "They knew each other's sorrows, joys, and troubles—helping each other in bad times as well as good, in every possible way."[206] He also praised the "literaries" held at the school as "among the most important events. Such crowds we had—the house would be jammed. Recitations, songs, dialogs, and debates composed the programs. Almost everyone took part. There were some pretty heated debates at times." "Those literaries," he said, "were among the happiest events of our lives."[207] The literary in Liberty Township in Beadle County "drew crowds almost every evening" and when it was too cold to ride horses, the settlers set out on foot to attend.[208] One pioneer woman, as if trying to dispel the myth of prairie privation, wrote to her brother and sister in New York that "we have had lyceums in our schoolhouse all winter had real nice times we had a paper, singing speaking and so on."[209]

Another woman recalled that book sharing in the "book-hungry land" of Dakota Territory brought many visitors to her house.[210]

The local lodges of the nation's rapidly growing fraternal societies were also ubiquitous in Dakota Territory and the locus of much community interaction.[211] In 1888, there were 621 members of the Knights Templar of Dakota, 735 members of the International Order of Odd Fellows, and many members of the Order of the Eastern Star of South Dakota.[212] The largest fraternal order, however, was the Masons. In 1888, the Masons had over 4,000 members and had established one hundred lodges across Dakota Territory. In 1888 alone, the Masons added 512 members.[213] Among Masonic officers were South Dakota statehood promoters George Hand (Grand Master), George Kingsbury (Senior Grand Warden), William Beadle (Grand Marshall), O. S. Gifford (Grand Master), Arthur Mellette (Grand Treasurer), and Andrew Lee (Grand Senior Deacon).[214] General Beadle, the architect of Dakota Territory's common school system, was a "member of all regular Masonry including the 33d degree of Scottish Rite."[215] More than half of the delegates to the 1885 and 1889 constitutional conventions were Masons, including Alonzo Edgerton, the president of both conventions.[216] While the Masonic temples of Dakota often attracted the more prominent civic and social leaders, the panoply of clubs and social and religious organizations in the territory offered multiple avenues for community involvement and social interaction.

ORDER

Fraternal lodges, social and civic events, literary societies, lyceums, and other communal activities provided a method, two historians of the Midwest have found, for "maintaining character in a disordered environment."[217] Through their community activities and political efforts the Dakota pioneers sought to build a workable social order and to minimize the uncertainty of life and the sources of disorder in their new prairie environment. The notion of "settling" connoted a desire to transcend the difficulties of migration, and the act of organizing a homestead manifested an ambition to become rooted in the land. The rectangular survey of homesteads lent order to the landscape itself, as did the organization, surveying, platting, and naming of town sites; establishment and naming of counties; designation of county seats; and planning and building of railroad lines.[218] Material improvements to homesteads, including the replacement of sod houses with wood structures and the addition of barns and fences, were also a high priority. Settlers also planted trees in the effort to organize prairie life and replicate the more orderly life they had left behind. "Since most of the early Dakotans came from the forested regions of Western Europe or the Lake States to the east," W. H. Droze noted, "they immediately sought to restore their forested environment."[219] Beyond these material improvements and their various efforts to become settled in the landscape, the settlers also brought with them a cultural, legal, and constitutional heritage that they saw as the basis of their new life, and they hoped to organize, as quickly as possible, the community activities they had previously known.

While farms and towns, communal activities, and the basic elements of New England and midwestern culture constituted the thick outward layer of social organization, the most fundamental organizing principle of Dakota life was the family. Joseph Ward, one of the leading ministers in the territory, underscored the "authority of the ultimate unit, the family," which was "held most sacred."[220] Americans of this era, Jackson Lears has noted, "placed their highest hopes for the preservation of moral order on the family itself," and the pioneer families of Dakota were no exception.[221] The typically young settlers in Dakota were quick to marry and to raise large families, and their family bonds and devotion to the domestic hearth were strong.[222] One son of the Dakota prairie fondly recalled his father's dedication to his family, his hard work, the hardships he endured, and how he "loved his neighbors, his country, and his God."[223] Pioneer mothers were the primary caretakers of children on the prairie and "kept homes orderly, perpetuated traditions, [and] conserved values."[224]

Threats to orderly family life in Dakota were not dismissed lightly. In 1883 the territorial legislature made the use of "obscene or lascivious" language in public or in the presence of women or children a misdemeanor.[225] Believing in alcohol's reputation as a "destroyer of the home," many settlers supported prohibition.[226] By 1887, all but a few Dakota counties had banned liquor using a local-option law. A majority of voters supported statewide prohibition in an 1889 referendum.[227] In an act symbolizing the need to protect republican practices and institutions from disruption, Dakota Territory banned liquor sales on Election Day.[228] One proponent of settlement in Dakota explained the link between temperance, republican virtue, and the proper instruction of the young: "To all earnestly desiring 'health, wealth and happiness' for themselves and [who] are willing to unite with us in advancing the cause of temperance, in sustaining public virtue and fostering education we say—Come to Dakota!"[229] Drunkenness was stigmatized while sobriety and industriousness met the prevailing social standards of republican virtue. According to one study of social life on the plains, "being a good provider for one's family, staying sober, being a good helpmate, and being a good farmer all ensured acceptance by the community."[230]

While social stigmas and communal expectations could shape personal behavior, Dakotans were also strong supporters of the social ordering that accompanied the rule of law and generally supported a legalistic culture. They established courts, relied on the Anglo-American common law tradition, codified and organized the varied territorial statutes, created a bar association in 1885, and spent much of the 1880s debating the proper constitutional order for the future state.[231] The East River areas of southern Dakota were not known to be wild and disorderly. Observers proudly distinguished between the rowdy years after the territory was first organized and the later settlement period, when Dakota settlers were known to "maintain law and order as well as even the Puritans did."[232] Watertown, for example, prided itself on its "law-abiding, order-loving, church-going people."[233] One study of social conditions in Dakota at the time of statehood concluded that the "vast majority of the people of the state were law abiding citizens."[234] Both public executions and private, extralegal violence were extremely rare in Dakota Territory.[235] The midwestern mix of Yankee, German, and Scandinavian culture that predominated in Dakota Territory "regarded due-process of law as a dependable regulator of social problems" and was generally not amenable to lynch law.[236]

The process of laying the foundation of social order in Dakota is perhaps best captured by the contemporary philosopher Josiah Royce, who was born in an unruly California mining camp and thus had the benefit of viewing a social transition from primal disorder to organized settlement in the West. In 1883, at the high point of the Dakota boom, Royce was asked to write a history of California (after the person originally tasked with the project died), which became the famous *California: From the Conquest in 1846 to the Second Vigilante Committee in San Francisco: A Study of American Character* (1886).[237] Having witnessed the early chaotic moments of rampant individualism in California history, Royce described a landscape "scarred by unsightly diggings, saloon brawls, vigilante committees establishing order with rope and gun."[238] But he also noted the state's evolution from the "chaos of unrestrained individualism to a measure of disciplined order."[239] After realizing the perils of the early stage of "irresponsible freedom," according to Royce, the mining camps began "in every way to insist upon order. The coming of women, the growth of families, the formation of church organizations, the building of schoolhouses, the establishment of local interests of all sorts, saved the wiser communities from the horrors of lynch law."[240] Royce used the California experience to shape his philosophical thinking and to emphasize the social benefits of cooperation, sharing, community, patriotism, and duty to one's fellow citizens. "We are all but dust save as this social order gives us life," Royce wrote.[241] When individuals chose to "serve the social order," they would find that they were serving their "own highest spiritual destiny in bodily form."[242] In keeping with Frederick Jackson Turner's frontier ideals, Robert Hine noted, Royce believed that in the "spirit of the pioneer's 'house raising' lies the salvation of the Republic."[243] The social ordering that Royce found to ultimately prevail in California was the norm in Dakota.

The settlers who peopled Dakota did not arrive with intellectual blank slates, nor did the social order they created emerge out of a formless state of nature. The Dakota pioneers borrowed heavily from the culture of American republicanism and its English antecedents. The New Englanders and midwesterners who constituted the bulk of the boom migration to Dakota celebrated the history, figures, and symbols of American democracy. The honor afforded to this tradition was particularly heartfelt for the many Dakota pioneers who served the Union cause during the Civil War, which deepened patriotic fervor in the North and further entrenched the democratic ideals for which they fought. More specifically, the Dakota pioneers embraced the republican principles of civic virtue, patriotism, physical work, agrarian fundamentalism, and dedication to the commonwealth, and they abhorred corruption and self-interestedness. The goals of republicanism were pursued in the political realm, reinforced in community activities, and cultivated in the schools. The dominant republican ideals articulated in political discourse were not always upheld and at times were impaired by the austerity of prairie life, but they were the cultural currency in which Dakota pioneers traded. The other imposing institutional force in the life of settlers, which buttressed republican social and political structures and inculcated personal virtue, was the local Christian church.

CHAPTER 3

GOD'S COUNTRY

Our God will order all right—we trust—in Him.

Dakota pioneer, 1885

One of the most conspicuous physical features of the territorial landscape was the Christian church, often one of the first buildings constructed in a territorial town. As one Dakota settler observed in 1889, along with the schoolhouse and the grain elevator, the "spires of the churches" were the "first indication of a town."[1] Territorial immigration commissioner P. F. McClure observed, "Towering church spires on the prairie, like signal-lights of the harbor, point out each city, town or modest village."[2] Church spires were treated as an "index to the moral character of a community" in Dakota Territory.[3] General William Beadle recalled that the rural churches of the Norwegian immigrants were a testament to their Christian devotion, evidence that they were "true to their faith" and a sign that they were "faithful farmers."[4] In 1888, one year before statehood, the *New York Independent* reported more than a thousand churches in Dakota Territory.[5] One county boasted in its immigration literature that it was home to eighteen churches.[6]

From the pulpits of these Christian churches came sermons that provided a higher purpose to settlers' sometimes arduous lives. One pioneer woman became, through scripture readings and prayer services, a "witness to her salvation," and the experience brought a "revival to her own soul."[7] Religion "gave people a sense that others shared their assumptions about earthly society as well as the meaning of life," a feeling that diminished the isolation of prairie living.[8] The clergy, according to one Lutheran pioneer, "gave great inspiration to the people on those lonely prairies, and life took on new meaning as they found satisfaction in religious beliefs."[9] A woman in Dakota Territory lamented the sorrows in her life but recognized that "in that better home beyond the river of death we Shall feel no Sorrow if we live as we ought to in this world. How Sweet to die and leave all cares behind us. Peaceful rest." Lonely for her family in the East, she looked toward the day when "we will meet where partings never take place."[10] Another Dakotan received a letter from his brother in Norway that read, "If you are still alive, I hope you are well. If not we will meet in heaven." Apparently unsure that this final meeting would take place, the brother then clarified that the heavenly reunion would take place only if everything was "well with your soul."[11]

Faith in the Christian afterlife on the part of this immigrant Norwegian and many other settlers shaped behavior on the frontier. Earthly virtue would, they believed, bring eternal peace. A settler in Wessington, hoping that his children's children would work toward a Christian heaven, counseled them to "live in this life that you may hav the reward of the good & fathful in the life that is beyond now."[12] Living a Christian life in preparation for Heaven entailed certain duties and obligations to God and man. Among the most basic requirements was attending church to hear the Word. A young Dakotan recalled, "Father and mother were always quite rigid in their insistence upon the proper observation of the Sabbath. No ball games, picnicking, fishing, or hunting were allowed."[13] Another settler remembered: "Grace at the table, reading from the Bible, and morning prayers were never neglected nor overlooked. No matter what strangers spent the night with us, the Bible was read and everybody knelt for prayer before the stranger felt free to leave. No work was too urgent for this service to be dispensed with."[14] Since most Dakota settlers became farmers in wide-open rural spaces, religious devotion took on added significance. Robert Swierenga, noting the "vital place of religious practices and beliefs in the lives of rural folk," has concluded, "Rural life truly was church centered."[15]

The settlers' plan for the next world and respect for the Sabbath indicate the influence of religion in their lives. O. E. Rolvaag recalled that for the "pioneers, there was no force other than the church which could draw mind and thought away from the struggle for survival."[16] One settler later recalled of the pioneer generation: "They had convictions; they knew what they believed and believed it heart and soul."[17] General Beadle said "with all confidence that South Dakotans were never so sincerely and so generally religious in faith and practice" as during the boom.[18] Arthur Mellette explained that the "citizens of Dakota are a God fearing people, and have not been backward in making provision for the moral and religious welfare of their families. . . . Religion takes deep root in this free soil, and the large church attendance bespeaks the interest manifested by the people and shows their spirit in the work."[19] Delegates to the constitutional conventions of the 1880s voted to designate "Under God the People Rule" as the state motto for southern Dakota.[20] The choice of town names such as Epiphany, Faith, Eden, Mission, and Sinai also reflected Dakota settlers' religious inclinations. In the 1880s southern Dakota settlers even considered naming their future state "God's Country."[21]

During a presidential address to the State Historical Society long after the boom, former governor Charles Herreid made an observation that would have been obvious decades earlier—the settlers of Dakota "were a religious people."[22] Herreid's statement might have been directed at some of the progressive historians of the early twentieth century who increasingly marginalized the role of religion in American history. In the past two decades, historians have started to again emphasize the role of religion and ethnicity in the politics of the late nineteenth century and have criticized the progressive historians' focus on economic conflict.[23] This renewed emphasis on religiosity is further justified by the experience of territorial Dakotans.

Settlers' religious practice and belief, in tandem with their ethnic background, influenced political action. Paul Kleppner has explained that political orientation often depended on an individual's connection to religious and ethnic groups, which gave meaning to the "inchoate world of politics."[24] Religious and ethnic loyalties shaped political behavior and were important influences and points of contention in the political culture. Richard Jensen found that "religion was the fundamental source of political conflict in the Midwest," the place of origin for most Dakota settlers.[25] Frederick Luebke's analysis of the Great Plains noted that ethnically English and Scandinavian groups generally supported the Republican Party, while Catholics voted Democratic.[26] Jon Gjerde has also examined the political conflict that accompanied the Catholic immigration to the rural Midwest, a region primarily Protestant.[27] Whereas historians of an earlier era saw social friction chiefly in the form of "farmers opposing bankers," recent studies take note of such conflicts as "Catholics against Protestants."[28] Interdenominational friction signals the importance settlers attached to religious beliefs.

The role of Christianity in the lives of Dakota settlers provides another example of the territory's reliance on the borrowed republican traditions of New England and the Midwest. The "most powerful" factor shaping the culture of the American colonies, according to David Hackett Fischer, was religion, which the American founders thought would instill republican virtue.[29] In line with the Founders, historians have also emphasized the coexistence of and interrelationship between the republican and liberal political traditions and Christianity.[30] These powerful religious currents persisted long after the American Revolution.[31] Abraham Lincoln, the iconic voice of the Midwest, famously drew upon the religious impulse.[32] The shared traditions of various Christian denominations served as another bond among midwestern communities, common articles of faith that became, according to Andrew Cayton and Peter Onuf, the "tendons of trans-local communities."[33] New Englanders and midwesterners carried the Christian cross with them to the towns and homesteads of Dakota Territory.

Religious devotion helped order social life in Dakota Territory. Religion linked Dakota settlers to long-standing Christian traditions, gave meaning to settlers' lives, acted as a social stabilizer and source of community interaction, and provided moral guidance. In the "heavily churched landscape" of the upper Midwest, Robert Ostergren has noted, the "church was physically symbolic of its role as the keeper of culture and of continuity with the past."[34] In his study of rural Illinois, John Mack Faragher has noted that as "forces of order, churches reinforced the basic cultural assumptions, guiding tender consciences and influencing personal behavior at home and at work."[35] Religion brought "social discipline and influence for decency and peace," according to T. Scott Miyakawa, and fostered a stable social order that depended not only on the Constitution or the U.S. Supreme Court but also on "the village church."[36] One Dakota clergyman saw his ministry as providing the "mortar for the foundations for future generations."[37]

Churches also acted as centers of community activity where settlers worshipped together and socialized.[38] By encouraging community inter-action and dedication to principles higher than personal self-interest, the churches reinforced key ingredients of republicanism. Frederick Luebke concluded that churches on the plains "frequently provided the nucleus of ethnic life and functioned as substitutes for the array of social and cultural societies that were available in urban centers."[39] Most Dakota settlers carried on their lives, in word, deed, or physical location, within the orbit of this religious nucleus.

Preserving the social order involved regulating such social vices as drinking and gambling and promoting "decorum, decency, and morality," according to Louis B. Wright. "Christian folk" in the West did their best to maintain "standards of morality in the hinterland." Churches served as "moral courts" that sought to enforce a code of conduct and generally reduce the problem of "license and lawlessness" in an area where legal institutions were still developing. By promoting civilization in the form of schooling and manners, "churches labored persistently on the side of the angels of cultural light"; their success, Wright concluded, "was far greater than cynics have been willing to admit." The Christian churches in the West "always fought to re-establish traditional civilization and their conservatism usually prevailed."[40] Christian ministers promoted a stable social and moral structure in a foreign and forbidding land. The Christian church, Avery O. Craven once explained, "gave a conservative touch to an otherwise unsteady order."[41] John Newton McLoney, product of an Ohio and Iowa upbringing and of an education at Grinnell College and Yale seminary and a veteran of preaching in Maine, was the minister of First Congregational Church in Sioux Falls from 1879 to 1884. His words were "strength to the weak-hearted, restraint upon the wayward, edifying to any whose faith needed support, comforting to the down-cast," and they led "careless or skeptical minds to the contemplation of eternal things and human duty and human destiny."[42]

By the time of the Great Dakota Boom, of course, the unity of Chris-tendom had long since ended. The Christian Church had divided into multiple denominations with distinct theological traditions, and the tendency toward division and subdivision accelerated in the Midwest during the nineteenth century. The united Lutheran church of Europe, for example, splintered into twenty-one different synods in the United States.[43] Because of the existence of multiple Christian churches and the strong commitment to them, interdenominational friction was inevitable, especially between Catholics, who represented the unified European Christian church of old, and Protestants, who began the revolt against the old regime. The friction between Catholics and Protestants demonstrates the passionate commitment to religion in Dakota Territory and in the rural Midwest in general. The settlers cared enough about religion to quarrel over theological distinctions that have since lost much of their significance. Protestant-Catholic tensions also underscore the potency of the republican tradition, for many Protestants feared that Catholics were a threat to republican government. They believed that Catholic commitments to papal pronouncements and an old European institution allied with oppressive monarchies were inimical to the American republican tradition of independent citizenship and self-rule and that the Catholic presence threatened the unity of the commonwealth. American Catholics, in turn, often responded to these suspicions by trying to demonstrate their commitment to the American republican tradition.

Protestant-Catholic friction also highlights an exclusionary aspect of the republican order created in Dakota Territory. The republicanism embraced by Dakota settlers included many of the virtues of the American democratic tradition, but it also conferred social privileges on Protestants, who tended to dominate Dakota politics. The Anglo-American Protestant majority in Dakota was certainly viewed as the natural holder of political authority. This majority took few formal steps to marginalize minority groups, often welcomed immigrants, and held a vision of republicanism that was generally expansive, but an element of social exclusivity could be found in territorial affairs.

In the political leadership of Dakota Territory, two religious denominations stand out, highlighting the influence of the English heritage. The Congregationalists and Episcopalians who migrated to Dakota Territory were the descendents, respectively, of the Puritan settlers of New England

and the Anglican settlers of Virginia, who once battled each another in England during the English civil wars.[44] Lynwood Oyos describes the leaders of the Episcopal and Congregational churches in the two decades prior to statehood as representative of Dakota Territory's "dominant Yankee Protestant heritage."[45] The upstart Sioux Falls politician Richard Pettigrew pointed to the power of these churches when he complained about the "ring" of political leaders associated with the "Episcopal and Congregational caucuses."[46]

In his magisterial work *Albion's Seed*, David Hackett Fischer traces the migrations of four English subcultures or "folkways" to America, including the Puritan transplantation from East Anglia to New England.[47] These New England Puritans built their communities around the Congregational church, and the influence of the descendents of these New England Yankee Congregationalists could be readily detected in Dakota Territory. The first Congregational church in Yankton "looked as if it belonged on a New Hampshire common"; its "New England frame structure, with clapboard sides, gabled roof, and modest steeple" conformed to a design that came to be known as "prairie Gothic."[48] By 1888 there were two hundred Congregational churches in Dakota Territory, and the Congregational Conference circulated news of the church's progress in *The Pilgrim Herald*.[49] During his work with the Sioux, Congregational missionary Stephen Riggs translated the Bible and John Bunyan's *Pilgrim's Progress*, which first appeared in the 1670s, into the Sioux language.[50]

Dakota Congregationalists were active in politics. One of the most influential figures of the formative years of Dakota Territory was the Congregational minister Joseph Ward, who "maintained a close New England connection" while becoming known as "the father of Congregationalism" in Dakota.[51] Like many of the Yankee-Unionist-Protestant founders of Dakota, Ward was a Civil War veteran and a graduate of Phillips Academy in Andover, Massachusetts, Brown University, and Andover's Theological Seminary.[52] In 1879, when he helped launch the movement for Dakota statehood, the principal leaders were members of Ward's First Congregational Church and were designated "latter-day Pilgrims" by one historian.[53] In the early years of statehood, one minister noted with pride the election of Congregationalists to political office. He added that

"South Dakota churches exert a wholesome, persistent influence upon our public life" and lauded the "growing tendency to elect Christians of high morals to our federal and state offices."[54] One of the two U.S. senators chosen from the new state of South Dakota was James Kyle, a Congregational minister from Aberdeen who graduated from Congregationalist Oberlin College in 1878, studied law, attended the Western Theological Seminary, and entered the ministry in 1882. He moved to Dakota Territory in 1885 to become a pastor at Ipswich, a prominent jumping-off point for Dakota settlers, and then moved to Aberdeen in 1889 to serve as pastor at Plymouth Congregational Church.[55] When the prominent statehood proponent Bartlett Tripp died, his eulogist praised his ancestors, who helped form the "Pilgrim and Puritan migration," and his worthy and prayerful Congregationalist childhood in Maine, which "consecrated him to good citizenship and noble manhood."[56]

The Episcopalians were as prominent in Dakota Territory as the Congregationalists. When the Episcopalians established their first church, the same year Dakota Territory was established, they immodestly called it the "Mother Church of the Dakotas."[57] The church's founder, the Reverend Melancthon Hoyt, traced his lineage back to Simon Hoyt, who migrated from England to Salem, Massachusetts, in 1628. Born in Connecticut in 1809, Reverend Hoyt attended Yale University, was a member of the first graduating class of Yale Theological College, and then quickly began his work building churches in the West.[58] Hoyt and other Episcopalians were active in politics and civic affairs in Dakota. The historian Herbert T. Hoover argues that the members of the Episcopalian church in Dakota Territory "became as much a political caucus as a religious group."[59] Howard Lamar similarly noted that a "large number of the leading figures in Dakota were Episcopalian."[60] Historians believe a notorious defrauder of Indians was found innocent of corruption charges due to his connections to the influential Episcopal church in Dakota.[61] President Grant's "peace policy" toward Native Americans allowed the Episcopal church to appoint many Indian agents.[62] Hoover notes that this appointment "privilege brought enormous economic benefits to Episcopal caucus leaders and their friends at Yankton," since by "far the best full-time jobs in the territory existed at Indian agency jurisdictions."[63]

The Episcopalians also had important supporters on the national level. John Jacob Astor funded the construction of Calvary Cathedral in Sioux Falls, which displayed pieces from three historic crosses, including ones carried by William the Conqueror and Richard the Lion-Hearted.[64]

In addition to old-stock American settlers who were members of the Congregational and Episcopalian churches, Dakota Territory also saw a large influx of foreign-born Scandinavians who were dedicated to the Lutheran church. One poem dubbed the God-fearing Norwegian emigrants "Viking Abrahams" who had "left the fjords and mountain scenes behind" to settle on the Dakota prairie.[65] O. E. Rolvaag described these Norwegian settlers as "strongly inclined toward religion."[66] The "America letters" they mailed back to Norway included powerful expressions of their continuing piety.[67] A Norwegian Lutheran minister in Renner instructed young people "in the Norwegian language, and they committed to memory, more or less thoroughly, Luther's Catechism."[68] At the turn of the century, 55 percent of South Dakotans were foreign-born or were the children of foreign-born parents, and many of these immigrants were Scandinavians who held tightly to their cultural heritage.[69] Old World religious customs and sanctions persisted on the prairie.[70] Norwegian Lutherans maintained a solidarity and cultural unity in America that stemmed from their origins in Norway's "self-enclosed rural enclaves where shared values had reinforced and perpetuated a common life style."[71] The most powerful influence on Norwegian culture was the "stern, pervasive Protestantism of the state church."[72]

Old World Lutheran unity did not persist on the prairie, however. Lutherans divided into synods organized along ethnic and theological lines. Some Norwegians, for example, joined the Eielsen Synod, which promoted lay preaching and questioned the hierarchical organization of the Lutheran church.[73] More Norwegians affiliated with Hauge's Synod, which stressed the "importance of small groups of Lutheran Christians meeting for prayer and edification by hearing and studying the Bible and Bible-based books."[74] The Norwegian Synod, the largest Lutheran sect nationally, split in the 1880s over the issue of predestination. At least eighteen South Dakota congregations left the Norwegian Synod to join the Anti-Missourians in the 1880s. The Anti-Missourians then joined the

Norwegian-Danish Conference and the Norwegian Augustana Synod to form the United Norwegian Lutheran Church in America. German immigrants to Dakota Territory joined the Iowa, Ohio, Missouri, and Wisconsin synods.[75]

The rebellions and cleavages within the Lutheran church reveal the hold of religion on the lives of the settlers and the earnestness with which they debated theological matters. According to one study, the differences between Lutheran synods generated intense debates among early Dakotans, and the "religious and theological discussions in pioneer homes sometimes became quite involved and lengthy, lasting far into the night." These discussions included the doctrinal foundations of Christianity: "Which Precedes in Christian Experience, Repentance or Faith?" "Faith or Works, Order of Precedence and Relative Worth"; "Can a Man of His Own Accord and Strength Repent?" "Can a Christian in This Life Be Wholly Sanctified?" "Free Will or Predestination?" One Lutheran settler remembered that "because of differences of religious beliefs, debate and discussions were not infrequent and sometimes lacked the Christian spirit of tolerance and grace."[76]

Lutheran ministers had great influence in their communities and often preached strong messages. The first priority of many Norwegian immigrants was finding a pastor to preach the Word and bring spiritual order to their new lives on the prairie.[77] The Lutheran pastor was often the most educated person in a settlement and a revered source of moral authority; "he and the immigrant church tended to awaken and foster the nationality and consciousness of the immigrant settlers."[78] Pastors led their congregations in the singing of such rousing hymns as "A Mighty Fortress Is Our God." Written by Martin Luther, the hymn proclaimed that standing alone in the world was "losing," but with the Lord, one "wins the victory in every field of battle."[79] Other Norwegian hymns, such as "Lord, Bestow on Us Thy Every Blessing," simply asked for God to be with the Dakota pioneers:

> Lord, bestow on us Thy blessing
> Let Thy face upon us shine;
> May we all, Thy grace possessing

Walk within Thy light divine.

Come and visit every heart

And They peace to us impart.

Father, Son, and Spirit hear us

Be Thou now and ever near us.[80]

The large population of Norwegian immigrants was outnumbered by the German immigrants, who were also denominationally splintered. Both Germans from Germany proper and Germans who farmed in Russia immigrated to Dakota and were "highly religious," according to Howard Lamar.[81] The Germans from Germany tended to be divided between Catholic and Protestant faiths, the former from the south and from the Rhineland and the latter, mostly Lutherans, from the north.[82] Denominational divisions between Protestant Germans were on display in the small town of Tolstoy (named by Germans from Russia), home to German Lutheran, Congregational, Methodist, Baptist, and Adventist churches.[83] Whatever their denominational affiliation, the immigrants' dedication to their churches and their contemplation of the Christian Heaven attest to the salience of religion in their lives. A hymn sung by German Catholic pioneers at funerals in Dakota Territory reflects the pioneers' attentiveness to the next world:

Why are you weeping, friends and brothers?

We will see each other again,

On the day of the Last Judgment.

Fear only God and nothing else,

And nothing else.[84]

The prominence of Protestantism among the Dakota settlers from the Midwest and New England and among European immigrants evidences the subordinate role of Catholics in Dakota Territory and, more generally, serves as a reminder of the exclusionary aspects of the Protestant republican political order. Following the surge of Catholic immigration to the United States in the mid-nineteenth century, American Catholics were increasingly scrutinized for their alleged foreign loyalties. Nativist and anti-Catholic sentiment escalated during the 1850s, the decade prior to the establishment of Dakota Territory. The outbreak of the Civil War, occurring the year Dakota Territory was formally created, momentarily refocused American politics, but concerns about Catholicism persisted. Northern abolitionists, in addition to advancing the anti-slavery cause, were often anti-Catholic, a tendency reinforced by a papal tilt toward the Confederacy. Republicans viewed Catholics as their "primary enemy in the North" and tended to place Southern rebels and Catholics in the same threatening category.[85] John McGreevy notes that the "idea that American Catholics, like southern Confederates, threatened the foundations of the nation-state became a truism in some religious and intellectual circles."[86] The Civil War only heightened religious zeal. During the Civil War, for example, Congress voted to put "In God We Trust" on the nation's coins.[87] "To the cultural leaders of the North," according to one study, "the Civil War was a holy war."[88]

During the critical years of Dakota Territory's development, anti-Catholic sentiment flourished in the nation at large. In 1875 Republican president U.S. Grant, the former Union war hero and a one-time nativist Know-Nothing, stoked the fires of anti-Catholicism during a famous reunion speech to veterans of the Army of the Tennessee in Des Moines. Grant's speech condemned aid to "sectarian" education, a term commonly understood to mean Catholic schools.[89] After the speech, some Catholics worried that Grant was beginning "what Bismarck and his friends are trying to do against us in Europe," and some feared that the president had "inaugurated a Kulturkampf."[90] Republicans subsequently used a "national campaign of anti-Catholic bigotry" against the Democratic Party, home to most Catholics, as the political effectiveness of waving the bloody shirt of the Civil War waned.[91] Sparked by Grant and fueled by other lesser spokesmen, a "surge of anti-Catholic sentiment" ensued in the 1870s and 1880s.[92] By the 1880s, according to one prominent analysis, religious conflict had precipitated a "crisis in Protestant-Catholic relations."[93]

While the boom era in Dakota coincided with a resurgence of anti-Catholicism in American politics, the general phenomenon dates back to the Reformation of the sixteenth century. When Protestants began to break away from the Christian Church headquartered in Rome, they published derisive critiques of Roman Catholicism. The ensuing religious wars between Protestants and Catholics in Europe only deepened the sectarian divide. The English who settled North America were primarily Protestant, and they trumpeted their break with Roman Europe and continued to denounce what they saw as the corruption, tyranny, and anti-republican tendencies of Catholicism. "The settlers who came to America," Ray Allen Billington noted, "carried with them to the new land the same hatred of Popery which characterized the England of that day," and these attitudes "intensified" in the colonial hinterlands.[94] As more Catholics migrated to the United States, the majority Protestant population feared that they would be disloyal and attempt to reassert Roman control over the new American republic.[95] At the time Dakota Territory was settled, renewed religious conflict in Europe brought another "influx of refugees from Europe's quarrels to America."[96] Germans, for example, who became the largest foreign-born population in Dakota, were deeply divided by Chancellor Bismarck's Kulturkampf against the Catholic Church in Germany.[97] The first Catholic bishop of South Dakota, Martin Marty, was forced to leave his native Switzerland when Protestants took over his Jesuit high school, during which incident "Marty was able to see the smoke of cannons and hear the sounds of gunfire."[98] The ouster of the Jesuits from Switzerland marked the beginning of religious conflicts that convulsed late-nineteenth-century Europe.[99]

As Dakota approached statehood in the 1880s, a nativist revival was fully under way and was particularly strong in the Dakota pioneers' places of origin. John Higham found that the fears of a papal-led takeover of the United States were strongest in "Midwestern rural areas."[100] In Iowa, which sent many settlers to Dakota Territory, the American Protective Association was formed in 1887. The anti-Catholic APA, Higham noted, "absorbed many of the other nativist societies which had sprouted in the eighties and dominated the gaudiest wave of religious nativism in fifty years"; it was also influential in Nebraska and Minnesota and would ultimately claim 3,000 members in the state of South Dakota.[101] The governor of Nebraska and a U.S. senator from Minnesota were informed that arms were allegedly being shipped to priests in Michigan and Nebraska in coffins or in boxes labeled "holy wine."[102] In preparation for a rumored Catholic assault, one "rural schoolteacher in Minnesota went about heavily armed for weeks to defend himself against the anticipated massacre."[103]

The instigation of political Populism in the late nineteenth century also involved a strain of anti-Catholicism. Some Populists correlated the centralized authority of the Catholic Church with the power of centralized economic monopolies.[104] As the organizational structures of the later Populist movement began to congeal in the late 1880s, an anti-Catholic movement emerged that was "tinged with more hysteria and suffused with a deeper nativism than the religious friction of the mid-seventies."[105] Populism would derive energy from Protestant evangelism.[106]

As noted earlier, the settling of Dakota Territory also coincided with a large influx of Scandinavian Lutherans, many of whom held anti-Catholic views.[107] Catholic bishop Martin Marty nervously wrote in 1885 that "Swedes and Norwegians are arriving like armies."[108] In his study of nativism, John Higham noted that anti-Catholic "sentiment throve among foreign-born Protestants from . . . Scandinavia" who particularly "hated the Irish," an ethnic group known for its loyalties to Catholicism.[109] The Irish reputation for unruliness surely grew as rumors spread of an Irish Catholic invasion of British Canada to be launched from Dakota Territory.[110] Just after statehood, an anonymous circular entitled "A Terrible Discovery! A Catholic Conspiracy!" was written in "Scandinavian and scattered over the state" of South Dakota. The circular denounced Bishop Marty's support for U.S. Senator Richard Pettigrew and equated a vote for Pettigrew with "a vote for Catholics and for Catholic supremacy in America."[111]

In 1883, the year Dakotans wrote their first constitution, American Lutherans celebrated the four hundredth anniversary of Martin Luther's birth.[112] Luther had deemed the pope a "bloodthirsty, unclean, blasphemic whore of the devil" and helped write "history" books that, among other lurid tales, described the piling of six thousand children's heads in a nunnery fish pond during the reign of Pope Gregory I.[113] In O. E. Rolvaag's novel *Peder Victorious*, the famous character Beret fights to preserve her family's Norwegian heritage on the Dakota prairie and castigates her son Peder for fraternizing with Irish Catholics, "those people" of another, "dangerous" faith. Another Norwegian settler in *Peder Victorious* insists "that before he'd let any of his marry a Catholic he'd see him buried alive!" The prospect of such a wedding causes a "terrible rumpus" and "awful commotion" in the settlement. Beret denounces the "wickedness" of Peder's consorting with an Irish Catholic girl and tells him, "If the day should come that you get yourself mixed up with the Irish, then you will have lost your mother—that I could not live through!" Beret declares, "You can't mix wheat and potatoes in the same bin."[114]

Reflecting such sentiments, Protestants tended to hold the positions of power in Dakota Territory. Seeming a bit overwhelmed, Bishop Martin Marty wrote in 1885 of the "protestant sects" whose "number is legion."[115] Catholics in Dakota tended to be "rural people," while many Protestants came from established communities in the Midwest, understood the workings of territorial government, generally ran the business enterprises on small-town Main Streets, and "naturally became leaders in the different settlements."[116] Howard Lamar noted that the leaders of the statehood movement tended to be "Protestant" and of "Old American" origin.[117] Gary Olson has similarly concluded that Yankee settlers "were perhaps more important than all the others in shaping the cultural patterns and institutions" of Dakota and that these patterns were the result of "the essential transplanting of New England's political, economic and social values and ways of doing things."[118] Lynwood Oyos notes that "Yankee merchants" and "members of the Eastern establishment . . . became the Territory's politicians, educators and cultural advocates"; for example, Dakota "Congregationalists brought with them their New England Puritan heritage."[119] In subsequent decades, social and economic life in the Dakotas continued to be strongly influenced by men who tended to be "Yankee or Scandinavian, Protestant, and Republican."[120]

Fraternal orders with an anti-Catholic history were also influential in Dakota territorial politics during the late nineteenth century, the "golden age of fraternity."[121] The Masons, known to be a "wholly middle-class, Anglo/Nordic, Protestant organization," were especially influential in Dakota Territory.[122] The first Masonic lodge in southern Dakota was organized in Yankton in 1862 on the second floor of the capitol, where it held meetings close to the territory's levers of power. The Reverend

Melancthon Hoyt, the first Master Mason of the lodge, was an Episcopal minister generally regarded as the "father of the early Episcopal
Church in Dakota Territory."[123] In 1881, George Hand, the Grand Master
of the South Dakota Masons and a leader in the constitutional conventions, praised those who "gather around this altar, with hearts and hands
intent upon building up in this new land the great moral temple of Free-
masonry." Masonic camaraderie could be exclusive, however. As John
Higham noted, "Masonic lodges, being tinged by an anti-Catholic heritage," provided a number of members for anti-Catholic groups in the late
nineteenth century.[124]

Prominent political issues in Dakota Territory also caused Catholic-
Protestant friction. Catholics tended to be less supportive of prohibition,
for example, which caused conflicts between some Protestant groups and
Catholics.[125] Protestant temperance advocates targeted imbibers in general, but the movement also carried obvious "anti-Irish overtones, given
the common association of Irish and whiskey."[126] By the 1880s it was
"quite evident that an aggressive temperance sentiment pervaded all
parties" in Dakota Territory.[127] Only a few counties failed to ban liquor
sales under a local-option law, and a prohibition statute was adopted by
territory-wide vote in 1889.[128] One minister, speaking to a crowd in Yankton, reportedly "consigned the German population of the place to the bot-
tomless pit for its stand against prohibition." In another speech against the
"liquor traffic," this one made before German immigrants many of whom
were Catholic, the minister exclaimed, "Ye dogs, ye vipers—that's what
our Savior called such cattle as you are when He was upon the earth."[129]
One Dakotan who wrote to Bishop Marty accused him of "selling liquor"
and warned that he was "liable to be arrested" for such activities.[130] While
the territorial Episcopalian bishop William Hobart Hare supported, as a
concession to Catholics, an exemption for sacramental alcohol in prohibition legislation, the Methodists, the State Prohibition League, and the
Woman's Christian Temperance Union opposed such a waiver. A leading Methodist minister in Dakota rejected the exemption's obeisance to
Catholic tradition: "I would also suggest that it might not be an unpardon-
able sin in this age of advanced light to differ 'from the customs of the
Catholic Church.'" The minister denounced bringing the "cup of death"

and the "monstrous evil" of alcohol to church "altars."[131] The Congregationalists and Scandinavian immigrants similarly supported prohibition, and the establishment Masons opposed drinking until the 1930s.[132] The issue of prohibition would also prove to be a divisive issue during the constitutional debates in Dakota Territory.

Education proved another source of social friction. Late-nineteenth-century conflicts over schooling in national politics paralleled developments in Dakota, where matters of religion and education intertwined. Dakota immigration commissioner P. F. McClure said that the "interest displayed in educational matters is always an index of the religious and moral culture of a community"; in Dakota, he continued, churches and schools "occupy the first cares of every new community."[133] Education, unlike any other issue, according to John McGreevy, "quickly generated both anti-Catholicism and Catholic belligerence, and at the state and local levels debates over education blazed their way through electoral politics."[134]

In the 1870s, schools became a prominent issue for the Republican Party at the national level. Republicans planned to use an expanded public school system to remake the defeated South and to promote a generic Protestantism by ensuring that "sectarian" schools (understood as Catholic) did not tap public coffers.[135] President Grant made a vigorous commitment in 1875 to withhold public aid from "sectarian" schools, and Speaker of the House James G. Blaine took up the cause by touting a national constitutional amendment to that effect.[136] Blaine "fully appreciated the wide political appeal of the nativist and anti-Catholic rhetoric that accompanied the President's proposal."[137] *The Nation*, which favored the Blaine amendment, noted that it was designed for use in a "campaign to catch anti-Catholic votes."[138] In his election campaign for the governorship of Ohio in 1875, Rutherford B. Hayes instructed his staff to keep "the Catholic question" front and center and informed Blaine of the electoral advantages this strategy produced.[139] In keeping with these political currents, anti-sectarian school funding provisions were included in the Dakota constitutions written during the 1880s.

Support for Blaine, who hoped his campaign against sectarian schools would propel his bid for the presidency, was strong in Dakota Territory.

George Kingsbury, a well-known civic leader and territorial newspaperman, thought James Blaine "a great leader and an able statesmen." The 1884 Dakota convention of the Republican Party, the territory's dominant party, supported Blaine, and there was "no dissension on that score."[140] When choosing a representative to attend the national Republican convention, "delegates were instructed to vote for Blaine."[141] Most of the Republican delegates at the 1888 convention also supported Blaine: "The convention was stirred to wild enthusiasm by the speaker's reference to prominent presidential candidates, and especially by the name of Blaine."[142] In 1889, the year statehood was achieved, a new national organization sought to revive the Blaine amendment.[143] At a Republican convention held in Aberdeen in 1892, the attendees once again nominated Blaine. Edwin Torrey recalled the critical moment: "It was then that a leather lunged pest in the gallery broke up the meeting. 'Nominate Blaine!' he yelled. Nearly every man in the hall was at heart a Blaine man, though for expediency's sake he had kept his sentiment to himself. 'Nominate Blaine' was a blast upon the bugle worth a thousand men. It was all over in a minute more. Blaine was nominated by acclamation, and the audience melted away midst shrieks and laughter."[144]

The Blaine boomlet, the burst of anti-Catholicism nationally, and the intense criticism of sectarian education all occurred at the same time as the Catholic population in Dakota Territory was growing most rapidly and Catholic schools were being built. In 1879, when Martin Marty became prefector apostolic of Dakota Territory, a precursor to being named bishop, there were twenty Catholic churches and twelve priests in Dakota.[145] In 1884, when the Great Dakota Boom was fully underway, Marty reported that he oversaw eighty-two churches and forty-five priests.[146] During this period, the Catholic Church encouraged its priests and parishioners to build Catholic schools, and by 1885 one publication noted the existence of "many parochial schools of the Catholic Church" in Dakota Territory.[147] When Marty departed South Dakota in the early 1890s, he left behind Catholic churches, sixty-eight priests, and "many Catholic schools."[148] Six Catholic hospitals and several Catholic high schools were also founded, and the Benedictine, Mercy, St. Joseph, St. Vincent DePaul, Presentation, and St. Francis sisters established orders in the state.[149] By the early twentieth century, there were 79,000 Catholics, 177 Catholic churches, eighty-two priests, forty-four elementary schools, and eight Catholic high schools in the state of South Dakota.[150]

Part of the impetus for the organization of Catholic schools was the strong Protestant imprint on the public or common schools. One study highlighted the influence of the New England "Puritan forefathers" on education policy in Dakota and the creation of the territory's "common schools." Just as the "colonists fashioned their schools upon old English patterns," the "pioneers of Dakota, too, outlined their system after those of eastern states, for they had known no other contact with school organization." The author noted the "similarity between New England and Dakota by reference to outstanding men" and compared the organizers of Dakota schools to "Edwards, Mather, Cheever, Poymont, Lancaster, Phillips, Barnard, and Mann."[151] General William Beadle, the undisputed leader of the common school movement in South Dakota, was a Michigander, a Mason, a Republican, a Union war veteran, and a member of Joseph Ward's influential Congregational Church in Yankton, which carried on the tradition of New England Puritanism in Dakota.[152] While serving as education superintendent, Beadle advocated the New England township system for schools.[153]

Early education statutes also underscored the efforts of old-stock American leaders to maintain their linguistic dominance. The territorial legislature adopted a provision in 1879 stating that "no district money was to go to any school where the English language was not the exclusive language taught."[154] Two years later, the legislature passed a modified law preventing schools from teaching in any language other than English for more than one hour a day.[155] In the late 1880s, Wisconsin and Illinois enacted complete bans on instruction in any foreign language, angering many German immigrants.[156] Such prohibitions were designed to "harass sectarian schools which often provided instruction to immigrant communities in their native language."[157] While German and Norwegian immigrants were generally welcomed to Dakota Territory, Yankees and midwesterners expected them to speak English.[158]

Catholic leaders in Dakota Territory advocated the building of Catholic schools in part to avoid the Protestant-dominated education system.

With the exception of some Lutheran and Episcopalian elementary schools, "most Protestants were content to let the Territory shoulder the financial burden of elementary education," while "Catholic communities definitely wanted a religion-oriented education for their children."[159] The Councils of Baltimore, which Bishop Marty attended in 1884, encouraged the publication of Catholic newspapers and books and also made Catholic education mandatory for Catholic children.[160] A Catholic pastoral letter emphasized that it was not "desirable or advantageous that religion should be excluded from the school" and promoted the opening of Catholic schools.[161] Catholics faced the threat of excommunication for not sending their children to Catholic schools.[162]

To the chagrin of Catholics, Protestant ministers in South Dakota were often the strongest proponents of public schools and often served as teachers and administrators within the school system.[163] The strong Protestant influence in public school policy caused concern among some Catholics and "intensified the belief among Catholic immigrants that the government and the public schools were Protestant dominated"; as a result, among Catholic settlers' collective priorities, the "erection of parish schools was second only to that of building a house of worship."[164] Bishop Marty advised priests that "to keep up and propagate a good spirit, you ought to have at least one Catholic school in the district."[165] Territorial statutes also forced common schools to adopt the Protestant-leaning McGuffey textbooks, and "no other text-books could be lawfully used" without specific permission from the territorial superintendent.[166] Such textbooks, according to one study, had been known for their "strong and universal" anti-Catholic sentiments.[167]

Conflict over education stemmed in part from the Bible battles of the late nineteenth century, which found parallels in Dakota. In 1869 a non-Protestant majority on the Cincinnati school board voted to abandon Bible reading in classrooms, triggering a "national upheaval" and an "anti-Catholic media frenzy" that helped spur the large-scale "anti-Catholic movement" of the era.[168] Similarly, when Boss Tweed secured partial public funding for Catholic schools in New York, Protestants demanded that public aid to sectarian education be banned and that sectarian teaching in public schools be prohibited, but that the Protestant tradition of Bible reading was not to be considered sectarian. One prominent Presbyterian minister in Dakota Territory denounced the "schemes the Romanists engineer through the New York legislature."[169] In 1872 Iowa and Illinois, whose constitutions provided guidance to Dakota's constitutional drafters, amended their constitutions to prohibit public funds from being spent on sectarian education.[170] Missouri, Alabama, and North Carolina adopted similar constitutional prohibitions.[171] In 1875 prominent Republican politicians including U.S. Grant, Rutherford Hayes, James Garfield, and James Blaine called for a ban on aid to sectarian schools and generally sought to exploit anti-Catholic animus.[172] The following year, Congress required that Colorado Territory adopt a constitutional ban on aid to sectarian schools in order to gain entry into the Union and required similar "anti-sectarian boilerplate" for all subsequent states, including the Dakotas.[173] Congressional leaders also had strong reservations about the admission of New Mexico, then considered a "Catholic land" occupied by a "Catholic people."[174] Some critics in the 1870s feared that Catholics were taking over the schools in New Mexico and demanded that officials "outlaw any sectarian influence in the public schools."[175] When South Dakota was admitted to the Union in 1889, Congress still refused to admit New Mexico due to its Spanish Catholic heritage and because "its attitude towards the American system of free schools was more or less uncertain."[176]

The laws governing public schools in Dakota Territory similarly reflected Protestant concern about the influence of Catholicism on education. The territorial assembly passed a law in 1883 guaranteeing that Protestant activities such as Bible reading would not be considered a "sectarian" activity and would not, therefore, be excluded from the common schools.[177] The 1887 territorial code included similar provisions prohibiting "sectarian" activities in schools but exempting Bible reading.[178] Dakota legislators' specific designation of Bible reading as a "non-sectarian" activity indicated their Protestant proclivities and their support for a "generalized Protestant morality," which they did not consider sectarian.[179] Richard Baer has explained that Catholics did not distinguish between Bible reading and "sectarian" activities: "For Catholics, who were not in favor of individual interpretation of Scripture, the simple reading of Scripture (especially from the King James Version) commonly practiced in the 'public' schools was anything but a religiously neutral activity. It was an establishment of a majority's religion against a minority's."[180] Horace Mann, for example, a leading advocate of the common schools during the early nineteenth century, did not think his own generic Protestantism "sectarian": "He fervently believed that religion should be taught in the compulsory common schools, but it should be of a nonsectarian variety—a religion that he thought was common to all Christians, but that, when all was said and done, looked almost identical to his own Unitarianism."[181]

During the final adoption of the Dakota constitution, the *Dakota Catholic* decried the "anti-Catholic" tendencies of public schools and concluded, "Too often 'freedom from sectarian control' in our public schools, practically is made to mean the careful exclusion of every thing Catholic."[182] The first constitution drafted for South Dakota in 1883 barred funding for "sectarian" schools, as did the subsequent drafts in 1885 and 1889. The 1889 federal Enabling Act creating the Dakotas also required the new state to create "a system of public schools, which should be open to all children and free from sectarian control."[183] Senator Henry Blair of New Hampshire saw the act as completing the unfinished work of the failed Blaine amendment.[184] When Blair had earlier sought federal legislation similar to the Blaine amendment and it had failed, he blamed Jesuit priests, whom he deemed a "Black Legion" and an "enemy of this country" whose goal was "destroying the public school system."[185] When Congress passed the Enabling Act, Senator Blair saw the law's ban on public aid to sectarian schools as the "very essence" of the Blaine amendment.[186]

Exclusionary attitudes toward Catholics in Dakota Territory could also be detected in the debates at the constitutional conventions of the 1880s. The individuals who gave the opening prayers during the days of the 1883 convention in Sioux Falls are revealing. Invocations were given by Congregational, Episcopalian, Presbyterian, Methodist, and Reformed Church ministers, but none were given by Catholic priests.[187] During the debates over taxation during the 1885 constitutional convention, some delegates were concerned about exempting church property because it might aid the Catholic Church. John D. Hicks noted that certain "delegates declared that the only reason why the customary exemption was opposed was an unworthy desire to cripple the Roman Catholic Church."[188] One delegate conceded that the Catholic Church had "a good deal of property" but asked delegates to "divest yourselves of all prejudice" on the matter.[189] Another delegate advocated a "liberal exemption" for church property despite the fact that the Catholic church might benefit.[190] President Grant also helped popularize the taxation of church property during his 1875 anti-sectarian school speech in Des Moines. According to Ward McAfee, the measure was "popular with those who assumed that the Roman Catholic church would suffer the most under taxation."[191] Philip Hamburger notes that Grant used this "anti-Catholic" taxation proposal to "stir the basest passions of his fellow Americans."[192] Despite minor rumblings in the Dakota constitutional conventions about the taxation of Catholic church property, however, no action was taken.

Late-nineteenth-century federal Indian policy also sparked conflict among the leading religious figures in Dakota Territory, and these disputes were fueled by fear of Catholic influence. In keeping with President Grant's "peace policy" toward the Indians, various Sioux reservations were assigned to particular religious denominations that would appoint missionaries to serve as administrators. In Dakota Territory, reservations were allotted to the Episcopalians, the Catholics, and a joint Congregational-Presbyterian organization. Presbyterian records indicate a willingness to cooperate with fellow Protestants such as the Congregationalists, but "Roman Catholics were mentioned only as 'Romanist' opponents."[193] When Catholic bishop Marty visited the Pine Ridge and Rosebud reservations to conduct missionary work, "Episcopalians working under Bishop William Hobart Hare would get federal officials to run him out, but he would return in secret."[194] One study concludes that the "conflict between the Protestant mission groups and the Roman Catholics was nothing less than flagrant bigotry."[195] Another account notes that, during the missionary work on reservations in the 1880s, "there was no spirit of ecumenism [among religious groups], especially not with Catholics."[196] Bishop Marty "faced and participated in vigorous, sometimes vicious, interdenominational competition for souls in Sioux

Country."[197] Catholic missionary efforts at Sisseton and Flandreau, for example, "were stifled by competition from Congregational ministers and Episcopalian priests."[198]

After the failure of Grant's "peace policy," the federal government directly funded Indian schools, many of which were run by Catholics, further arousing Protestant anger.[199] Bishop Marty concluded that, unlike the Protestant Indian schools, the Catholic schools had been successful and that therefore the federal government would be willing to provide additional funds if the schools could be expanded to other reservations.[200] When criticizing the federal aid given to "Roman Catholic schools" on the Pine Ridge reservation in Dakota, opponents deemed them "sectarian bodies" and called for "Congress to prohibit the further use of Indian trust funds for sectarian schools." Opponents found the federal government's contracts with "sectarian" schools "grossly inequitable" and specifically highlighted aid to Catholic schools in the Dakotas.[201] When reporting on the dispute over federal spending on "sectarian schools," the *Washington Post* cited funds provided to the Catholic Church.[202]

In defending Catholic-run Indian schools, the *Catholic Sentinel* feared Indian children would otherwise be sent to government schools that "are often bitterly anti-Catholic" and subject to "Protestant Propaganda."[203] Another account of the battle over the funding of Indian schools concluded in 1902 that "bigotry was at the root of the propaganda against sectarian Indian schools, although it masqueraded under the guise of patriotism and deep concern for the preservation of the principle of 'separation of Church and State.'"[204] Bishop Marty complained in 1885 that "Protestant missionaries in the west are amply and gloriously supported by their coreligionists in the East," while "Catholics can not ever get the surplus of our rich Catholics on reasonable interest."[205] In 1891 Marty wrote to a bishop with the Bureau of Catholic Indian Missions in Washington that he was busy "defending our Indian schools against the combined power and craft of Protestant church and State."[206]

Episcopalian bishop Hare, leader of one of the most politically powerful churches in Dakota Territory, led criticism of the federal Indian funds being spent on Catholic schools, and his protests triggered much of the national reporting and commentary.[207] Bishop Hare believed that these funds were being "abused" and were used to promote the "aggrandizement of Rome."[208] Hare, according Gerald Wolff, "harbored and nurtured special antipathy for the Roman Catholic Church."[209] Bishop Hare's personal papers include pamphlets of anti-Catholic groups that denounced "Popery" and "Romanism" and viewed the Catholic Church as an "un-American" institution whose rituals dated back to "barbaric times" and whose priests were "under the orders of a foreign superior." "The Catholic Church," the pamphlets declared, "is the persistent enemy of the American public school system."[210]

As an Episcopal bishop, Hare represented an eastern cultural heritage transplanted to Dakota Territory, and, unsurprisingly, he maintained a hostile attitude toward Catholics. His biographer describes him as the "best Anglican type" and an "English churchman of gentle breeding" who "sprang both from the New England Puritans and the Pennsylvania Friends whose beliefs and standards have played so important a part in the religious and political life of America." The Episcopalian Church, Hare said, had "put itself on the Protestant and not on the Roman side of the great line of cleavage" following the upheavals that beset Christendom in the sixteenth century. Hare's church stood against religious extremism, including the "excesses of Rome." Catholics, according to Hare, "huddle together in the dark, shut off from modern thought, cherishing dear but exploded theories and legends, reviving antiquated customs, and seeking to impose them as laws upon others, thus binding living men to-day in the cerements of the dead past."[211] Hare's views were in evidence when he learned that a Catholic priest had almost performed a Catholic service in an Episcopal church. Hare admitted that the "mere thought of a priest of Rome addressing the Virgin in prayer at the Cathedral altar [was] painful to me."[212]

Hare indicated his republican concerns in commenting on clippings that discussed "Catholicism" and "Jesuitism and the central rule of Rome," which could not "be the religion of the citizens of a free country."[213] He also saved clippings that referred to the "colossal usurpations of Papal tyranny" and quotations from William Gladstone criticizing "Papal Supremacy."[214] Gladstone's pamphlet criticizing "Catholicism as a formidable enemy," according to John McGreevy, became "hugely popular" in the late nineteenth century, and New York publishers rushed it into print.[215] Bishop Hare also collected the writings of the National League for the Protection of American Institutions, founded in 1889, which denounced aid to Catholic Indian schools and called for the revival of the Blaine amendment.[216] Despite his recurring clashes with the Catholic Church, Hare asked that evidence of interdenominational friction be "carefully excluded" from Doane Robinson's history of South Dakota, a fact that may explain why this social conflict has previously failed to become a prominent research topic in Dakota history.[217]

Religious and ethnic differences in Dakota Territory affected social life and such basic rituals as marriage. According to one account, Norwegian Lutheran "families were tight-knit and if a family member associated too closely with someone of another denomination or nationality it was very upsetting."[218] Ethnic or religious intermarriage was discouraged, and "pastors warned their flocks not to associate too closely with outside groups."[219] If a man asked a German farmer for his daughter's hand in marriage, one story had it, the "first count against the suitor was that he was an Irishman," one of the surest signs of Catholicism.[220] Despite their ethnic bond, Germans who adhered to differing Lutheran and Catholic faiths, according to Frederick Luebke, "would have remarkably little to do with each other."[221] For Germans and Norwegians, endogamy (marrying within one's own group) was the general rule. Catholics were also instructed not to marry "heathens, Jews, or members of any sect who are not at all or not validly baptized."[222] Catholics in Dakota Territory were also counseled to join Catholic fraternal orders such as the Knights of Columbus, to be skeptical of the rituals of such fraternal societies as the Masons, to send their children to Catholic schools, and to generally promote the Catholic faith.[223] Ethnic and religious clumping was common practice. As John Hudson has emphasized in his analysis of North Dakota, the "Dakota frontier was not a melting pot."[224] This ethnic and religious solidarity explains the origin of the old saw holding that a mixed marriage in the Dakotas was a union of a Catholic and a Lutheran.

Understanding the skepticism or outright hostility of Protestants and the influence of the American republican tradition, Bishop Martin Marty tended toward "liberal" Catholicism, or the molding of the Catholic

Church to fit American culture, institutions, and history. In 1889, on the centennial celebration of George Washington's inauguration, Bishop Marty explained that the Catholic Church's "highest authorities have repeatedly expressed their special admiration for our American republican forms, and despite the occasional whisper of malicious slander, the children of the Church stand foremost as the faithful supporters, as in the hour of danger they were the enthusiastic defenders of the American Republic." Marty thought it "most proper that Catholics take enthusiastic part in the coming Centennial celebration of the establishment of our constitutional government."[225] He instructed German Catholics in Dakota "to be proud preservers of their cultural heritage and linguistic proficiency," but he also urged them to become Americanized, use the English language, and embrace the "duties of citizenship."[226] Marty, according to one account, "was singularly successful in staying aloof from the rivalry then existing in the American Catholic Church between the Germans and the Irish, the so-called 'conservatives' and 'Americanizers.'"[227] During these years, Marty allied himself with the archbishop of St. Paul, John Ireland, who oversaw Dakota Territory and was the "foremost Catholic liberal of the late nineteenth century."[228] Marty, in short, sought to work within the established republican order and firmly professed American pragmatism: "The American is reasonable in his judgments; he is not intolerant; he does not believe that he knows and understands everything; he willingly listens and accepts things from others. . . . The American is an empirical man of experience, not of theory. He seeks effectiveness, results."[229]

Marty's embrace of pragmatism and the accommodations he made to American republicanism are reminders that denominational tensions should not be overstated. Centuries separated the Catholic-Protestant wars of the sixteenth century and the Dakota settlement boom. Dakota anti-Catholicism was also a far cry from that of the Massachusetts Bay Colony, where the discovery of a Catholic priest would result in his "perpetual imprisonment," or even that in 1850s America, where a dozen Catholic churches were burned.[230] Although religious and ethnic rifts occurred over such matters as schooling and prohibition in Dakota Territory, there were also positive signs of religious and ethnic comity.

Consideration of a provision to target the Catholic Church for taxation during the constitutional conventions of the 1880s, for example, resulted in its rejection. At the end of the novel *Peder Victorious*, Beret does, after a period of protest, allow her son to marry the Irish Catholic girl.[231] Beret may have wanted to preserve her family's Norwegian Lutheran heritage, but her objections faded, and ultimately, love prevailed.

European immigrants, despite tensions over prohibition and language, were also folded into the social order of Dakota. General Beadle thought the German and Norwegian immigrants "well qualified to share honorably and effectively in the making of the commonwealth."[232] A Dakota memorial to Congress favoring statehood maintained that the "foreign population" was "engaged in agricultural, mechanical, business, and professional pursuits, and no class of citizens is more desirable."[233] One territorial leader praised the Norwegians, the "hardy descendents of adventurous Vikings," for adapting well to "all our institutions, courts, schools, political conventions and offices as though to the manor born."[234] Germans and Norwegians, historians have noted, were favored immigrants and viewed as sturdy yeomen prepared for republican citizenship.[235] Statehood movement leaders also worked to include the foreign-born in the process of ratifying a constitution, and several foreign-born immigrants served as delegates. Delegates of the 1883 constitutional convention ordered a thousand copies of the constitution printed in German and a thousand in Norwegian.[236] After the 1885 constitutional convention, 20,000 newspaper supplements explaining the convention were printed in German, 20,000 in "Scandinavian," and 10,000 in Russian (for the German immigrants from Russia).[237] Such outreach indicates the unifying effect of republicanism in Dakota Territory and suggests the erosion of ethnic differences over time. O. E. Rolvaag later quipped that he had "actually succeeded in getting the 'Yankees' to see that the Norwegians are good people, and that the country has not lost anything in getting us here."[238] Long before Rolvaag's comment, however, leaders in Dakota Territory were well on their way to this realization.

Periodic religious friction in the territory underscores the importance of Christianity. The religious zeal of many Dakotans was a major force in their daily lives and structured their view of the world. Dakota Territory was settled long before what Phillip Rieff called the "wake for Christian culture" was held and the "long period of deconversion" had started.[239] Devotion to Christianity, Dakotans believed, was critical to the creation of the virtuous citizenry upon which the republic depended. Many of the ministers and political leaders of Dakota were Protestant, however, and thus favored the inculcation of Protestant virtue and feared the effect of Rome-centered Catholicism on the republican order. The republican polity created in Dakota Territory, despite its great achievement in implanting a republican political culture, was not open to all citizens on the same terms, and Catholics could at times serve as the object of social hostility because of their religious beliefs. Protestant suspicion of Catholicism suggests two central components of the political culture of Dakota Territory: Dakotans took their religious convictions to heart, and they feared forces that might interrupt or undermine the creation of a republican polity. Protestant-Catholic friction, however, should not be seen as a major departure from Dakotans' republican achievements, which were significant. Another of these republican achievements, which should not be diminished by denominational tension, was the successful formulation of an organic law for a future state, a process that replicated the founding moment of the American republican tradition.

CHAPTER 4

"THE ORGANIC LAW OF A GREAT COMMONWEALTH"

The blessings of a free government can only be maintained by a firm adherence to justice, moderation, temperance, frugality and virtue and by frequent recurrence to fundamental principles.

Sioux Falls Constitution of 1883

On July 4, 1889, the weather in Sioux Falls was fair and clear.[1] On the 113th anniversary of the Declaration of Independence, the city was already home to 12,000 people, approximately the population of Boston at the time of the American Revolution.[2] During the 1889 Fourth of July celebration, Sioux Falls "entertained the largest crowd of people ever assembled at any one place in Dakota." The railroads ran special trains that transported an additional 9,000 people into the city, and horse-drawn carriages rolled in, carrying another 6,000.[3] At sunrise, the city woke to the thunder of a forty-two-gun salute fired by the Sioux Falls Light Artillery company, the clang of the city's church bells, and the wail of steam whistles. At 10 A.M., a holiday ceremony commenced, featuring speeches, music, an invocation by the Episcopalian bishop William Hobart Hare, a reading of the Declaration of Independence, and the singing of "Hail Columbia." The festivities also included a parade, a baseball game at Base Ball Park, a band contest, tub races on the Big Sioux River, a greased-pole-climbing contest, a greased-pig contest, sack races, three-legged races, bicycle races, wheel-barrow races, horse races, and a grand balloon ascension featuring a man who would leap from the balloon basket in a parachute—all part of what the *St. Paul Pioneer Press* called a "monster celebration."[4] The balloon ascension had to be delayed due to strong Dakota winds. When it was finally attempted, the wind caused an errant spark that sent the $450 balloon up in smoke, "a kind of ascension not fully satisfactory to the 5,000 spectators."[5]

At noon, after marching in the parade, the seventy-five delegates of the South Dakota constitutional convention gathered at Germania Hall, which had been built in 1880 by the local Germania Verein (meaning "unite") to "foster art, to awaken the mind to liberty, to create a love for all that is good and beautiful, to encourage social intercourse and to aid in preserving the fruits of German culture." The hall was festooned with American flags and red, white, and blue bunting, and each delegate's name and home county were printed on a piece of white board in front of his assigned desk. County maps were posted on the walls, and parliamentary rules, statistical data, and volumes of Dakota history rested on delegates' desks.[6] Four large stars hung on the walls, symbolizing the four new states, including South Dakota, that were on the verge of entering the Union. The prayer that opened the convention was given by the minister of the First Congregational Church in Sioux Falls. The blessing of the Congregational Church, the original Puritan church in the New World, symbolized the transmigration of New England institutions and culture, after a period of evolution in the Midwest, to Dakota Territory. The delegate elected president of the convention, Judge Alonzo Edgerton, was born in New York, had long been active in Minnesota politics, and was a Civil War veteran and a member of the Congregational Church and the Grand Army of the Republic. Edgerton thanked the delegates for the honor they had bestowed on him and "expressed the joy which all felt that the rights so long denied and due the people of this great commonwealth were about to be realized." After they adjourned, many of the delegates proceeded to the baseball games, the various races, or a prohibition meeting.[7]

The 1889 constitutional convention in Sioux Falls represented the culmination of a decade-long quest for Dakota statehood. As the Great Dakota Boom unfolded during the 1880s and farmers filled the prairies of Eastern Dakota, the territory became ever more ripe for statehood and self-rule. A long tradition of American republicanism undergirded the movement for statehood. For a decade, civic leaders in Dakota had been frustrated by the defects in the territorial system of governance and by a national political environment that stymied the statehood crusade. At long last, after constitutions written in 1883 and 1885 failed to spur congressional action, Dakota leaders were able in 1889 to frame a constitution and join the Union as a state.

HERITAGE

All three of the constitutional conventions held in Dakota Territory during the 1880s were steeped in the precedents and symbols of the American democratic tradition. The delegates ritually invoked the Revolution, the Founders, and past American heroes and glories. They even had intricate debates over the meaning of the Northwest Ordinance of 1787 and the treaty with France granting Louisiana to the Americans. Delegate Gideon Moody said the "country is a hundred odd years old, and we will try to reap the benefit of the experience of those who have gone before us."[8] Perhaps more than any other experience, the delegates invoked the American Civil War, in which so many of them had done their duty for the Union. At the end of the 1885 constitutional convention, the delegates even sang "Marching through Georgia" to celebrate the completion of their work.[9] With the sergeant at arms' "fine baritone ringing out the old war song," the other delegates joined in "with a sympathy which none but a soldier can feel, and which was apparent in many glistening eyes and quivering lips."[10] Statehood advocate Hugh Campbell, when speaking to a campfire of the GAR post in Yankton, was compelled to first honor those "scattered survivors of that band of young men and boys, who twenty years ago shouldered their muskets to fight for the flag and the preservation of the union." Campbell combined the historical precedents of the Revolution and the Civil War, averring that the statehood advocates were "animated by the same spirit which actuated the men of '76 and the men of '61."[11] At an organizational convention in Huron in June 1883, B. G. Caulfield invoked the "old moorings of the constitution" and the "ancient customs of this republic" in the face of congressional opposition to Dakota statehood.[12] At the 1885 convention, Judge Edgerton hoped the delegates possessed the same wisdom as the Framers of 1787, but doubted that ascending to such glorified heights was possible. "It may not be said of us as it frequently is of the framers of the constitution," he said, "that they built better than they knew," but observers might "be able to say 'They built as well as they knew.'"[13]

Besides drawing on the American democratic heritage generally, the constitution makers specifically pursued republican ends. In particular, they insisted that patriotism and service to the interests of the commonwealth trump private scheming and profiteering, and they obsessed about ending corruption and promoting agrarian ideals. The convention delegates' chief goal was to subordinate personal interests to the "common interest and general welfare" and to adhere to the duties of virtuous and civic-minded statesmen.[14] Judge Edgerton advised delegates during the 1885 convention to draw on "judgment and patriotism," "prudence and discretion," and the "light which experience can furnish us and all the judgment and wisdom which nature and education have endowed us with" when they wrote the "organic law of a great commonwealth."[15]

Edgerton's use of the term "patriotism" indicates the importance the delegates assigned to republicanism and public-spiritedness when framing the constitution. The summons to the 1883 constitutional convention cited support for statehood by "a quarter of a million patriotic, liberty loving, God-fearing people," all motivated by "pure and simple patriotism."[16] During the debate at the 1883 convention, delegate W. W. Brookings urged that there "must be patriotism in the work—not partisanship."[17] Conversely, political posturing, self-interestedness, and partisan bickering were viewed as unpatriotic. One statehood advocate declared the 1883 convention a success because it was "strongly non partisan, public spirited and patriotic."[18] When discussing a prominent visitor to the convention, Judge Gideon Moody said that though some feared "politics was his governing motive," they soon discovered "it was patriotism rather that swelled his breast."[19] Statehood promoters hoped for a future in which the age of territorial "intrigues," "log rolling," "lobbying," "partisanship," and "political factions" could be transcended by the patriotic citizens of a self-governing Dakota commonwealth.[20]

Delegates to the 1880s constitutional conventions expended their greatest energy trying to prevent corruption in the future state government. Weary of carpetbag territorial appointees and their collaboration with railroad interests, the delegates pushed for stringent limitations on outside influences on the legislature. In keeping with the long-standing republican obsession with eliminating political corruption, they incorporated several anti-corruption elements into the future state's fundamental law. They hoped a responsible state government controlled by locally elected citizens would bring an end to the despised territorial system, which they blamed for causing "lasting and remediless injury to the institutions and future of the commonwealth."[21]

The statehood movement also embraced the republican fondness for agrarianism. Fundamentally, the statehooders believed that securing self-government would give them greater control over their economic destiny. The leaders of southern Dakota could then promote an agricultural economy based on the work of small yeoman farmers instead of the more industrialized model of the northern section. The north was viewed as dominated by "speculators and large holders," whereas the south consisted of "small farmers, small merchants and mechanics and all that class of industries which grow up in a country, consisting of homesteaders, pre-emptors and actual resident farmers." In the north, the large-scale bonanza farms were controlled by out-of-state owners, were worked by employees brought in from city "slums" with "no stake in the country," and depended on the Northern Pacific Railroad, which strongly influenced northern politics. To escape this corrupt system, to live as "independent men," and to enjoy the fruits of small-scale yeoman agriculture, statehood was necessary.[22] The call for the 1883 constitutional convention flatly stated that northern Dakota was in the "hands of large capitalists and extensive operators and speculators," in contrast to the "homeholders and steady going citizens" of the south: "No commonwealth could be satisfactorily managed wherein two elements so diverse might be joined."[23] Throughout the constitution-writing process of the 1880s, the voice of agrarian idealism was consistently heard.

In addition to the American democratic tradition, republican ideas, and agrarianism, statehood advocates maintained an intense respect for

Dakota Territory, 1884. Beinecke Rare Book and Manuscript Library, Yale University.

Christianity. At a June 1883 conclave called to debate the merits of a constitutional convention, Episcopalian minister Melancthon Hoyt, the "oldest pioneer clergyman of Dakota," blessed the work of the convention and called on God to bless conventioneers so that "they may glorify Thy holy name and perpetuate the best interests of the citizens of this territory."[24] The call for the 1883 constitutional convention cited the support of a "God-fearing people" for statehood and self-governance.[25] On the first day of the 1883 constitutional convention, J. N. McLoney of the First Congregational Church in Sioux Falls prayed that "Thy perfect wisdom may direct the deliberations of this body" and that the convention be "full of what may redound to the glory of the commonwealth."[26] Recognizing the interrelationship of republicanism and religion, a minister during the 1885 convention reminded delegates that God had "taught the great republics of the world to lean upon their God."[27] Religiosity and constitutionalism met directly every morning of that convention.[28] The *Jamestown Alert* noted that the 1883 constitutional convention had "prayers every morning" and "no one knows but that what is now a political gathering may be transformed into a great religious event."[29] This degree of Christian influence upon state constitutions was recognized by U.S. Supreme Court Justice David J. Brewer a few years later in a Supreme Court opinion. Finding "a constant recognition of religious obligations" in state constitutions, Brewer concluded that "they affirm and reaffirm that this is a religious nation."[30]

The use of Christian imagery and the adoption of the state motto also indicated the Christian preferences of the constitutional framers. When the 1883 convention was grappling with whether to have voters simultaneously elect state officers when ratifying the constitution, delegate Robert Dollard said, "We are much in the position of the children of Israel who paused on the banks of the river in sight of the promised land. We have constructed the bridge; now shall we cross it?"[31] The *Spearfish Register* wrote of the Dakota constitution: "In rearing this monument let every one build over again his own house as in the days of dismantled Jerusalem . . . under the guidance of a kind God, [the constitution] will defy the storm of centuries to come."[32] Since statehood would end the rule of territorial appointees and weaken railroad influences, delegate Hugh Campbell said it was equivalent to escaping the "hands of the Philistines."[33] During the 1885 convention, the report of the committee on the state seal and coat of arms recommended a motto for the new state: "Under God, the People Rule." An amendment to change the motto to "The People Rule" failed 10–73. The vote on the report (without the

amendment) passed with only one negative vote. A constitutional pre-
amble was also adopted that began, "We, the people of Dakota, grateful
to Almighty God for our civil and religious liberty."[34]

From heavy reliance on the republican and Christian traditions of
the United States flowed consensus on rudimentary questions when the
constitutional framers of Dakota convened. The absence of debate on
these questions at the constitutional conventions, according to Gordon
Bakken, indicated a "consensus of silence on certain of America's fundamental principles." Bakken believes that the Dakota framers' "recurrence
to fundamental principles confirmed the faith of the Founding Fathers
in the state-making process."[35] The Dakota constitution's bill of rights,
noteworthy for the degree of consensus it generated during the convention and for its extensive use of the American constitutional heritage,
even included a provision stating that the "blessings of a free government
can only be maintained by a firm adherence to justice, moderation, temperance, frugality and virtue and by frequent recurrence to fundamental
principles."[36] The Dakota framers worked squarely within the American
political and constitutional tradition.

TRANSCENDING THE TERRITORIAL SYSTEM

The statehood advocates and framers of the South Dakota constitution
relied on republicanism and the history of U.S. democratic practices
when they criticized and rebelled against the territorial system. Few
western settlers favored the territorial system, which limited their exer-
cise of republican rights. Under the territorial system, the president of
the United State chose the governor and judges for the territory, and Congress established the territory's organic law. Any statutes passed by the
territorial legislature could be vetoed by the federally appointed governor or preempted or repealed by Congress.[37] Deepening Dakotans' anger
toward the territorial system were the length of the gestation period from
territorial status to statehood and a particularly villainous territorial governor. Gideon Moody captured the sentiment of many delegates during
the 1885 constitutional convention when he prayed for the coming of a
"self-governing" "commonwealth" that would uphold the "manhood" of

Dakotans, and when he denounced the "evils of living under a government that is clearly one held at the will of a foreign tribunal."[38]

In 1880 Nehemiah Ordway was appointed governor of Dakota Territory, and he quickly set in motion plans for plunder and revealed his contempt for republican ideals. Ordway made his first visit to Sioux Falls in 1880, where he wooed the editor of the *Sioux Falls Pantagraph* on the veranda of the Cataract House hotel until one in the morning. Ordway explained the connections he had forged in Washington during his long service as sergeant at arms in the House of Representatives, and his role as "banker" to many congressmen. These connections, on both sides of the political aisle, he claimed, afforded him control of federal appointments in the territory. He now offered to make the editor of the *Pantagraph* postmaster of Sioux Falls. Ordway said he wanted to make a fortune in the territory and needed to build a strong political combination that should include a co-conspiring newspaper in Sioux Falls. "I will make similar arrangements in other localities," Ordway said, "and we can organize affairs so as to have everything our own way." The governor also bribed legislators, threatened vetoes of legislators' bills if they resisted his plans, compelled settlers seeking county seats to give him land, installed his son as territorial auditor in order to control finances, and moved the territorial capital from Yankton to Bismarck in order to benefit from real estate speculation.[39]

The settlers' disgust with figures such as Ordway and with the territorial system in general was effectively summarized by the prominent Congregational minister Joseph Ward, who argued that the people in the territories were "treated, not simply as aliens, but almost as enemies" and were "not regarded as a part of the common country, but as a dependency, a province." Promoting local control and statehood would make Dakotan democracy "pure" by ending the "demoralizing influence of Federal patronage," which excluded "decent" men from political life and brought in a breed of "toadying" hacks equivalent to those "that appeared in any remote Roman province in the bad days of the Empire." In critiquing the territorial system, Ward invoked the Founders and the freedoms sought by the American colonists, compared the treatment of Dakota to the treatment of Kansas before the Civil War, and cited the work of William Penn, who "went far to confirm the 'right of the free Saxon people to be governed by law of which they themselves were makers.'" Ward's citation of historical antecedents went beyond the obvious. He also relied on the Northwest Ordinance of 1787, the 1803 Treaty with France, the *Dred Scott* decision, and the organization of state government in Michigan in 1835 "without an enabling act from Congress," which Congress approved in 1837. Drawing a contrast with the appointed spoilsmen in the territory, Ward praised the "virtue and intelligence," "enterprise and sturdy vigor" of territorial residents, who had "borne the first shock of savage uprisings" and now sought statehood for the "sake of the common weal." The territory's settlers, Ward declared, were exemplary republican citizens, and no other group in the nation exceeded their "loving reverence for the Fathers of the Republic." He called for an end to federal territorial policy and for Congress to create states that were "truly republican, and in entire harmony with the spirit that created the present Union."[40]

Under the territorial system, the transition to statehood depended on passage of an enabling act by Congress. During the peak years of the Great Dakota Boom in the 1880s, however, Congress was in no mood to help Dakota. Congress, John D. Hicks noted, was "absorbed in politics" and was "indifferent to all else."[41] Yet settlers continued to fill the Dakota plains, making the delay of statehood that much more offensive. During the 1880s, Dakota Territory had twice the population of Iowa and Wisconsin when they were admitted to the Union, three times the population of Michigan and California, four times the population of Missouri and Colorado, five times the population of Ohio and Illinois, and six times the population of Indiana and Nevada.[42] Throughout the boom, the *Yankton Press and Dakotaian* begged Congress to listen to the "claims of the three hundred thousand disfranchised residents of the republic."[43]

Congressional opposition to Dakota statehood stemmed from a simple logic. The creation of two new states from Dakota Territory would likely bring with them four new Republican senators and additional Republican congressmen. Between 1881 and 1883, the Republicans held the presidency and both houses of Congress and thus had the opportunity to approve statehood for the Dakotas, but Senator Eugene Hale of Maine objected because of the failure of the city of Yankton to pay off certain railroad bonds (some of the bondholders were in Maine).[44] During the six years following the 1882 elections, the federal government was divided along partisan lines, and thus the Democrats could block statehood for the Dakotas. The *Boston Daily Advertiser* and other national newspapers based their criticism of congressional Democrats for blocking statehood on the experiences of other, less-populated territories: "To say that a territory which contains 80,000 farms is in danger of dwindling into a second Nevada is manifestly absurd."[45] The *Advertiser*'s emphasis on the agrarian stability of Dakota contrasted with the experience of Nevada, which had been granted statehood after only three years' territorial status despite its small and transient mining population.[46]

Those in Congress with little sympathy for Dakota statehood could point to dissenters in the territory to bolster their arguments against admission. Two factions based in the north, often working in tandem, led efforts to stymie the momentum toward statehood and undermine the legitimacy of the movement. Territorial officeholders such as Governor Ordway and some of his newspaper allies worked particularly hard to block statehood, which would end Ordway's governorship and his ability to profit from territorial machinations.[47] Ordway's allies at the influential Northern Pacific Railroad also opposed statehood, which might lead to the passage of tighter railroad regulations by a state legislature more attuned to the interests of Dakotans.[48] The *Chicago Inter Ocean* concluded that it was the "ringsters, tricksters, and small-fry politicians" in the north who opposed statehood.[49]

Those Dakotans actively seeking statehood and battling with opponents in the north also sought division of the territory, especially after Ordway engineered the removal of the capital to Bismarck. The more settled, agrarian, and republican southern section favored separation from the north because southern leaders viewed the north as too subservient to political combinations, railroads, and bonanza farms. Statehooder Bartlett Tripp deemed the north "one great wheat field rented and cultivated in large tracts, while the south is a pastoral and agricultural region divided into small farms, occupied and cultivated by the owners of the soil."[50] Territorial appointees and their allies such as the Northern Pacific were seen as the main opponents of statehood and division. The

Yankton newspaper claimed the Northern Pacific was "bending every energy to throttle the division movement."[51]

In September 1883, during the first constitutional convention in Sioux Falls, the Ordway forces organized a counterconvention in Fargo to protest and delegitimize the statehood and division efforts of the south. The effort did not have the desired effect. Less than 50 of the 109 delegates attended the counterconvention, and there were doubts about the credentials of some of the delegates who did appear. When the delegates assembled, contrary to Ordway's plans, some of them even expressed support for division of the territory.[52] Of the Fargo convention the *Pioneer Press* said, "Nobody seemed to know what it was called together for." The newspaper deemed the Fargo convention "scarcely representative" and "almost without occupation," while it found the Sioux Falls constitutional convention meeting at the same time much more "earnest" and legitimate. The only objection heard at the Fargo convention that drew any consensus was the concern that southern Dakota would appropriate the name "Dakota." Representatives from the south, however, consistently expressed their willingness to make concessions on the name issue.[53]

Even some northern newspapers threw cold water on the Fargo convention. The *Grand Forks Herald* argued that northern Dakotans would ignore the Fargo convention, which it labeled "a Bismarck capital scheme, pure and simple."[54] The *Fargo Republican* was perhaps the most stridently critical of the Fargo convention, which it said was "originated by the Bismarck ring" and "scheming politicians." The newspaper opined that the masses opposed the Fargo convention and that the "ringsters" were using the loss-of-name issue as "a cover for an attempt to place the people of north Dakota in an attitude of opposition to division and to thwart the efforts of the southern section."[55] The Fargo newspaper concluded that statehood opponents were simply trying to create the impression that territorial residents did not favor division and statehood.[56]

SEEKING CONSENSUS

The efforts of opponents of statehood to create the impression of disunity within the territory steeled the statehood advocates' resolve to promote consensus. The probable resistance of Congress and the heartfelt desire to end their territorial status concentrated statehooders' efforts to achieve unity and bipartisanship. During the 1883 convention, delegate Thomas Sterling made a plea commonly heard during the conventions to oppose "doubtful measures" and promote "unanimity."[57] Statehood advocates consistently appealed to the minority of Democrats in the territory to join them as a sign of consensus. During the 1883 convention, delegate Abraham Boynton of Lincoln County, the oldest member of the Democratic territorial central committee, revealed "he had been accused by members of the committee as being made a Republican tool by working to get a Republican territory into the union."[58] Frank Ziebach, another Democrat, worried that he would be accused of "being used as a cat-spaw to rake the chestnuts out of the fire for the Republican monkey."[59] Republican statehood advocates were in turn criticized for appealing to Democrats to achieve statehood and for rumors that they had offered future state offices to Democrats, an act one newspaper deemed a "sinking of principle . . . beneath the manhood of true men" and a "betrayal of party interests" in the cause of "currying favor with the Democratic members of the next Congress."[60] Statehood advocates also sought to avoid divisive issues such as prohibition and female suffrage and any unorthodox constitutional provisions that might cause dissent. The *Yankton Press and Dakotaian* emphasized the need to avoid "experimental clauses," for this was "no time to inject radical issues into fundamental law when so much depends upon" a favorable congressional response.[61]

The safest method of avoiding untried experiments that might foster uncertainty and dissent was to borrow from existing constitutions, a common practice in the West.[62] The committee formed to promote adoption of the 1883 constitution openly declared that the charter had "no claims to originality" and was "a compilation of the best sections of all constitutions of the several states."[63] The committee assured citizens that the constitution of every other state was available during the convention debates, that they were consulted and discussed in open debate, and that the framers sought to avoid "new and unconstrued provisions" in order to win congressional approval. "Every material line and section then of our constitution," the committee announced, "will be found in the laws of the later and more modern constitutions of the states."[64] L. W. Lansing, delegate to the 1885 convention from Hand County, doubted that a constitution could be assembled "from scratch" in a short period of time, but soon discovered that "with plenty of copies of the constitutions of other and older states . . . it was largely a matter of editing and selection."[65] The excessive borrowing, however, did not translate into the absence of reform provisions. Voters were urged to compare the 1883 constitution with the latest reform-oriented constitutions, especially the Illinois constitution of 1870 and the Pennsylvania constitution of 1875.[66] After the 1883 constitutional convention, the *Yankton Press and Dakotaian* called the resulting charter a "combination of the best elements to be extracted from the constitutions of thirty-seven states with enough in the way of new points to indicate that our people are abreast with the spirit of progressiveness."[67]

Another potential pitfall awaiting the framers was the growing frustration and resentment of many Dakotans with the inertia and politicization of the statehood process. At times, such passions generated calls for more drastic action. Some statehood advocates, led by Hugh Campbell, argued that Dakota should simply assert its right to statehood and elect a government regardless of whether Congress passed an enabling act. Campbell cited U.S. Supreme Court cases, past actions of Congress, the rebellion of the original thirteen colonies, the Northwest Ordinance, and the assertiveness and impatience of other states in earlier decades.[68] Between 1836 and 1848, Congress had indeed simply admitted Michigan, Iowa, Florida, and Arkansas without first authorizing these states to organize a government. California, Oregon, and Kansas had also written constitutions and organized their governments without congressional action. Gordon Bakken has noted that the "absence of enabling acts corresponded to the congressional democratization of the territorial system itself," a trend that created "great latitude for territorial action."[69] Despite these precedents, whether the delegates of the Dakota conventions should unilaterally adopt a constitution and immediately elect a government that would then take power remained a persistent tactical question for the statehood movement to answer. Some sober leaders counseled against such notions of popular sovereignty, which Union veterans of the Civil War found particularly distasteful.[70] In the end, the powerful temptation to elect a state government and declare statehood was resisted in the name of promoting consensus and pacifying Congress, but not without heated discussion and the invocation of the most sacred symbols and precedents of American democracy.

The debate over the perils and principles of popular sovereignty reached fever pitch over one particular clause in the constitution. At the 1885 convention, during consideration of the report of the committee on the bill of rights, Hugh Campbell introduced an amendment, taken verbatim from the Pennsylvania constitution, stating that the people should "have the right at all times to alter, reform, or abolish their forms of government." President Edgerton, Joseph Ward, and others opposed such a "revolutionary" clause, which they thought would only incite opposition in Congress. In response, Campbell cited Patrick Henry, the Declaration of Independence, and the Founding Fathers. "I hope the time will never come," Campbell said, "when the people of Dakota will have less spirit than did their fathers." Campbell reminded the convention of the Democrats' treatment of the people of Kansas in 1860, "turn[ing] out their legislature and forc[ing] down their throats the Lecompton constitution." Campbell paid little heed to the concerns of the Democrats in Congress, whom the opponents of his provision, he said, treated like "demigods" and "czars." As Judge Edgerton was calling for the vote on Campbell's provision, a motion was made to adjourn. When the vote on the measure deadlocked at 36 to 36, the leaders of the convention quickly adjourned the convention in hopes of defusing the situation.[71]

When the convention reconvened the next morning, what the *Pioneer Press* called an "exceedingly heated discussion" continued about Campbell's amendment. Judge Edgerton criticized the invocation of Patrick Henry, noting that Henry called "upon Virginia to rise in revolt against the mother government" and sought separation from, not inclusion in, a political regime. Counseling against "revolutionary methods" and urging the convention to move ahead "peaceably," Edgerton pointed out that the clause in the Pennsylvania constitution in question had originally been adopted in 1776 during a critical moment of the American Revolution and that he did not want to "snuff gunpowder again." If "ever the bugle calls again," he said, "the old soldiers will fall in, but it must be to rally around the old flag," not to embrace disorder and disunion. Invoking his Civil War service, Edgerton advised the body to avoid revolutionary strife. During Edgerton's speech, according to the *Pioneer Press*, Campbell "sat nervously fingering law books at hand," taking umbrage at the remarks. With the convention on the brink of a "wordy conflict" amid "great confusion," a wise delegate moved to refer the resolution to a committee. The motion passed unanimously.[72] The committee later reported a more subdued provision which declared that the people had the "right, by lawful and constitutional methods, to alter or reform their forms of government."[73] In the end, the *Pioneer Press* reporter concluded, the debate probably did "more good than harm by calling the attention of the public at large to the fact that South Dakota is in earnest in the matter of securing division and admission."[74] The delegates made the pragmatic decision that would advance the cause of statehood.

The most potentially divisive issues addressed during the conventions were prohibition and women's suffrage. Statehood leaders consistently worked to avoid including a prohibition provision in the constitution and, insisting that statehood must come first, called on temperance advocates to save their energy for a legislative battle once statehood was achieved. Since the constitution was a "struggle and contest against power, against corruption in high places, against great corporations," and therefore "a struggle for life and death," it required the "unanimous and undivided support of the people." It was "suicidal" to divide voters over the prohibition issue.[75] Although many statehood leaders were also temperance men, they agreed to subordinate the prohibition question to the quest for statehood. The Reverend Joseph Ward argued that statehood must come first because to include prohibition would "array the whisky ring of the whole country against the admission of south Dakota."[76] The decision of certain temperance advocates to defer prohibition helped ensure that the convention remained "a thoroughly harmonious body."[77] To include prohibition in the constitution, the *Pioneer Press* opined, would have been "to give it its death-blow before it is fairly born."[78]

The prohibition issue was closely linked to the question of women's suffrage. When a temperance convention convened during the 1883 constitutional convention, it endorsed the plan of the Dakota Woman's

Christian Temperance Union to promote women's suffrage as "a weapon of defense against the saloons."[79] Politically active women could, it was argued, help "in the labor of arresting the advance of crime and corruption." Other women's suffrage advocates simply appealed to gender equality. The framers heard a plea for suffrage from Marietta M. Bones, vice-president of the National Woman Suffrage Association. Bones advocated including women's suffrage in the constitution instead of submitting the question to a popular vote, because she did not think the masses truly understood the benefits of women's voting rights and were "as ignorant of the advantages freedom would be to them, as were the slaves in the south: who, had they endorsed the action of John Brown at Harper's Ferry in their interest this country would have been saved the horrors of a terrible war." Using the language of republicanism, Bones argued that women sought the "higher duties and obligations of American citizenship" and that without women's voting rights, Dakota would not have "a republican form of government."[80] One unknown correspondent to the *Pioneer Press*, however, counseling Dakotans not to simultaneously pursue statehood, suffrage, and prohibition, wrote that the "great mass of the women of Dakota do not want the ballot; nor do the people of Dakota want to have every community and town rent with strife and passion over the question of prohibition and temperance." The correspondent argued that such extraneous measures "only tend to divide and exasperate the people, creating divisions and factions, without any appreciable good." Advocates of maintaining consensus and avoiding the "gauntlet of all criticism of our enemies" ultimately prevailed, and both prohibition and suffrage were left out of the final drafts of the three constitutions written during the 1880s.[81] These provisions were, however, prepared for popular plebiscite upon the achievement of statehood.

FRAMING THE FUNDAMENTAL LAW

Safeguarding against political corruption is one of the strongest pillars of republican theory. In keeping with this tradition, delegates to the constitutional conventions in Dakota Territory expended great energy attempting to craft a document that limited the potential for corrupt practices. With the political corruption of the post–Civil War era fresh in their memories, statehood advocates were acutely aware of democracy's shortcomings and consciously sought to transcend them. These efforts were spurred on by the strong reaction to the national scandals preceding the statehood period, the "Indian ring" in Dakota Territory during the 1870s, the corruption of territorial governors such as Ordway, and the ripening stench of Grantism. When Carl Schurz was named Secretary of the Interior in 1876, he launched a high-profile campaign to eliminate corruption in the Indian agencies.[82] By the time the South Dakota constitution was adopted, as John D. Hicks noted, the nation was "conscious and ashamed of its political corruption." Because of railroad influence on legislatures in other states and in Dakota, constitution writers were well aware of the need for reform.[83] The territorial appointees sent from Washington were also a constant source of outrage and a reminder of the need for reform. During the 1883 constitutional convention, delegate George Hand declared that the "territory is in the hands of as unscrupulous a set of scoundrels as ever disgraced a people, and I came here to help rid you of the incubus."[84]

Similar to legislative reformers in other constitutional conventions in the West, the Dakota framers worried about how to constrain the "human drive to act selfishly" among legislators. The constitutionalism they embraced, reflecting republican tradition, included an underlying pessimism "about human nature and democratic political processes."[85] Their anti-corruption efforts focused particularly on the legislature. The Dakota constitution would include restrictions on legislators' ability to compete for state contracts, a prohibition on legislators' holding other offices created while they served in the legislature, and bans on corrupt solicitation and "lobbying," which were punishable by fine and imprisonment.[86] A Yankton newspaper, when commenting on the 1883 constitution, noted the inclusion of "punishment for bribery, even in its most simple form," a provision that was "the outgrowth of an experience which has taught us that the public can only be protected by the most stringent requirements."[87] The constitution also mandated a large House and Senate membership, which was thought to make corrupt conspiracies and combinations more difficult and to eliminate the "evil effects of small legislative bodies."[88]

Fears of future legislative corruption and lack of reform-mindedness prompted the framers to include restrictions on legislators' behavior in the constitution and not to leave such questions to future legislatures of uncertain virtue or will.[89] As one South Dakota delegate put it simply, the "object of Constitutions is to limit the legislature."[90]

The constitutional framers also adopted provisions designed specifically to limit the "lavish" spending of previous legislatures.[91] Many delegates were especially critical of the "unusually large appropriations" made by the 1883 territorial legislature under the direction of Governor Ordway.[92] During the 1883 constitutional convention, delegates were also reminded of the legislative scheming that underlay Ordway's plan to move the capital when, on September 15, 1883, Judge Edgerton issued his decision declaring the removal unconstitutional. The Yankton newspaper, hailing this decision as a blow to the "official vultures who feed upon the carcass of public spoils," concluded that the Bismarck ring could no longer "fatten upon the wages of sin."[93] To restrict legislative opportunities for spending public money, the length of the legislative session was limited, strict limits were placed on state indebtedness, state loans and donations were banned, aid to corporations was outlawed, state ownership of private stock was prohibited, and county, town, city, and school district debt was capped at 5 percent of assessed property valuation.[94] Taxation was limited to two mills per dollar, but two additional mills could be levied to retire state debt.[95] Even the often critical *Bismarck Tribune* commented that the 1883 constitution bore "decided evidence of careful precaution" and was "economical in its provisions for expenditures."[96] Legislators could not receive railroad passes or "any other valuable thing" from corporations (a violation precluded legislators from running for reelection), and the governor's appointment and pardoning powers were also curtailed to limit political favoritism.[97]

Anti-corruption efforts also focused on the disposal of public lands reserved for education purposes. Congress had long set aside the sixteenth and thirty-sixth sections of each township of federal land to be used to finance education, but by the time of the Dakota statehood movement, concern was growing that new states sold these lands too cheaply to speculators.[98] As early as the 1882 convention of the Citizens

Constitutional Association, Dakotans were calling for constitutional protections for school lands to prevent the "waste and fraud" and "combinations and fraudulent schemes" seen in other states.[99] General William Beadle spearheaded efforts to establish a constitutionally mandated minimum sale price for these school lands. Beadle's plan to institute a $10 per acre minimum for school lands seemed "preposterous" at the time it was proposed because premium Iowa land was then selling for $2.50 to $4.00 and "no state had ever required a limitation higher than 'double minimum,' that is, two dollars and fifty cents per acre."[100] The Beadle plan prevailed, however, and became a model reform measure adopted by other western states. In addition to curbing corruption, the Dakota school lands law also promoted the agrarian agenda by granting preferential credit terms to settlers who acquired school lands.[101]

RAILROADS

In *Nature's Metropolis*, a masterful study of the economic relationship between the urban center of Chicago and the "Great West," including Dakota Territory, author William Cronon explained how Chicago shaped the settlement of the late-nineteenth-century boom areas. By the 1850s, Chicago had eclipsed St. Louis, which had long been the economic center of the West and the destination point of farm goods shipped via the Mississippi River. The rise of Chicago and the elongating spurs of its railroad network altered the manner in which prairie farmers sold their crops.[102] As railroads worked their way westward across the plains, according to Cronon, established farmers in Illinois, Wisconsin, Minnesota, and Iowa "swept out into Kansas, Nebraska, and Dakota Territory," settled these new lands, and ultimately sent carloads of wheat and corn streaming back into Chicago.[103] As Chicago's railroads delivered more settlers to Dakota Territory and the broader Great Plains, the nation was introduced to a new frontier, which Hamlin Garland later called the "middle border."[104] The railroads out of Chicago spurred and hastened this introduction. One contemporary said flatly, "Dakota has been made by the railroads."[105]

The main railroad arteries into southern Dakota were the Chicago & Northwestern and the Chicago, Milwaukee & St. Paul railroads.

According to one history, the Great Dakota Boom was "triggered by the intense rivalry" between the Chicago & Northwestern and the Milwaukee Road.[106] Each railroad built a transportation network designed to profit from shipping the agricultural bounty of Dakota to markets in the East.[107] Both railroad companies also promoted the agricultural prospects of Dakota to potential settlers and helped to recruit new immigrants from Europe. The Milwaukee Road's agents in Liverpool "portrayed America as a land of riches and plenty. To the politically oppressed they revealed the American West as still the 'home of the free.'"[108] During the boom, these roads built lines across southern Dakota to the Missouri River and routinely brought in settlers from New England and the Midwest and immigrant farmers from Northern Europe and returned to the East hauling Dakota grain.

The Milwaukee Road and the Chicago & Northwestern were not land grant railroads. Only a small amount of land in southern Dakota was granted to one railroad, the Winona & St. Peter, in Deuel and Codington counties. None of the nation's five major transcontinental railroads passed through southern Dakota. In 1871 Congress made the last railroad land grant just as public opinion began to turn against the railroads and some critics began to argue that such grants conflicted with the agrarian policy of distributing federal land to homesteaders.[109] By the time of the Dakota boom, congressional opposition to additional grants of federal land to railroad companies had become intense.[110]

Well before the exhaustion of federal land-grant largesse, however, the Northern Pacific Railway was organized, and it ultimately became an influential opponent of Dakota statehood. In 1864, Congress had granted fifty million acres to the Northern Pacific to build a transcontinental line from Lake Superior to Puget Sound.[111] A prominent historian of the legal history of railroads has deemed the congressional land grant to the Northern Pacific "particularly generous" and "unusually lavish."[112] Such grants placed the railroads in charge of distributing large parcels of land, thereby affecting landholding patterns in the plains states the rail lines crossed. Railroads were granted 20 percent of the land in Kansas, and in North Dakota 24 percent.[113] The land grant process was so generous that, in the end, the federal government gave out to the railroads a swath of land larger than the territory occupied by the entire German empire.[114] The railroads' large-scale landholdings conflicted with republican ideals and caused economic and political tensions in the West, including Dakota Territory. During the 1880s, Dakota statehood advocates saw the Northern Pacific and federal officeholders allied with it as their primary enemies. The railroad feared that a state government, sans malleable territorial officials, would be more difficult to control and thus more likely to pursue regulatory measures the railroad opposed.[115]

While the Northern Pacific was the target of statehooders' anger, Dakota farmers also bristled at railroad shipping rates. The cost of shipping Dakota wheat to Chicago by rail could consume one-half the price received by the farmer for his crop.[116] From certain points in Dakota, it was cheaper to ship wheat to Liverpool than to Chicago or the Twin Cities. A grain dealer in Milbank in southern Dakota who sold his wheat in Minneapolis had to pay the full cost of transporting it all the way to Milwaukee. Even the conservative *St. Paul Pioneer Press* recognized the "miserable oppression" of Dakota farmers who shipped their products to eastern markets. Those "who would submit quietly to such outrage," said the paper, "must be either more or less than men."[117] Complaints about shipping rates were linked to complaints about railroads' political power in the territory.[118] Governor Ordway's unpopularity stemmed in part from his alliance with Northern Pacific officials. Ordway's replacement, Louis Church, was appointed by President Cleveland upon the advice of James J. Hill, president of the Great Northern, another railway that ran through northern Dakota.[119] Concern about the railroads inspired agrarian activism in Dakota, helped spur the organization of the Farmers' Alliance in the Midwest, and supplied political support to the late-nineteenth-century antitrust movement.[120] Concerns about the power railroads wielded would echo through the halls of the Dakota constitutional conventions.

THE JUDICIAL MOMENT

When they began their work, the constitutional framers of southern Dakota faced the choice of whether to regulate railroads. Some other states had been reluctant early in their economic development to regulate or otherwise discourage the development of railroads.[121] But the delegates in Dakota Territory had little doubt which track they would take. Many Dakota settlers hailed from the Midwest, where state controls on railroads had been a political reality since the agrarian protests of the 1870s. In keeping with the midwestern heritage of many at the conventions, the constitutional framers did not hesitate to pursue railroad regulation. This decision was consistent with the direction of public policy in the 1870s, when state governments became much more critical of the privileges and grants offered to businesses and of corporate practices in general.[122]

In the late 1860s, the state of Illinois began to experiment with "Granger laws," promoted by the popular farmers' organization known as the Grange and designed to regulate railroads. In the Illinois constitutional convention held during the winter of 1869–70, railroad regulation was a prominent issue. Delegates framed a railroad provision of "unprecedented stringency" and submitted it to the voters, who adopted it overwhelmingly. It declared that railroads were public highways and thus subject to government regulation and that legislatures could set maximum rates that railroads could charge shippers and could prohibit rate discrimination and line consolidation. Historian George H. Miller noted that the "railway article of the proposed Illinois constitution was in accord with the trend of American constitutional thought during the 1850s, 1860s, and 1870s" and "that its example was followed by Michigan in 1870 and by Pennsylvania in 1873."[123] James Ely has similarly found that an increasing number of midwestern states during this period, including Iowa, Minnesota, and Wisconsin, were inspired by the "elaborate railroad provision of the Illinois Constitution of 1870" to regulate railroads.[124] Wisconsin, in particular, became known for its stringent railroad regulatory provision known as the Potter law of 1874, which served as "a powerful symbol of western radicalism."[125] The railroads helped challenge the constitutionality of these laws.[126] In the "Granger cases" of 1877, including *Munn v. Illinois* (the lead case), the U.S. Supreme Court upheld the power of states to regulate railroads, reasoning that they were "clothed with a public interest" and thus subject to legislative control.[127]

An important legacy of these efforts to regulate railroads was the "adoption of detailed railroad provisions in state constitutions," for which the "pioneering Illinois Constitution of 1870 served as a model for other jurisdictions."[128] During the constitutional debate in southern Dakota, the Illinois constitution was consistently held up as a model. The adoption of railway regulations in southern Dakota in the 1880s could hardly be considered "radical," according to George Miller, because such regulations were already so "deeply imbedded in American tradition and law."[129] The *Munn v. Illinois* decision was handed down just a few years prior to the organization of a serious statehood movement in Dakota Territory. Regulating railroads was not an extraordinary measure for the transplanted midwestern farmers in Dakota Territory and thus not deemed a risky or experimental scheme during the constitutional conventions. It is not surprising, therefore, that the constitutional conventions of the 1880s adopted restrictions on railroads with minimal dissent. Not until the late 1880s did the U.S. Supreme Court begin to reject railroad regulatory measures as an unconstitutional interference with property rights.[130]

The restrictions on railroads adopted in the southern Dakota conventions reflected midwestern republican antipathy toward the concentration of economic power and forces seen to disrupt an agrarian economic structure. A large number of farmers in Dakota Territory came from states such as Iowa, Wisconsin, Minnesota, and Illinois, which constituted the core region of Grange activity and anti-railroad sentiment. These midwesterners embraced what Gerald Berk deems a "regional republicanism" that sought to preserve an economic order of decentralized farms not dependent on larger economic forces.[131] This midwestern republican tradition drew upon the "cultural resources of civic humanism articulated by the founders," among other antecedents, and sought to subordinate certain economic activities to the needs of the commonwealth and a yeoman-centered agricultural order. Railroad rates were thus made "subject to substantive republican norms, namely, decentralized market development."[132]

These republican sentiments extended beyond railroads to the activities of corporations in general, which the South Dakota framers also sought to restrict. The constitution prohibited the extension of any "special" charters to particular business entities, required corporations to be organized under "general" incorporation laws, and limited a corporation's activities to those designated in its charter. The constitution provided for the revocation or annulment of corporate charters and allowed minority shareholders to aggregate their shares in order to elect a member of the board of directors and prevent a "ring" from choosing all of the corporation's directors.[133] The constitution also prohibited the extension of public credit to any corporation.[134] Bank charters were limited to twenty years, and when that period expired, if the bank did not renew its charter, it could retain its corporate character only to sue and be sued. Bank stockholders were also subject to double liability.[135] The 1885 convention also adopted a homestead exemption for debtors that shielded their homes and a "reasonable amount of property" from seizure by creditors, a measure that favored the yeoman over the banker.[136] Corporate activities that could impair economic competition were also the subject of scrutiny. Following national trends, many constitutional delegates in Dakota were concerned about corporate consolidation and "trusts" and therefore adopted a provision limiting corporate mergers that would create monopolies.[137] Many of the provisions regulating corporate activity were borrowed from the Illinois and Pennsylvania constitutions, which had been amended specifically to address the undue influence of corporations.[138] Noting dubious business schemes of earlier decades, one delegate said: "We have come here from other states where we have been scorched. Those that have been once burned are afraid of the fire."[139] The framers of the Dakota constitution, though they could make few claims to originality, were hardly stooges of the corporate class and were well versed in recent precedents of constitutional reform and their grounding in republicanism.

CONSTITUTIONAL CONVENTIONS

During the winter of 1881–82, advocates of statehood in southern Dakota organized the Citizens Constitutional League to advocate the inclusion of certain provisions in the future state's constitution, including prohibition, restrictions on taxation, protections for school lands, and provisions "against railroads and other monopolies."[140] These issues were considered at an organizational meeting in Canton in June 1882 that included many "temperance men."[141] The Canton meeting formed an executive committee tasked with organizing a larger convention in Huron to discuss the extent of popular support in southern Dakota for writing a constitution and moving toward statehood.[142] On March 13, 1883, the executive committee issued the call for a convention in Huron, but, to facilitate consensus, the committee concluded that "special issues" discussed at the Canton meeting, including prohibition, should "be reserved for future and separate action."[143] Governor Ordway handed statehood advocates another source of outrage to help energize their efforts when he vetoed the bill passed by the legislature authorizing the constitutional convention.[144]

In June 1883, four hundred delegates convened in Huron to determine whether southern Dakota should proceed to write a constitution. The outcome of the debate was never in question, and an ordinance calling for a constitutional convention was quickly adopted.[145] The Huron convention set the 1st of August as the date for an election of delegates to a constitutional convention to begin in Sioux Falls on September 4. The Huron delegates invoked the Declaration of Independence, the U.S. Constitution and Bill of Rights, the Northwest Ordinance, the treaty with France ceding Louisiana, and the "ancient customs of this republic" to justify their move toward statehood.[146] According to the *Pioneer Press*, a "large majority" of the newspapers in the territory supported the statehood movement, but dissent could be found in the north and in the Black Hills. Some opponents questioned the wisdom of an effort that could be construed as an assertion of statehood without congressional approval, while others doubted whether a Democratic Congress would ever be receptive to statehood. Wisely, the Huron delegates decided to abandon any notion of establishing a state government without congressional approval and agreed to postpone inclusion of prohibition in the constitution. The convention recognized that "a Democratic congress backed by an all-powerful whiskey ring" would likely block admission under a "prohibitory constitution."[147] Convention delegate Bartlett Tripp, accusing "enemies" of Dakota of spreading the idea that the convention was "revolutionary," deemed the convention a "patriotic" affair. The "old flag was flaunted aloft," Tripp proclaimed, "and the wings of the great American bird were extended wide in the eloquent perorations of those embryo western statesmen," who simply wanted "a new star upon the old flag."[148]

When delegates to the first constitutional convention in Dakota Territory assembled in Germania Hall in Sioux Falls in September 1883, the walls were freshly frescoed and calcimined, the wood was newly painted, carpets were laid, and the old kerosene lamps had been replaced with gas chandeliers. A rostrum and desk were placed in the front of the hall for the use of the convention's president. The American flag and other decorations festooned the hall. The public was allowed to observe from the gallery.[149] During the convention, a newspaper noted that the "gallery of the Germania hall is well filled every day."[150] Large regional newspapers such as the *St. Paul Pioneer Press* and *Chicago Inter Ocean* sent correspondents to cover the proceedings.[151]

At noon on Tuesday September 4, 1883, the delegates began their work. After a prayer, the delegates were sworn in, Arthur Mellette was unanimously elected temporary chairman, and the committee on rules and the order of business was appointed. The delegates hoped to complete their work in roughly two weeks. After the organization of committees on the various topics to be addressed in the constitution, the committees would begin their work and then send reports to the full convention for acceptance, revision, or rejection. Under this plan, the *St. Paul Pioneer Press* reported, the delegates hoped that their "work may be greatly expedited."[152] On the second day, the convention elected permanent officers, including the Democratic lawyer Bartlett Tripp as president. Tripp's election was deemed "a bombshell in the ranks of the small squad of obstructionists hanging around the edge of the convention," because it underscored the partisan unity of the statehood forces and the willingness of the Republican majority to work with the Democratic minority.[153] The *Sioux Falls Daily Leader* praised Tripp as a "Dakotaian of the Dakotaians" and, stressing the unity and mission of the convention, proclaimed, "We are all Dakotaians, and we are all members of a Union with a great big capital U."[154] The *Yankton Press and Dakotaian* predicted that Governor Ordway would be flustered by Tripp's selection, for it signaled the "complete harmony" of the convention.[155] Delegates also sought to appeal to the Democratic Congress by choosing Tripp, whom the *Bismarck Tribune* deemed "a rock-ribbed, never-surrender Democrat."[156] The *Tribune* also reported that the "utmost harmony and

desire to expedite the business of the convention prevails."[157] One statehood leader later recalled that the 1883 convention was one of "toleration
and harmony" and that only one objection was made to the rulings of the
chair, which was quickly sustained by a vote of the delegates.[158]

On day three of the convention, the committee assignments were
announced, chairs were asked to announce committee meeting times
and places, and all the committees proceeded to meet in the evening.[159]
A large amount of time was set aside for committees to complete their
work, and some moved quickly.[160] By day eight, about half of the committees had reported their proposed provisions.[161] The work of the delegates and their virtue was widely praised in newspaper reports. Even the
Bismarck Tribune saw the delegates as "making as fine a body of men as
ever assembled in any legislative body."[162]

CORPORATIONS

Almost immediately, mirroring the concerns of Dakota farmers, the convention considered the issue of railroads and corporations generally. The
delegates included thirty-one farmers, an occupational group outnumbered only by the convention's forty-two lawyers. One newspaper noted
that the "number of farmers, newspaper men and solid citizens generally
present showed the movement to spring from the people."[163] The organization of the Farmers' Alliance in the 1880s also helped to spur the
concern over railroads and to ensure that farmers' voices were heard. On
day five of the convention, the *St. Paul Pioneer Press* reported "a strong
desire among the delegates who are farmers to deal with corporations
of the character of railroads, telegraph, etc. They say these corporations
should pay the same rate of tax as private individuals, should not be
allowed to consolidate, and should receive no aid that is not given private parties." Arthur Mellette, soon to be the last territorial governor and
later the first governor of the state of South Dakota, served as chairman
of the committee on corporations, which was "hard at work" all afternoon and evening of day five, drafting its provisions. The *Pioneer Press*
reported an "assiduity in the work of these men that commend them as
patriots. They are earnest and unflinching."[164] On day seven, a resolution

was referred to the corporations committee asking it to consider a provision to require the state legislature to pass laws setting maximum railroad rates and for the election of railroad commissioners who would insure that railroad laws were observed.[165] On day eight, some delegates thought that the tasks of the corporations committee were becoming "so complicated and numerous" that the size of the committee should be increased by six members, but this motion was defeated when committee reported it could handle its work.[166]

On day nine, the corporations committee issued its unanimous report, a juncture "anticipated with more than ordinary interest." Corporation-owned property was to be taxed like all other property, the state was prohibited from becoming a stockholder or assuming corporate liabilities, and the granting of subsidies was prohibited.[167] On day thirteen, when the corporations committee report was debated, there was, according to the *Yankton Press and Dakotaian*, "some hot shot fired at the railroad corporations of the country."[168] Delegate A. S. Jones of Hutchinson County offered an amendment to the report that required the legislature to pass laws regulating railroad rates and prohibiting unjust rate discrimination. Democratic delegate Abraham Boynton argued that the matter should be left to the legislature's discretion, believing it was not "wise to proceed on the ground that our legislature will be corrupt, to be bought up, like sheep."[169] J. C. Elliot of Grant County, however, worried that the south, like northern Dakota, was "falling also into the grasp of powerful corporations." Leading members of the convention, including corporations committee chairman Mellette, agreed with Elliot and supported the Jones rate-regulation amendment, which passed by a lopsided 53–18 vote.[170] In the end, the 1883 constitution made certain that railroads were deemed common carriers and that the legislature had the power and constitutional obligation to regulate them.[171]

CORRUPTION

The issue of railroad regulation was linked to fears that railroads and other interests exercised excessive influence over the territorial legislature. As a result, the framers took several steps to prevent corruption in the legislature. During the debate on day eight over the legislative committee's report, delegate Hugh Campbell denounced the previous legislature, which he termed "damnable, and a blotch on the name of Dakota," and condemned legislative "logrolling" by the governor.[172] The committee on the legislative section of the constitution sought to make it a crime for legislators to trade votes or for state officials, including the governor, to "wield official power in favor of or against any pending measure in the legislature."[173] The republican ideal embedded in these provisions envisioned a future legislature making decisions based on the public interest, not based on the logic of vote trading or due to outside pressures and influence.

In response to the perceived profligacy of federal appointees and the territorial legislature, delegates also limited public indebtedness. Counties, cities, and towns were prohibited from incurring debt levels exceeding 5 percent of assessed property valuation.[174] When a committee report was amended to prohibit local governments from extending aid to individuals or corporations, a few delegates worried that this provision would limit the economic development opportunities of local governments that might seek to promote railroad construction. Proponents of the provision, however, argued that railroads built with public money were not worth the trouble.[175] Delegate Gideon Moody thought that loans and grants by local governments would "open the doors to all sort of robbery of the people; that the people generally were constantly being attracted by some ignus fatus that never realized." Delegate B. G. Caulfield considered it good for "towns and cities to guard against indebtedness." After rigorous debate, amendments to allow local governments to offer grants and loans failed.[176] Spending on public works projects by local governments was capped at $500,000, and the *St. Paul Pioneer Press* characterized such provisions as "instances of the safeguards that are thrown around the powers usually granted legislatures by constitutions."[177]

BILL OF RIGHTS

The constitution's bill of rights represented the most obvious embrace of American democratic traditions. The debate over this provision also forced the delegates to directly address the perils of popular sovereignty. The lengthy bill of rights adopted by the framers borrowed heavily from earlier bills of rights and set forth common guarantees of liberty such as freedom of the press and religion and the right to trial by jury.[178] Many of these rights had also been set forth in the Northwest Ordinance governing the establishment of midwestern states and were repeated in the organic acts establishing western territories.[179] On day ten of the convention, when the report of the committee on the declaration of rights was considered, Hugh Campbell offered an amendment guaranteeing to the people the right to "abolish" their form of government in such manner as they thought proper.[180] Gideon Moody offered a similar amendment but with different wording.[181] Delegates Mellette and Robert Dollard opposed the amendment as "impolitic," and others thought it unnecessary; as a result the amendments to insert "abolish" were withdrawn.[182] The final report issued by the declaration of rights committee did not include the word "abolish" and instead settled for the phrase "right to alter and reform."[183]

During the bill of rights debate, the right to a jury trial was also called into question by delegates who feared that jurors were too often subject to corrupt influences. Gideon Moody called juries "a relic of barbarism," "a source of great injustice and corruption," and a "shield behind which rascals hide." While Moody based his argument on republican fears of corruption, defenders of the jury system recognized juries as bulwarks against the abuse of republican citizens. Delegate Hand said that the right to a jury "is something that belongs to the humblest citizen. It may be a shield for rascals, but it is a shield also for honest men." The right to trial by jury was ultimately preserved by the framers after a debate that demonstrated that they could differ as to the proper means to republican ends.[184]

SUFFRAGE AND PROHIBITION

The convention also grappled with the controversial issues of suffrage and prohibition. On day five, the committee on elections reported provisions that limited women's suffrage to school elections. The *Pioneer*

Press noted that this report "pretty effectually and satisfactorily does away with the problem of women's suffrage."[185] The decision was not made without a fair hearing, however. The Woman's Christian Temperance Union met during the convention, and the vice-president of the National Woman Suffrage Association, who was described as "an omnipresent member of the lobby," vowed to fight against statehood if women were not given the right to vote.[186] On day three, the NWSA spokeswoman asked to speak to the convention, and when given the rostrum, she lamented that women had "no more authority in self government than have the paupers and idiots." She pointed to recent elections in Wyoming made less "boisterous and riotous" by the participation of women.[187] On the ninth day, a motion to allow women to hold any office but vote only in school elections failed 16–114.[188] Reasons given for the failure of suffrage varied, but for those statehood advocates who sought to avoid constitutional provisions likely to jeopardize the document's popular adoption, the failure of suffrage was a relief.

Prohibitionists also pressed their case, but many delegates were similarly determined not to imperil the constitution by appending to it an alcohol ban sure to alienate large blocks of voters.[189] When on day eleven prohibition was debated, "for the first time blood was discovered in the eyes of some" delegates. The *St. Paul Pioneer Press* reported that "considerable feeling was evinced at times," and the mood of bipartisanship was endangered by some delegates who blamed the Democratic attendees for blocking prohibition.[190] When one delegate rejected the insinuations of his pro-temperance colleagues by proclaiming, "I am neither a drunkard or a rum seller," another delegate responded, "But you're a Democrat." Delegate A. B. Melville and others sought to preserve unity, however, by avoiding consideration of the prohibition issue and thus not "breaking faith with the Democrats." Delegate Melvin Grigsby considered the implications of prohibition for the entire statehood project. How, he asked, would "a Republican people with prohibition fare with a Democratic congress? We would be defeated. Money and whisky are both used freely in Congress." Gideon Moody also urged pragmatism, asking his colleagues to avoid deal-breaking measures to insure that "our work does not end as idle wind." Robert Dollard reminded his colleagues of the "solemn compact" made during the Huron convention to avoid consideration of prohibition and promote consensus. John Gamble reminded his fellow statehood advocates that Governor Ordway wanted the convention to adopt measures such as prohibition that would cause great division in the convention and in the statehood movement.[191] Arthur Mellette asked the central question: "Which is the paramount issue, prohibition or statehood?" When President Tripp addressed the issue, he said he was saddened that prohibition had caused the "first harsh word yet spoken" during the convention and asked delegates to "assert your manhood" and vote against the liquor ban.[192] During the votes on prohibition, "bouquets rained from ladies in the crowded gallery" who supported the measure, but the vote to include prohibition on the fall ballot with the constitution was defeated 64–38.[193] Delegate W. W. Brookings quipped that the ladies should "keep their bouquets to decorate the grave of their cause."[194] After the vote, a "large and enthusiastic" crowd at a Sioux Falls church denounced the result and called on people to vote against the prohibitionless constitution. The demonstration led some observers to think the constitution would "be snowed under."[195]

ELECTING STATE OFFICERS

Convention delegates at the 1883 convention also struggled with the question of whether Dakotans would elect a new state government at the same time they voted on ratifying the new constitution. Whereas some of the strongest statehood advocates sought to elect a slate of officers regardless of what Congress determined Dakota's fate to be, others sought to steer a conservative course and not alienate Congress or cause unneeded criticism of the statehood movement. On day twelve of the convention, a "field day for debaters," an equally divided convention debated the issue of electing officials to administer the future state.[196] Delegate Robert Dollard argued that Oregon provided a precedent for electing a state government without congressional approval. In response, opponents of electing officers "displayed more than ordinary zeal and used extraordinary language, reflecting in one or two instances upon the motives of those who favored the propositions." The debate was "growing very intense, when the president called upon the convention to proceed more dispassionately."[197] Those who opposed the election of a slate of officers included prominent delegates Moody, Campbell, and Mellette, and Richard Pettigrew.[198] On day thirteen, the delegates voted by a twenty-four-vote margin to elect a slate of officers but stipulated that the officers would not take power until congressional approval had been granted. The delegates hoped that the election of a government-in-waiting would "keep the fire burning on the altar of Statehood."[199] On day fourteen, however, still concerned about maintaining unity and avoiding any substantive objections, the convention decided to leave the decision of electing state officers to the convention's executive committee, which then postponed the election. The *St. Paul Pioneer Press* reported that observers thought this decision was "wise" because the election measure was the "only objectionable feature of the convention's whole proceedings."[200] The delegates had decided, once again, to avoid a potentially fatal pitfall for the constitution.

During the fall 1883 ratification campaign, the primary objection raised by opponents of the constitution was a provision relating to railroad taxation. The convention had granted the legislature the authority to tax a railroad's "gross earnings" instead of its property holdings, then the preferred method of taxation.[201] The delegates recognized that because property held by the Northern Pacific Railroad was exempted from taxation by federal law, the only method of collecting taxes from the railroad was through a gross earnings tax.[202] In an unsigned document, opponents of the constitution denounced the gross earnings tax as a sellout to "monied corporations," which might escape the taxes imposed "equally upon every kind and character of taxable property." Instead of specifically taxing railroad property, these opponents argued, the constitution left taxation decisions to the legislature, which was subject to corruption and undue railroad influence.[203]

The executive committee of the constitutional convention rejected the "nameless and fatherless circular," written by "men afraid to subscribe their names to, or admit the authorship of, such a paper."[204] The committee argued that the constitution's railroad taxation provision, borrowed from Illinois and Nebraska, was stronger than Iowa's provision. "No one has ever accused Iowa of being under the domination of railroads," the committee noted; "she has had upon her statute books the strongest agrarian legislation against railroads of any state in the union, unless it be Illinois and Wisconsin." The committee argued that the provision was also stronger than its counterparts in the constitutions of Wisconsin, Minnesota, and Nebraska, all of which had the benefit of borrowing from the recently amended anti-railroad constitutions of Illinois and Pennsylvania. Even the Pennsylvania convention of 1873, the committee found, "thought it necessary to provide this section only," and the Pennsylvania convention had met "under the cry of 'reform,'" when a "whole class of leading Republicans of that great state had come out and denounced the party of that state as under the control of rings and monopolies" and "produced what in many respects were the most radical changes in organic law that any convention had ever made." The committee reprinted the railroad taxation provision of every other state constitution in the Union in order to demonstrate that Dakota's provision was strong and not a product of special interest meddling. It also noted that delegates Thomas Sterling and William Pierce, "two of the strongest anti-monopolist members of the convention," supported the provision.[205] In the end, proponents of the constitution effectively rebuffed the critics' claims, which were probably designed to derail the constitutional process itself and not to protect farmers. Opponents of the constitution wisely understood, however, that the most effective arguments against ratification were those that appealed to agrarian sympathies grounded in republican fears of corruption.

Consensus

Despite the dubious postconvention objections lodged against the railroad taxation provisions, the 1883 convention succeeded in transcending divisive matters that could endanger the statehood movement. The delegates purposely elected a Democrat as their president in a symbolic move to promote unity, successfully delayed addressing issues such as suffrage and prohibition that were recipes for discord, and chose not to presumptuously form a government and risk riling the critics of statehood. As the

St. Paul Pioneer Press put it, the constitution avoided "pet schemes" and "wild innovations" and thus provided no "pretext" for opponents to use to delay statehood. The Democratic Congress would have to find some other "subterfuge" for blocking statehood.[206]

On day fifteen, transcription of the constitution was complete and the delegates assembled to affix their signatures. They adjourned at 11 P.M.[207] The *Pioneer Press* reported that the delegates' work was "praised upon every hand" and noted the absence of "self-seeking or political wire-pulling" during the convention and the presence of a "number of quiet, intelligent farmers and business men" and other "brilliant young men" who bolstered the effort.[208] The newspaper praised the final document as having "been prepared with all the nicety of care that 135 of the brainiest men of South Dakota could give it"; as containing the "best safeguards against the undue power of corporations, bribery, executive usurpations and the power of creating debt and excessive taxation"; and as having borrowed the best provisions of the Illinois, Pennsylvania, and Nebraska constitutions.[209] The convention ordered 10,000 copies of the constitution to be printed and distributed to voters and, in order to appeal to the main body of European immigrants, also ordered 1,000 copies printed in German and 1,000 printed in Norwegian.[210] A message attached to the constitutions to be distributed to the public stated that the delegates conducted "careful research into all authorities and precedents" and that their actions were justified by the "formal enactments and decisions by the highest authorities known under our courts and constitutions." The circular urged voters to "lift yourselves out of bondage into the condition of freemen, exercising all your own rights of self-government, w[h]ere no one can bridge [*sic*] your enjoyment of life, liberty and the pursuit of happiness."[211] No manifestation or symbol of American democratic practice was spared from the public appeal.

The 1883 constitutional convention in Sioux Falls was a victory for the advocates of statehood. The absence of the Ordway and railroad forces and the delegates' deliberate pursuit of unity helped the process succeed. Statehood advocates avoided creating opposition by excluding prohibition and suffrage provisions from the constitution and by resisting the temptation to create a state government-in-waiting. Although detractors did make their voices heard through newspapers sympathetic to the north, their motives were subject to much suspicion. The *Yankton Press and Dakotaian* correctly argued that the opposition to the constitution "emanated from the Ordway ring and has been pushed by his captains and lieutenants" and by the "northern capital syndicate."[212] Despite this dissent, the constitution was endorsed by a popular vote of 12,336 to 6,814 in November.[213] After the ratification, Bartlett Tripp, apparently seeking to redress doubts about the low turnout and the number of opposition votes, noted that vote margins on the frontier were often narrow because of the many and varied objections that could be leveled against such a long document; he cited the defeat of constitutions in Iowa in 1845 and in Wisconsin in 1846. Tripp also noted that the Iowa constitution of 1846 had passed by only four hundred votes, the Missouri constitution of 1865 by only eighteen hundred votes, and the Nebraska constitution of 1866 by only a hundred votes.[214] Democrats in Congress were still not amenable to Dakota statehood, however. The executive committee of the 1883 convention never called for the election of state officers because political conditions in Washington were not favorable.[215] Although the statehooders' efforts were for the moment stymied, the stream of settlers into the territory continued, and movement leaders continued to press their claims and build popular support.

THE 1885 AND 1889 CONSTITUTIONS

Advocates of statehood were not deterred by the passive attitude of Congress. In 1885 the territorial legislature again passed a bill authorizing a constitutional convention, and this time the measure was not vetoed by the territorial governor, now Gilbert Pierce.[216] An election of delegates for a second constitutional convention was held on June 30, 1885.[217] In September 1885 a convention again assembled in Germania Hall in Sioux Falls to write a constitution.[218] For the 1885 delegates, the constitution drafted in 1883 served as a great "labor saver." "Many of its articles were transplanted" to the 1885 document, with "hardly any material changes made." The delegates' "disposition was to respect the text of the constitution of 1883."[219] The 1885 convention ordered 250 copies of

the 1883 constitution printed for the delegates' analysis and deliberations.[220] One source notes that the 1885 constitution was derived from
the 1883 constitution, the Enabling Act, the U.S. Constitution, constitutions of other countries, court decisions, and "men of good authority,"
but that the "most important and most widely used source was that of the
constitutions and charters of all the states in the Union," copies of which
were procured for the delegates.[221] To underscore the reform-mindedness
of the document, the executive committee circular written in favor of
adoption of the 1885 constitution emphasized that the convention had
relied on the "last reform constitutions of Pennsylvania and Illinois, in
which are to be found the latest, best, and most stringent guards, against
the abuses of the power of corporations, special legislation, excessive
taxation, and the extravagant incurring of municipal, county and state
indebtedness, and the most careful and guarded protection of the school
lands and interests of the people."[222]

The 1885 constitution, like its 1883 predecessor, embraced railroad
regulation. The *St. Paul Pioneer Press* noted that the "convention has
blood in its eye whenever the subject of railroads are mentioned" and
that the "standing committees are whacking away at the railway corporations."[223] At the request of the increasingly influential Farmers' Alliance,
resolutions were offered calling for railroads to be declared "common
carriers and subject to legislative control," demanding that the legislature
be empowered to control railroad rates, and requesting that "all property
shall bear the burden of taxation equally."[224] The "granger element predominated" at the convention, the *Pioneer Press* reported, and helped the
convention work toward consensus on the railroad issue.[225] A subtitle in
a *Pioneer Press* article read, "All Agreed as to Railroads," and the report
of the corporations committee, which handled railroad provisions, "was
adopted with little or no debate."[226] The committee report was adopted
without change except for one section "amended [so] as to prevent the
consolidation of rival railroads by lease or otherwise."[227] As a result of
these provisions, the Dakota Territory Farmers' Alliance considered the
1885 constitution "a 'farmer's' document, [which] included solid provisions about rural issues ranging from retention of school lands to regulation of corporations. Especially pleasing were sections dealing with the

election of railroad commissioners and public control of transportation utilities."[228]

In addition to the railroad question, the 1885 debates repeated some of the discussions prominent during the 1883 convention. Prohibition and suffrage were again addressed, and this time the delegates decided, in lieu of inclusion in the constitution, to submit the issues for separate popular votes in the fall. The prohibitionists and suffragists "yielded gracefully" to this compromise.[229] The convention again debated whether to include a provision in the bill of rights protecting the right of the people to "abolish their form of government," which was borrowed from the 1870 Pennsylvania constitution.[230] Alonzo Edgerton defended the provision by citing Patrick Henry and the Declaration of Independence. Vowing not to bend to "czars and satraps," he invoked the Civil War and asked, "What did that Democratic Congress say to the people of Kansas?" It had "forced down their throats the Lecompton constitution," was the answer. "If such a provision be treason, I pray God I may always be a traitor."[231] Judge Moody downplayed the subversiveness of the "abolish" clause and characterized it as symbolic and as harmless as a "sort of Fourth of July declaration." Although the delegates voted to include the word "abolish" to the bill of rights 46 to 17, the measure was referred to committee, which settled for the less inflammatory phrase "alter and reform" instead.[232] The delegates again avoided the "revolutionary" temptation to declare statehood unilaterally, and thereby prevented opponents from arguing that they were endorsing divisive doctrines of "squatter sovereignty" or state's rights.[233] They did, however, provide for the election of state officers should Congress agree to statehood. The few changes to the 1883 constitution adopted by the delegates tightened the application of republican principles by allowing civil juries to reach decisions by a three-fourths majority; increasing the size of the House of Representatives to a range of 75 to 135 (versus 55 to 100 in 1883 constitution) and the Senate to between 25 and 45 seats (versus 25 to 33 in 1883); further constraining the taxing power and limiting state debt to $100,000 (it had been $500,000 in the 1883 constitution); and fixing executive salaries at a low absolute level (the 1883 constitution had allowed salaries to be subsequently changed by statute).[234]

The delegates adopted the 1885 constitution unanimously.[235] The day before the signing of the final document, the arrangements committee worked through the night, with "a large force of clerks being employed to transcribe the document." At 10:30 A.M. on the day of final adoption, Reverend Joseph Ward, arrangements committee chairman, "appeared in the doorway, carrying in his hands a large roll of manuscript which every one recognized as the organic law of the coming State of Dakota," and as he entered, he received "prolonged applause." At 10:39, the secretary began to read the document to the convention, which settled in to listen for errors. After a break for lunch, the reading resumed and was completed just after 5:00 P.M. Hugh Campbell then moved to approve the constitution, and it was adopted unanimously at 5:17 P.M. with every delegate voting. The hall echoed with loud and long applause, and the delegates then proceeded to the front of the hall to sign the document.[236] Four decades later, in an indication that the delegates viewed the convention as a defining moment, Arthur C. Phillips finally admitted that he momentarily distracted President Edgerton and pilfered the historic gavel used during the 1885 convention.[237]

With interest spurred by separate votes on the prohibition and suffrage questions, more voters turned out in the fall of 1885 than in 1883, and the constitution won popular approval 25,226–6,565. The government-in-waiting convened in early December in Huron, the temporary capital, but quickly adjourned without addressing any legislative matters. Congressional partisanship again blocked the path to statehood. According to John D. Hicks, "Politics again prevented admission. Dakota was Republican; the administration was Democratic."[238] Despite burgeoning popular support within the territory, the moment of republican fulfillment for the advocates of Dakota statehood was again deferred.

The treatment of western territories emerged as an issue in the 1888 national elections. That fall, with the defeat of incumbent Democrat Grover Cleveland and the election of a Republican president and a Republican House to work with the existing Republican Senate, statehood for Dakota was assured.[239] An Aberdeen newspaper headline proclaimed, "A Glorious Day for Dakota—Good Bye, Old Grover. Good Bye."[240] In Yankton, celebrants lit bonfires, set off fireworks, rang bells, sang songs,

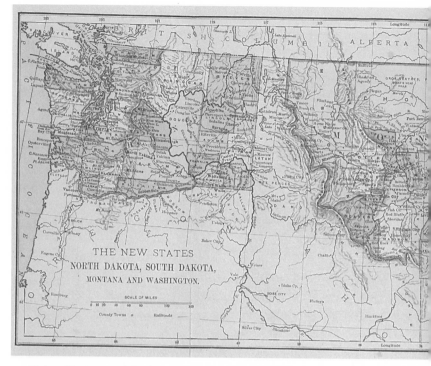

Dakota Territory and the three other "Omnibus States" that were admitted
to the Union in 1889. Beinecke Rare Book and Manuscript Library, Yale
University.

hoisted many flags, and were generally overtaken with "wild enthusiasm."[241] After the election and before the new Congress was sworn in,
the Democrats in the House, with nothing to lose, passed a bill admitting
the Dakotas, Washington, Montana, and New Mexico, but the Republican Senate, recognizing that the Democrats had slipped Democratic New
Mexico into the bill, demurred. The House finally gave way to Senate
demands, and New Mexico was removed from the legislation.[242] The two
Dakotas, Washington, and Montana were admitted to the Union in a new
Omnibus Bill. The final federal legislation called for a May election in
southern Dakota to determine the level of support for the 1885 constitution; if it was endorsed by popular vote once again, a convention would
meet to address technical changes, and another ratification vote on the

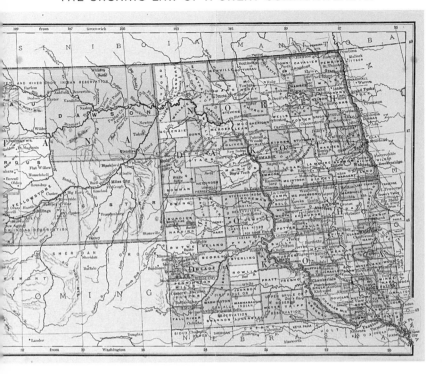

final constitution would be held in the fall.[243] The 1885 constitution was again ratified in May, and in accordance with the Omnibus Bill, four constitutional conventions began on July 4, 1889, in Sioux Falls, Bismarck, Olympia, and Helena.[244] When delegates once again assembled in Germania Hall in Sioux Falls during the summer of 1889, they avoided any changes to the constitution that might conflict with the requirements of the Omnibus Bill. The *Daily Argus-Leader* of Sioux Falls noted that the "delegates to the convention were elected not to make, but to patch a constitution."[245] The convening of the South Dakota constitutional convention on July 4, 1889, in Sioux Falls, the *Pioneer Press* wrote, would connect the republican aspirations of the Dakotas to those of the original American revolutionaries and would further inspire the other new "commonwealths" included in the Omnibus Bill with the "patriotic spirit and the wise and far-seeing statesmanship of the founders of the Union."[246] In the fall of 1889, the voters of South Dakota adopted the constitution by an overwhelming vote of 70,131 to 3,267.[247]

A PEOPLE'S MOVEMENT

The drive for statehood and the constitution-writing process in southern Dakota were the products of a popular democratic movement. Participants in the enterprise were immersed in the language, symbols, precedents, and practices of American democracy, civic republicanism, and political reform. Statehood advocates persistently called on citizens to promote the public interest, foster consensus, and combat corruption. The movement derived energy from territorial outrage over the corruption of unelected "carpetbag" appointees who frustrated the general will of the people. The movement ran with the grain of the American democratic tradition.

Viewing the statehood movement in South Dakota as democratic, broadly supported, and reform-oriented deviates from the interpretation offered by Howard Lamar in his 1956 book *Dakota Territory*. According to Lamar, the statehood movement was controlled by an "oligarchy" in southern Dakota that was economically "conservative" and dismissive of railroad and corporate regulations. Lamar criticized the convention delegates for their failure to adopt "radical innovations" and for being "conservative in their treatment of nearly every question." The "same men," he argued, were the "controlling forces" in all three constitutional conventions, and this "inner circle" went "unchallenged." The delegates, according to Lamar, were preoccupied with finding "methods to assure the popular ratification" of the constitution.[248]

Lamar's analysis, written during the age of progressive history and prior to the great wave of research into the prominence and persistence of political republicanism in United States history, overlooks the democratic heritage embraced by the advocates of statehood and the republicanism embedded in the movement. Lamar's portrayal of an economic oligarchy squelching the hopes of yeoman farmers is a reflection of what Paul

Kleppner calls a "strong economic determinist bias" that once "permeated American historiography," especially in the early twentieth century. This mode of interpretation privileged economic conflict over widely shared assumptions within the political culture and slighted the role of religion and ethnicity.[249] Lamar's criticism of the constitutional process in Dakota relied heavily on the interpretative framework of Charles Beard, who famously criticized the federal Constitution as a product of class conflict and the influence of economic elites.[250] In Dakota, however, a broad consensus among both convention delegates and many settlers prevailed on the major economic issue of the time, especially railroad regulation. Their treatment of railroads was not "radical" or particularly "innovative," as it proceeded from the recent regulatory history and constitutional precedents of several midwestern states. The constitutional conventions did not exclude critics of the railroads and were in fact open to a large number of delegates. Given Dakotans' frustration with their long-delayed entry into the Union, the delegates' focus on circumventing issues that might further delay statehood is certainly understandable and consistent with the exigent circumstances.

The numerous elections and conventions leading to statehood, the unanimous approval of constitutions by convention delegates, the diversity in the delegates who served in the constitutional conventions and the territorial legislature, and the popular vote counts in favor of the constitution also indicate public support for the document and undercut the notion of an oligarchy controlling the statehood movement. Dakota Territory certainly had its strong personalities and vocal leaders, but this should not be taken as evidence of a lack of popular support for those leaders or for statehood.[251] As Jean Baker has noted, "to see only the control of leaders is to distort the degree of consensual fraternity" in a political movement.[252] Debates over economic questions and the potential economic motivations of some social actors should not lead one to assume the existence of a singular have-versus-have-not struggle or to overlook the existence of common political principles. While the quest for material gain was certainly a strong component of life during the late nineteenth century, Americans, as Boyd Schaffer once noted, also shared many political assumptions and imagined and strove for a republic grounded in "equity, good will, freedom and abundance."[253] Recognition of this striving and the strength of the republican impulse is the best lens through which to view the Dakota statehood movement and its effort to craft a constitution.

Full consideration of the symbols of American democracy and the elements of the republican tradition at work in Dakota Territory reveals the participatory nature of the constitutional process. While natural leaders certainly emerged in the statehood movement, and while those leaders often reflected the prominence and social advantages of old-stock Americans, the procedural steps toward statehood were open to widespread public involvement. The earliest statehood clubs, for example, were organized on the democratic Grange model in order to promote popular participation. The road to statehood also proceeded through several stages open to the public. A convention to discuss statehood was held in Canton in June 1882, a convention to determine whether to call a constitutional convention was held in Huron in June 1883, delegates were elected to a constitutional convention to be held in September 1883, delegates were elected to a constitutional convention to be held in September 1885, and delegates were yet again elected for the constitutional convention held in July 1889. Along the way, there were innumerable political acts common to the Anglo-American political tradition, including conventions, debates, public speeches, elections, referendums, community meetings, clashes of opinion in the numerous territorial newspapers, and the writing of ordinances, petitions, circulars, and editorials. The three constitutions were also subjected to a popular vote and passed each time, a result not always replicated in other ratification votes in the West.

On the preeminent economic issue of the day, railroad regulation, the statehood advocates and constitution framers sided with the drafters of the Granger constitutions of the Midwest, the original home of many Dakota settlers. The anti-railroad provisions of the 1883 and 1885 constitutions were largely borrowed from other states such as Illinois and Pennsylvania, which had adopted rigorous railroad regulations. Delegate Robert Dollard plainly described the 1883 constitution as "hostile to railroads," and one newspaper deemed it a "granger constitution."[254] The *Pioneer Press* also recorded the prominence of the "granger element" at the 1885 convention.[255] When reporting on the 1885 constitution, the *Bismarck Tribune* noted that the "subject of railroads whenever brought up excites much comments. Its [*sic*] like a red flag."[256] The railroad regulations adopted by the convention were widely supported by the delegates.[257]

The adoption of railroad regulation indicates the influence of farmers within the constitutional conventions. Farmers' interests were also promoted more broadly by the increasingly potent Farmers' Alliance.[258] During the height of the statehood movement, the territorial Alliance was highly active, and the number of local Alliances grew from 256 in 1886 to 744 in 1888.[259] By the time of the 1889 constitutional convention, John D. Hicks noted, the "Alliance was able to dictate in the Dakotas," and its members possessed numerical control of the legislature.[260] Achieving statehood, which would deny Congress the power to nullify legislative enactments and which would displace federally appointed governors with governors popularly elected by Dakotans, would further enhance the political influence of farmers. The Farmers' Alliance, having already won victories in the territorial legislature, would thus benefit from laws passed by a sovereign state legislature.[261] The Alliance did not, therefore, object to the adoption of the 1889 constitution. Alliance president H. L. Loucks gave his blessing by attending the constitutional convention, and the Alliance described the constitution as a "farmers'" document.[262] With the aid of the Alliance, the document was widely supported in the fall election.[263] Given the large farm population of Dakota Territory and its political influence, Alliance opposition to the constitution could have scuttled its approval.

The presence of farmers at the constitutional convention underscores the social diversity of the delegates who attended the conventions and undercuts the argument that an economic oligarchy controlled the constitution-writing process. The adoption of the provisions regulating railroads with little dissent also indicates the strength of the agrarian sentiment. The 1883 convention included thirty-one farmers, and the largest occupational bloc at the 1889 convention consisted of twenty-four farmers, who even outnumbered the twenty lawyers in attendance.[264] The executive committee promoting passage of the 1885 constitution noted that the convention was "composed in a large degree of the farming and industrial element of the people."[265] One newspaper reported that at least seventeen foreign-born delegates, including seven from Germany and Norway, attended the 1883 convention, and another noted that among the constitution writers and Dakotans in general, "great care was taken to deal fairly" with foreign-born residents.[266] In addition to including strong agrarian and foreign elements, membership across the constitutional conventions was not dominated by one consistent group. Only one person attended all three conventions. The 1889 convention included only eleven delegates who had served in the 1885 convention.[267] The diversity and turnover in the constitutional conventions were comparable to those in the territorial legislature from 1862 to 1889, where 70 percent of legislators served only one term and only 15 percent served two terms.[268]

As part of his thesis that Dakota was controlled by an economic oligarchy, Lamar argued that the September constitutional conventions were timed to prevent farmers from attending because they would then be busy with harvesting.[269] Reports from 1883, however, indicate that the harvest was largely complete by the time the convention convened on September 1. On that day, one newspaper noted that "many farmers" in Yankton County had finished harvesting and had already begun preparations for the following year's planting.[270] On September 3 another newspaper reported that the final numbers on the wheat harvest had already been tabulated.[271] The 1885 constitutional convention did not meet until September 8.[272] On August 26, a farmer near Aberdeen wrote to his brother that he had finished cutting his wheat the previous week (after three weeks of work) and that his threshing would be done "this week."[273] On August 18, 1886, another farmer wrote to his sister that "what crops are good we are all done harvesting."[274] At least one delegate suggested a reason for holding the constitutional conventions in September. During the 1883 convention, Hugh Campbell said that it was necessary to organize the convention during the summer, write the constitution in the early fall, and hold a popular vote on the constitution in November in order to demonstrate to Congress, which convened in January, that Dakotans supported statehood.[275] Lamar's argument also suffers from the fact that many farmers actually did attend the constitutional conventions. While some farmers' harvests may have been delayed and threshing may have continued into September, and though it may have been easier for farmers with hired hands to attend the conventions, the lack of significant agrarian protest and the endorsement of the territory's most influential agricultural organization indicate the absence of serious objection to the timing of the constitutional conventions.

Turnout for the elections of delegates to the constitutional conventions could have been higher. But modest turnout for a delegate election prompted few worried comments from newspapers, nor did it cause much public concern. In 1885 the *St. Paul Pioneer Press* observed that some counties did not hold delegate elections because "there was no opposition to the nominations."[276] It also opined that lower turnout could reflect the fact that "people took it for granted that good men would be selected, or . . . there was a feeling prevalent in the community that the effort to secure statehood would not be successful, and therefore [voters] stayed away from the polls."[277] The delegate election for the 1885 convention, moreover, was held on June 30, well ahead of the harvest schedule, and farmer representation at the 1885 convention was strong.[278] The timing of the delegate election and the constitutional conventions may never have been ideal, given the day-to-day obligations of pioneer farming, but evidence of a conspiracy among economic elites to stifle farmer participation is exceedingly thin. Many farmers ultimately participated in the conventions, farm groups did not launch protests against the timing of the conventions, and the results of the conventions were supported by farmers.

Lamar's criticism of the constitution makers' efforts is also based on their failure to adopt "radical" reforms.[279] Although he does not define "radical," Lamar implies some variant of socialist reform.[280] Using radicalism or socialism as a standard to measure the success of the constitutional delegates creates an unfair burden given the absence of any significant radical or socialist element in Dakota Territory.[281] Such a standard also obscures other important reforms. The delegates willingly adopted many reforms short of socialism, including railroad regulation, that fit squarely within the midwestern political tradition and that comported with the republican goal of promoting a decentralized agrarian economy and limiting corrupt influences on government.

Lamar also deemed prohibitionists and suffragists "reformers" and viewed the marginalization of their issues as evidence that economic elites dominated the constitutional conventions.[282] These issues, however, are more properly viewed as questions of social policy than as economic questions dividing rich elites from the poorer masses. Although liquor interests would certainly have seen prohibition, also supported by many would-be women voters, as an economic issue, this does not justify viewing prohibition as a reform issue undermined by an economic oligarchy. Many constitution makers who supported prohibition decided to postpone action on the issue in order to speed statehood and avoid generating unnecessary opposition—not out of subservience to economic powers. Delegate Gideon Moody viewed prohibition as a "dangerous rock in the channel" to be circumvented until statehood was achieved, when he, as a "citizen of the commonwealth," and other Dakotans could then determine the fate of the issue. Statehood leaders, moreover, were willing to put prohibition to a popular vote.[283]

Focusing on class conflict and the absence of socialism or "radical" reforms obscures the influence of republicanism in Dakota Territory, whose adherents sought to place certain constraints on the operation of the market. Envisioning a decentralized agrarian economy, most Dakotans sought railroad regulation and other reforms that promoted that vision and squared with the midwestern tradition of political reform. This approach, as Elizabeth Sanders has noted, was "distinctly Jeffersonian and republican."[284] Late-nineteenth-century protests against monopolies and railroads focused on the disruptive effect of large-scale economic entities on the decentralized economy and were "rooted in agrarian republican ideology."[285] Historians in the past several decades have increasingly recognized agrarian reformers' reliance on the republican tradition as a basis for constraining the market and have downplayed the older notion of deep-seated conflict between distinct economic classes.[286] When the Populists organized in South Dakota during the 1890s, they relied on republican ideals.

The ubiquitous reliance on republican ideas, language, references, and symbols in Dakota Territory during the 1880s indicates a broad-based consensus instead of a polity divided into economic classes.

Delegations to the constitutional conventions of the 1880s included a large numbers of farmers, and the Farmers' Alliance, which was highly organized in Dakota Territory at the time, openly praised the constitution. Far from ignoring railroad regulation at the behest of capitalists, constitution drafters borrowed the most stringent provisions of the midwestern Granger constitutions. The absence of "radical" reforms, which Lamar saw as evidence of oligarchic control of the statehood process, is better viewed as demonstrating consensus in favor of railroad regulations modeled on well-known provisions in midwestern constitutions. The rejection of prohibition and suffrage, which Lamar viewed as "reform" provisions, was primarily based on cultural objections and pragmatism, not the economic self-interest of statehood advocates. The statehooders sought to avoid provisions that a large number of Dakotans would likely object to and that could undermine the prospects of statehood and the realization of settlers' republican ambitions. The prominent statehooders that Lamar viewed as forming an "oligarchy" were often the most articulate defenders and purveyors of republicanism and the staunchest opponents of the shady alliance of territorial officials, railroads, and other interests, a combination much more deserving of retrospective opprobrium. Lamar's contrary interpretation, however, deserves a more elaborate explanation, given his well-earned reputation as a scholar of western history and because such an explanation reveals a great deal about the evolution of historians' thinking about the American West and Dakota Territory's place in it.

American and English history, civic and personal virtue, and the basic elements of republicanism were taught in Dakota's many public schools. This photograph features schoolchildren with their teacher in front of a schoolhouse located near Tyndall.

Dakota children were raised to be patriotic. Here children are costumed for one of the many patriotic celebrations held in Dakota Territory.

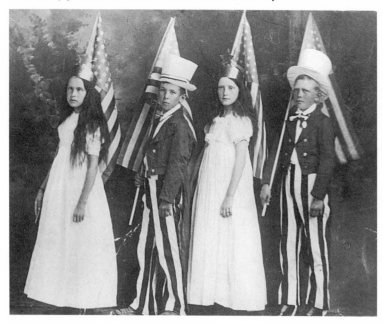

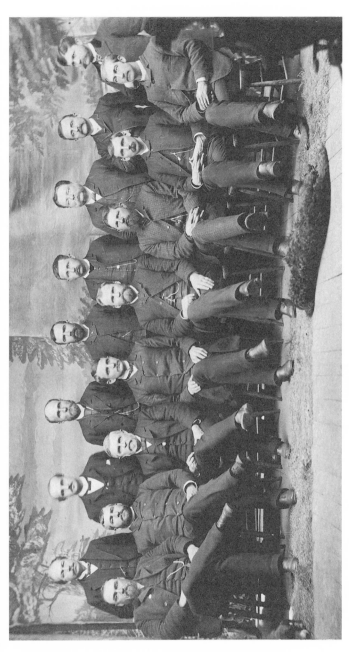

Participation in local government was a tenet of republicanism that found wide acceptance in Dakota Territory. This photograph features elected officials in Lincoln County, so named for the martyred president. Lincoln was the first president to be elected as a member of the Republican Party, the dominant political party in Dakota. Many residents of the Midwest, the region from which Lincoln hailed, and many veterans of the Union Army, which Lincoln commanded, settled in Dakota.

The Republican Party was the majority party in Dakota Territory because of the large number of New England and midwestern settlers. Photographed here are delegates to a GOP political convention in Bon Homme County in 1889.

Over 550 newspapers enlivened the public sphere in Dakota Territory. A printer stands in front of his shop in the town of Gary in Deuel County.

Congregational Church, Worthing, S.D.

The Puritan churches of New England came to be known as the Congregational Church, which exerted a strong influence on the culture of the Dakota prairie. This is the Congregational Church in Worthing, Lincoln County.

The Church of England, or Anglican Church, became the Episcopalian Church in the United States and included many members of the Protestant establishment. The Episcopalian Church in Yankton, Yankton County, pictured here, was dubbed the "Mother Church of the Dakotas." Yankton was the territorial capital until 1883. Several prominent territorial leaders were members of the Episcopal Church in Dakota.

Protestants were not always welcoming to Catholic settlers. This photograph features the Catholic church in Jefferson, Union County. The town was named for Thomas Jefferson, an advocate of religious freedom in the new United States and a critic of Catholic absolutism in Europe. Fears of a Catholic threat to republican governance were part of the inherited political culture of Dakota settlers.

For advocates of statehood in Dakota Territory, the writing of a constitution for the future state represented the culmination of all their efforts to promote self-rule and break the control of federally appointed territorial officials. These delegates to the 1885 constitutional convention met in Germania Hall in Sioux Falls, a reflection of the influence of German immigrants in Dakota Territory. Siouxland Heritage Museums, Sioux Falls, South Dakota.

A. J. Edgerton, featured in this photograph, was a prominent territorial leader. As president of the constitutional conventions, he was a moderate force and dampened the enthusiasm of those delegates who wanted to declare statehood despite the absence of congressional authorization. Edgerton believed that the conventioneers were writing the "organic law of a great commonwealth." Along with many other prominent leaders in the territory, he was a Civil War veteran, a midwesterner, and a member of the Congregational Church, the Grand Army of the Republic, and the Masons.

Railroads were a primary means for settlers to travel to Dakota Territory, but their economic power also caused some civic republicans concern. This is the Chicago & Northwestern depot in Highmore.

Grand Army of the Republic lodges were a prominent feature of civic life in Dakota Territory. Photographed here in 1890, the year after statehood, is a GAR parade in Sioux Falls. Siouxland Heritage Museums, Sioux Falls, South Dakota.

CHAPTER 5

THE INTELLECTUAL ORIGINS OF DAKOTA TERRITORY

Succeeding generations will quite properly ask new questions of the past.

Allan G. Bogue,
"Frederick Jackson Turner Reconsidered" (1994)

The story of Dakota Territory did not always include the influences of republicanism and Christianity nor a favorable assessment of Dakota's constitutional origins. The lone scholarly history of the territory to date is Howard Lamar's 1956 book, *Dakota Territory, 1861–1889: A Study of Frontier Politics*, which took a generally dim view of its subject. The individuals and scholarly trends that influenced Lamar explain his grim assessment. Understanding the intellectual origins of Lamar's *Dakota Territory*, written prior to the major developments in American historiography that inform this study, helps explain the need for a revised interpretation of the main political and social currents at work in Dakota Territory. A review of Lamar's long-term intellectual development and of his thoughts on the present direction of western history also yields important insights into the American historical profession in general. Considering the origins and limitations of Lamar's *Dakota Territory* in tandem with other developments in American historiography after its publication opens the door to a different view of the formative period of Dakota Territory and other parts of the American West.

Howard Roberts Lamar has enjoyed one of the most distinguished careers in the history of the American academy. Lamar taught history at Yale University for forty-five years and also served stints as dean of Yale College and university president. His most permanent contribution to the discipline of American history has been helping to reinvigorate the study of the American West. Lamar's scholarly works and the historians of the American West he trained have shaped the course of western historiography. The publication of *Dakota Territory* was a crucial first step in Lamar's intellectual development and has been recognized as an important contribution to western history.[1] This pioneering work by a major scholar helped spark a revival of western history. Reviewing *Dakota Territory* five decades after its publication, however, reveals the extent to which it was a product of its time and highlights the need to rethink the history of Dakota Territory in light of recent scholarship. Retracing Lamar's steps also offers an opportunity to reflect on the arc of western history, a trajectory that might give pause to the current generation of western historians.

Dakota Territory entered the stream of western history at a logical point in its development. At the time Lamar wrote the book, historians such as Earl Pomeroy were studying the American territorial system, and Lamar's reliance on and respect for Pomeroy are unmistakable. Lamar's *Dakota Territory* and his successor book, *The Far Southwest,* "became models for subsequent explorations of the relatively neglected subject of territorial politics," according to David J. Weber.[2] Lamar also waded into the Turner wars, although not as deeply as some historians. Frederick Jackson Turner's thesis focusing on the importance of the frontier in American development had once been a near-truism among American historians. By the 1930s, however, the frontier thesis had come under intense scrutiny, begetting what Allan G. Bogue called a "blood-drenched field" of historiography.[3] After such battles, Michael Steiner justifiably deemed "Turner the most influential as well as the most reviled historian since Karl Marx."[4] The impact of the historiographic turn against Turner is obvious in Lamar's book.

Few American historians now study the territorial system, but the echoes of the Turner debate can still be heard within the subdiscipline of western history.[5] The story of *Dakota Territory* can help historians understand the origins of this debate and the ideological underpinnings of many of the books on western history that line the library shelves. Lamar's scholarship subsequent to *Dakota Territory* and his reaction to the work of some of the students he helped to train also provide an important cautionary tale for those currently working in western history.

Lamar began his study of the West at Yale University in New Haven, Connecticut, not at a university farther west such as Wisconsin, where Frederick Jackson Turner and Frederic Logan Paxson had been training western historians for decades. Turner, in fact, promoted western history because he felt eastern institutions were too parochial and uninterested in the West, an attitude that did not quickly dissipate, despite Turner's complaint. When Lamar began teaching his course in western history at Yale, it was only "under the restriction that it was to be a small starred course only to be taken by history majors who had already had a number of 'regular' American history courses."[6] The skepticism of Yale professors toward western history certainly did not exempt Turner. Lamar later recalled that there "weren't any Turner defenders at Yale" during his years in graduate school in the 1940s.[7] Through his teaching, scholarship, and training of young historians at Yale, Lamar helped legitimize western history as a major field of historical inquiry.[8]

Lamar's road to studying western history took a winding path. Born and raised in Alabama, Lamar had deep southern roots.[9] He moved to Atlanta to attend college and in 1944 earned his bachelor of arts degree from Emory University, the flagship university of the South. At Emory he first studied the works of historians such as Frederick Jackson Turner and Charles Beard. In graduate school at Yale, Lamar read more by and about Turner, Beard, and other prominent historians in methodology courses.[10] He received his master's in history from Yale in 1945 and his Ph.D. in 1951.

Although Lamar wrote his dissertation about Dakota Territory, the history of the American West was not a high priority in the Yale history department. One of Lamar's professors at Yale was the historian George Wilson Pierson, who served as department chairman. Pierson was a "born easterner" who, Lamar recalled, "said that as far as he was concerned the American West began with the Hudson River." Pierson thought Turner had "botched" the interpretation of American history and "hitched his star to a covered wagon."[11]

In keeping with Pierson's sentiments, Lamar's book *Dakota Territory* was part of the reaction against the theories of Turner, who had in turn rejected the thinking of prominent late-nineteenth-century historians. When Turner began graduate school in the 1880s, many historians found the roots of American democracy in subcultures that had migrated to America from Teutonic Europe. In the 1890s, midwestern historians such as Turner attempted to challenge the dominance of the "Teutonic School" and eastern historians in general.[12] In graduate school at Johns Hopkins, Turner "staged a one-man revolt against eastern historians who ignored his section." Turner, along with Dakotan Hamlin Garland, helped spur a western cultural revolt against the East in the late nineteenth century.[13]

Finding the key to the nation's development in the democratic practices of the midwestern frontier, Turner presented his thinking in 1893 in a famous address in Chicago. As Walter Prescott Webb wrote, Turner's essay was "recognized as the most influential single piece of historical writing ever done in the United States."[14] Dixon Ryan Fox called Turner's paper the "most famous and most influential paper in American historiography."[15] By the 1920s, according to Ray Allen Billington, "much of the scholarly world worshipped at Turner's shrine," and his "scholarly disciples" treated the Turner theory as "Holy Writ." In the 1930s and 1940s, however, when Lamar was on the path to becoming a professional historian, the Turner "thesis endured a series of attacks."[16] Billington noted that "for two decades aspiring young historians made their reputations by leaping on the anti-Turner bandwagon."[17] Lamar similarly recalled that the "muted criticisms that first appeared during the 1920s— when Charles A. Beard noted that the frontier could not explain slavery, the growth of the city, the industrializing process, and the rise of labor— turned into a full-scale attack in the 1930s."[18]

From the 1890s to the 1940s, as various historians began to question historical "objectivity" and to emphasize that the events of the present determined how one viewed the past, the "New History" of James Harvey Robinson and Charles Beard gained adherents.[19] Beard's revisionist history of the U.S. Constitution, for example, had "political significance" for progressives who were seeking to reform the way political institutions functioned.[20] When writing *An Economic Interpretation of the Constitution* (1913), Beard insisted on giving history a practical meaning in the "living present" and breaking with the "sterile" history of old.[21] Forrest McDonald has noted the common belief that Beard's book sought "to undermine the prevailing veneration of the Constitution, which the Supreme Court was using to strike down progressive social and economic legislation."[22] Beard's book "became a new prevailing orthodoxy" in the 1930s and 1940s and, by the time of his death in 1948, had become a "sacred cow."[23]

Followers of Beard and critics of American society believed that the widespread acceptance of Turner's interpretation limited their ability to reform American institutions. The Turner interpretation of American history did not provide a "usable past" for these reformers, but instead a "useless past" to be transcended, according to Warren Susman. For Turner and other "conservatives," the "frontier had created the perfect small-town bourgeoisie: stable, reliable (i.e., Republican), uninfluenced by immigrant blocs and foreign radicals, the safeguard of the Republic." But a growing number of intellectuals in the 1920s and 1930s thought that the frontier heritage inhibited the growth of high culture, created "Puritanical" small towns governed by conformity, caused psychological trauma, and generally resulted in the creation of a "warped man in a warped culture."[24] The frontier, Susman notes, "became the scapegoat for all that was wrong with contemporary America," and the "revolt against this particular 'useless past' was part of a larger revolt against what was considered to be the Midwestern domination of American life and values."[25]

More generally, many intellectuals thought that Turner's thesis obscured a darker record of capitalist exploitation, class conflict, and imperialism.[26] "Left-wing scholars in particular," according to John Lauritz Larson, "felt ideologically excluded by the breadth and force of Turner's legacy."[27] Turner's "mystique of rural America" and his "Middle Western loyalties began to seem quaint" in the 1930s, according to Richard Hofstadter, and a new generation of historians began "gagging" on Turner's sentimentality.[28] Hofstadter noted that an "avalanche of criticism descended on the Turnerian structure, precipitated in large degree by the new ideological currents set in motion by the Great Depression."[29] During Lamar's formative years of education and at the time he began his dissertation, many intellectuals were targeting Turner.

Lamar's turn toward western history and the Turner debate was directly affected by Yale history professor Ralph Henry Gabriel. After Lamar discovered that another graduate student at a different university was also working on the subject of industrialization in Alabama, which was Lamar's initial research project, Lamar went into a "panic." He began his "hunt for a new dissertation" by meeting with Professor Gabriel, whom Lamar remembers as a "grand old affable, brilliant man in American Studies and history." Gabriel said, "Well, Lamar, born in the South, educated in the East, go West for your dissertation." Gabriel informed Lamar about the new collection of western materials donated to Yale by the insurance magnate William Robertson Coe. Gabriel instructed Lamar to visit the collection's curator, Archibald Hanna, and to see if the archive contained a research topic. Within four days, Lamar latched on to the story of Dakota Territory, and Gabriel agreed to serve as one of his dissertation advisors.[30]

In his famous book *The Course of American Democratic Thought*, published in 1940, Gabriel sounded themes consistent with the progressive history of the 1930s that would be found later in Lamar's work on Dakota Territory. In the post–Civil War era, according to Gabriel, the United States was "drifting toward monopoly capitalism." Similar concerns about economic power, social inequality, and class conflict would be embraced by Lamar. Gabriel also understood the gravity of the battles over the Turner thesis. Recognizing the "emotionalism" of the Turner debate and the "tenaciously held social beliefs" embedded in the Turner thesis, Gabriel believed that "more than a scientific hypothesis [was] at stake." "For the basic ideas of Turner," according to Gabriel, "were the doctrines of the American democratic faith."[31] At a minimum, Gabriel's writings surely highlighted for Lamar the importance of the Turner thesis. More specifically, Gabriel's directive to visit the Coe collection turned Lamar to the history of the American West. The result was Lamar's dissertation on Dakota Territory, completed in 1951 and published as a book in 1956 by Yale University Press.

Other direct influences on Lamar, though not as ideological as those linked to the Turner debate, include the scholarship of Earl Pomeroy and Walter Prescott Webb. Pomeroy's book *The Territories and the United States* (1947), originally a dissertation written at the University of California–Berkeley under Frederic Logan Paxson, heavily influenced Lamar's study of Dakota Territory.[32] In part because the first chapter of *Dakota Territory* discusses the workings of the territorial system in detail, Lamar's book is sometimes recalled as a territorial study.[33] One analysis categorizes *Dakota Territory* and Lamar's subsequent book, *The Far Southwest,* as "model analyses of territorial governance."[34] Walter Prescott Webb, a University of Texas historian who served as president of both the Organization of American Historians and the American Historical Association in the 1950s, also influenced Lamar. His book *The Great Plains* (1931) emphasized settlers' adaptation to life on the arid plains and was widely cited and discussed in historical circles at the time Lamar was writing *Dakota Territory*.[35] Webb was not a Turner disciple and took pains to distinguish the history of the plains from that of Turner's Midwest.[36] Lamar later recalled that Webb "influenced me a great deal in that he was so articulate and he gave me the first coherent image of the plains west."[37]

The scholars A. Whitney Griswold and John D. Hicks helped draw Lamar to the role of farmers in the politics of Dakota Territory. His sympathy for farmers' political efforts can be partially explained by his brush with Griswold, who was later president of Yale. Lamar took a course on agrarian thought with Griswold and recalled that Griswold "just was in love with everything Jeffersonian. He thought Jefferson was the true American."[38] In 1948 Yale University Press published Griswold's book *Farming and Democracy*, which revealed his thorough understanding of American agrarian idealism.[39] John D. Hicks, who served as a reader for Pomeroy's dissertation on territorial governance, published the influential *The Populist Revolt* in 1931, a favorable treatment of Populism that heavily influenced Lamar's thinking on agrarian Populist activities in the Dakotas.[40] After studying with Frederic Logan Paxson at the

University of Wisconsin (before Paxson left for Berkeley) under the "lingering spirit of Frederick Jackson Turner," Hicks eventually came to be considered "the dean of Populist historians."[41] Although not a critic of Turner, Hicks found more economic conflict in the American past than Turner had. From an early age, Hicks considered progressive reformers the "'good guys' and their conservative opponents the 'bad guys.'"[42] This "neo-Populism," which C. Vann Woodward said pervaded the New Deal era, also "bred a Populistic view of the past." According to Woodward, "American historiography of the 1930s and 1940s reflects a strong persuasion of this sort. The most popular college textbook in American history was written by a Midwesterner, John D. Hicks, who was friendly to Populism and the foremost historian of the movement."[43] The notion of farmers as an economic class battling with established economic powers was embraced by Lamar in *Dakota Territory*.

Another obvious influence on Lamar was George Wilson Pierson, his advisor at Yale. Lamar later described a "masterful" essay by Pierson that criticized the Turner thesis as "overlaid with sectional bias, and saturated with nationalistic emotion."[44] In his essay, Pierson acknowledged his intellectual debts to Charles Beard and thanked him "for criticism and encouragement."[45] Pierson conceded that Turner's "brilliant papers have been the Bible, and today still constitute the central inspiration, of an extraordinary and widely-held faith." Pierson sought to "re-examine, and then overhaul, what Professor Turner wrote" and perhaps "abandon entirely, the doctrine once taught us by a beloved man." Pierson maintained that American democracy had been enhanced not by the frontier but by the reforms of the Revolutionary and Jeffersonian periods, the abolition of primogeniture, the disestablishment of churches, public education, manhood suffrage, the reforms of the Jacksonian period, new state constitutions in the 1840s and 1850s, and elective judiciaries. Reasserting the role of the East in American history, Pierson thought Turner had missed the influence of "Anglo-American Protestantism": "Surely one cannot today dismiss the long evolution of Parliament, the history of Colonial legislatures, the methods of the New England town meeting, the self-government of Congregational churches, and the voting habits of trading-company stockholders without a thought." He concluded that

Turner was "too optimistic, too romantic, too provincial, and too nation-alistic to be reliable in any survey of world history or study in comparative civilization."[46]

Perhaps most important for Lamar's study of Dakota Territory were Pierson's comments on the significance of farmers in Turner's theory. "At last," Pierson wrote, "the Great Plains handed the individualist farmer his first defeat." This comment on the weakening of agrarian individualism on the Great Plains echoes Lamar's conclusion in *Dakota Territory* that farmers turned toward government for assistance. "What had happened to the ineradicably self-reliant, laissez-faire individualism of the Kansas frontiersmen to make them throw up their hands?" Pierson asked. "And whence came the inspiration and the very shape of the reforms they advocated?"[47] In *Dakota Territory*, Lamar argued that the inspiration came from the territorial experience, which involved heavy reliance on the federal government.

The emerging field of American Studies also affected Lamar's study of Dakota Territory. In the 1930s, several prominent universities began to organize American Studies programs, including Yale.[48] Along with endowing a Yale professorship dedicated to the study of Western history and donating his materials on the West to Yale's library, which Lamar used as the basis of *Dakota Territory*, the philanthropist William Robert-son Coe also helped fund Yale's new program.[49] Instead of becoming the new professor of western history, as Coe preferred, Yale historian David M. Potter became the head of the expanded American Studies program at Yale, and Lamar was tapped to teach western history, setting in motion his career as a western historian. One of the first and most widely known scholarly products of the field of American Studies was Henry Nash Smith's *Virgin Land* (1950), which began as a dissertation at Harvard and which Lamar found "very useful for background material" for his study of Dakota Territory.[50]

Despite later criticism from New Left historians, scholars in American Studies could hardly be dismissed as pro-American conservatives. Henry Nash Smith was openly a leftist who backed Henry Wallace for president in 1948, left the University of Texas for a more hospitable environment at the University of Minnesota, and said he embraced the "Marxist hope for peace at last after world revolution and the establishment of a classless society."[51] Smith, according to Neil Jumonville's understated characterization, was "critical of the capitalist development of the West."[52] According to Kerwin Lee Klein, Smith thought that "figurative words like frontier placed a 'veil' over the harsh face of reality, a mystifying effeminate garment of myth, metaphor, and social theory that the rational historian needed to rip away."[53] Leo Marx, an early leader in American Studies, recently recalled, "Virtually all of the scholars involved in founding American studies at Harvard were of a liberal or outright Left persuasion. This meant being anti-capitalist or at least highly critical of the capitalist system."[54] Smith later said that *Virgin Land* demonstrated how the powerful "ideology" of agrarianism served the "selfish interest of skillful manipulators," a sentiment embraced by Lamar in *Dakota Territory*.[55]

The intellectual currents of the age in which Lamar wrote can be readily detected in *Dakota Territory*. His arguments reflect the ongoing debate over the Turner thesis; Beard's emphasis on class conflict and his criticism of Turner; the sympathy for the plight of farmers evident in Griswold, Hicks, and Smith; Pierson's dismissal of the accomplishments of frontier democracy; and the skepticism of capitalism evident in American Studies programs and among New Deal intellectuals. Lamar classified the advocates of statehood in Dakota Territory as an "oligarchy" whose members were concerned only with their own class interests and were dismissive of farmers' concerns. Prominent statehood leaders, according to Lamar, "lacked any altruistic motives in their struggle for statehood," "had little faith in the electorate," and were "untouched or unimpressed by any radical political ideas or any program of social reform which were [*sic*] being considered throughout the country between 1880 and 1900."[56] He saw an "absence of true principles in the statehood fight."[57]

A Beardian concern with class divisions between capitalistic statehood advocates and yeoman farmers stands out in Lamar's interpretation.[58] Lamar noted that the distinct "class" of people in the territorial capital who constituted the governing "oligarchy" and advocated statehood were nonfarmers and middle class in "beliefs and habits." These leaders embraced the political philosophy "the business of government is business" (a not-so-subtle allusion to the Coolidge-era slogan ridiculed during the New Deal) and viewed "government as a wing of the business structure of the Territory." Instead of finding evidence of civic-mindedness, Lamar saw Dakota Territorial legislators as "a business-minded set of entrepreneurs, speculators, and promoters."[59] Consistent with Charles Beard's focus on economic interests and class conflict, Lamar later said of his study of Dakota Territory, "I think I looked for the economic motives and I found them."[60]

Lamar also recalled the specific Turnerian questions that animated his study: "Since my main interest was in political history, it became necessary to ask the question: Did free land and frontier conditions here produce democracy on the Upper Missouri? Was it a place where economic rugged individualism, political liberalism, and innovation flourished? Was it more American in its society than older parts of the nation?" In contrast to Turner's emphasis on the independence of frontiersmen, Lamar emphasized the federal "aid" and "subsidies" that benefited Dakota Territory and noted that the "territorial government became an economic-development agency of sorts."[61] One reviewer of *Dakota Territory* commented that the "frontiersman's dependence upon the Government in the trans-Mississippi West rather than operating as an individualistic entrepreneur developing democratic concepts is a theme currently emphasized in the writings of many western American historians."[62] Lamar concluded *Dakota Territory* by noting, "It is said"—obliquely referring to Turner—that the "first true American" was independent, democratic, and opposed to government involvement. By "contrast," Lamar wrote, the Dakota settler's experience caused him to turn to a government "partner to aid him."[63]

Contrary to Turner's conception of an organically developing frontier democracy, Lamar noted the "irony" of transplanted easterners within Dakota Territory advocating statehood. Lamar later quoted Earl Pomeroy on this point: "The colonial chafed against his colonial status but in a traditional way. Institutions and values changed less than geography, individual fortunes and techniques."[64] Echoing Pierson's emphasis on the pioneers' embrace of ideas in circulation long before the frontier era, Lamar noted that the Dakota statehood movement largely constituted "the age-old plea for 'home-rule' stated in the familiar language of liberty and democracy that has been voiced in various parts of the country since the American Revolution."[65] Instead of employing Turnerian democratic practices unique to the early stages of the frontier, Dakotans relied on "Eastern political techniques."[66] Lamar argued that the "politician-entrepreneur preceded the pioneer farmer," Turner's model democrat.[67] As opposed to Turner's emphasis on the growth of unique democratic practices on the frontier, Lamar generally saw Dakota Territory's political institutions as "imitative" of those in older states.[68]

Instead of upholding the yeoman ideal that Griswold described or embracing the Populist cause that Hicks celebrated, the leaders in Dakota Territory, by Lamar's reckoning, denigrated agrarian interests. Farmers were "held in contempt" by the statehood advocates, who considered them "dangerous." Lamar believed that the statehood leaders "feared all radical reforms" and were frightened by the power of farmers, who were much more "democratic than the Yankton oligarchy." As result, Lamar concluded, statehood was "never a people's movement." The "true revolution" within Dakota came only when farmers revolted against the proponents of statehood.[69]

By ignoring the concerns of farmers, according to Lamar, the territorial leaders helped spur the Populist movement and ultimately paved the way for the federal government's much larger role in farm policy, which was fully realized during the New Deal of the 1930s. The powerful influence of the territorial and federal governments in Dakota Territory "made it inevitable that the farmer should follow the pattern of action that he did" and embrace a form of "state socialism," a choice made more likely by the "political precedents" of the territorial period.[70] Unlike Turner, who detected democratic tendencies in the early stages of the frontier process, Lamar believed they came later: "The fact was that while opportunity (the safety valve?) always existed on the Dakota frontier, the chance for self-government, economic balance, and functioning democracy came at the end rather than at the beginning of the frontier period."[71]

Consistent with the analysis of the federal Constitution by Charles Beard, Lamar similarly critiqued the process of drafting a constitution for Dakota Territory.[72] The constitutional convention of 1883, Lamar said, was held during "sunny September harvest days," when farmers were preoccupied; hence "no radical innovations" were included in the document.[73] Lamar wrote that the Sioux Falls constitutional convention of 1885 was also held at the "height of harvesting season," and few rural people "could afford to be there." In "many cases the same men" who were involved in 1883 were involved in 1885, and thus the "controlling forces" were the "same" and the "inner circle" went "unchallenged." The delegates to the 1885 convention were more worried about finding "methods to assure the popular ratification" of the document than about "writing a new constitution"; they thus adopted the 1883 document "with only a few minor changes." The 1885 delegates were "conservative in their treatment of nearly every question."[74] In 1889 the "old guard" statehood advocates stymied a farmer revolt at the constitutional convention. "Conservatives" persuaded Congress to let the state into the Union on the basis of the 1885 constitution, and as a result, the "violent discontent" of farmers "could not find any outlet in constitutional changes."[75]

The tenor of Lamar's findings is not surprising, given the general intellectual trends of the age in which he wrote. Beard's well-known critique of Turner and American capitalism was bolstered by several other prominent intellectuals. In contrast to the brighter picture painted by Turner, another Wisconsinite, Thorstein Veblen, was a strong critic of capitalism, materialism, and concentrated wealth, and his writings heavily influenced early-twentieth-century social thought. Many of Veblen's writings found favor among New Deal intellectuals active in the 1930s.[76] C. Wright Mills's book *The Power Elite*, published the same year as Lamar's *Dakota Territory*, analyzed the narrow class of individuals who, Mills believed, controlled American institutions and echoed Lamar's criticism of a territorial "oligarchy," an "old guard," and an "inner circle."[77] The writings of Richard Hofstadter were also becoming more prominent in the 1950s. A critic of small-town culture and the businessmen whom Lamar saw as advocates of Dakota statehood, Hofstadter was fond of the anti-small-town writings of H. L. Mencken and Sinclair Lewis. Sounding a common theme among intellectuals of the 1950s, Hofstadter hoped that "cosmopolitanism" would ultimately displace the prevalence and provincialism of small-town culture in Turner's Midwest.[78] The publication of *Peyton Place*, released the same year that *Dakota Territory* was published, also popularized the supposed underside of small-town life.[79] The increasingly popular writings of Bernard De Voto also debunked the supposed fables of the West (after being at Harvard, De Voto said of his home in Ogden, Utah: "These people are not my people"). Wallace Stegner, whose book *Beyond the 100th Meridian* was published in 1954, similarly sought to "recover a Western past that had been obscured and nearly obliterated by the mythmakers."[80]

Other intellectual influences identifiable during the time Lamar was researching and writing, however, are hard to find in *Dakota Territory*. Yale historian David M. Potter, for example, was a fellow southerner, a fellow Emory graduate, a Lamar confidant, and a reader of Lamar's dissertation, but his influence on *Dakota Territory* seems minimal. Potter was a "firm and unwavering" "conservative," according to Michael Kammen, but he was also "tolerant, extraordinarily subtle, and nuanced."[81] Despite his unwillingness to embrace "democratic socialism," according to Robert Collins, Potter was "hardly the smug, uncritical 1950s intellectual of popular mythology. His concerns were important ones—the absence of community, the threat of mass culture, and the dangers of unbridled materialism."[82] Although a conservative, Potter was critical of Turner for not emphasizing the role of technology and industry in American history, so perhaps Lamar did take some cues about Turner's theoretical shortcomings from Potter's writings.[83] But in general, Potter and Lamar embraced distinctly different models of the American past. Potter believed that the consensus school of history he helped found in the 1950s was a reaction to the "excesses of the conflict school," the very school that Lamar embraced in *Dakota Territory*.[84]

To highlight the intellectual influences on Lamar is not to argue that he was a cork on the ocean of received opinion. He made many conscious choices in his scholarly career. Despite his southern roots, for example, he willingly abandoned his dissertation topic on the South and took up the study of the West in a department not known for its appreciation of lands beyond the Hudson River. Lamar also did not follow the scholarly direction of his fellow southerner and friend David Potter.

Lamar, in other words, was a flexible thinker who created a dissertation out of a newly opened archival collection and thereby prompted a broader exploration of the American territorial system.

Lamar's decision to emphasize economic conflict in Dakota Territory was not inevitable. He wrote his book on Dakota Territory during a time of ambiguity and flux in American historiography, conditions that created interpretative options for him.[85] He began his study at the tail end of the boom in progressive history, and by the time he was finishing his dissertation, the interpretative ground was shifting, although these changes probably came too late in the process of Lamar's research to make a decisive impact. Richard Hofstadter's *The American Political Tradition* (1948), for example, cast doubt on the notion that conflict was the defining feature of American history. Historiographers frequently note the displacement of the conflict interpretation with a "consensus" view of American history in the 1950s, which Peter Novick terms a "counterprogressive" tendency.[86] During this era, Lamar's student Patricia Nelson Limerick later noted, Ray Allen Billington and his allies also "rescued and refurbished Turner's 1893 ideas."[87] In 1951, the year Lamar completed his Ph.D., Merle Curti worried about "dark and wintry times" for scholars on the left who had been outspoken during the New Deal years.[88] Faced with signs of ambivalence in historical scholarship and growing political conservatism, however, Lamar ended up siding with the progressive point of view in his book, a decision reflecting his willingness to consider the evidence and take a strong interpretive stand.

Although rightly associated with the progressive school of history dominant in the 1930s and 1940s, *Dakota Territory* also signaled important intellectual trends. It helped revive and legitimize western history, especially at an institution not much given to studies of the West. Lamar's focus on the role of the federal government in American history also anticipated the prominent studies of the federal state published in the past few decades.[89] *Dakota Territory* also sounded themes that would again be embraced by the New Western historians decades hence. An emphasis on economic motives and class conflict is common in the new history. Unlike Lamar's work, however, some of the more recent histories of the West tend to be more strident. Despite his critical stance toward Turner in *Dakota Territory*, Lamar came to admire Turner's democratic vision. In an extended analysis of Turner published in 1969, Lamar wrote, "Just as Jefferson can be called democracy's spokesman, Turner deserves the title 'democracy's historian.'"[90] Admiring Turner's idealism, Lamar thought that as long as his vision persisted, "democracy would survive."[91]

Dakota Territory also reflects the limitations on historical scholarship in the 1940s. Although the consensus school was making its presence felt, Lamar conducted his research and wrote his dissertation before many of the significant twentieth-century trends in American history had developed. Although Ralph Henry Gabriel's work may be classified as intellectual history, the surge of interest in that field and in the role of ideas in history was only beginning when Lamar was writing. Historians such as Bernard Bailyn and Gordon S. Wood gave the history of republicanism a much higher profile in the decades after *Dakota Territory* was published.[92] Richard Hofstadter similarly made a strong case for the subordination of economic conflict to the influence of ideas in American history. Hofstadter was also much more critical of Populism than were the historians Lamar relied on in *Dakota Territory*, an interpretation that triggered criticism of Hofstadter and a raft of new publications about Populism. Unlike the historiography when Lamar wrote *Dakota Territory*, however, recent historical treatments of Populism have emphasized its republican nature.[93] In contrast to the focus on class friction in the 1940s, in later decades, historians focused on the persistent power of ethnic and religious identity as a source of conflict in American history. In another sign of his willingness to recognize new interpretative breakthroughs, Lamar later conceded that western history had not adequately dealt with ethnicity, religion, women, or laborers.[94] His embrace of these new strands of western history in the decades after he published *Dakota Territory* squared with his doubts about the "overallness" of Turner's thesis and proved his willingness to incorporate new groups into the story of the American West.[95]

During the course of his career following the publication of *Dakota Territory*, Lamar maintained a greater openness than some other western historians have shown to new evidence and research agendas *and* to Turner's older insights. At present, the interpretation of western history is shaped to a great extent by the New Western historians, some of whom studied under Lamar. Lamar's student Patricia Limerick, who deemed the "frontier" popularized by Turner "the F-word," found little of value in the "old Turnerian model of Anglo-Americans purposefully moving westward."[96] Donald Worster similarly thought that Turner was so blinded by "optimism" and his "patriotic impulses" that he could not see the "shameful side" of the West.[97] Worster condemned older western historians for their "moral complacency" and "blandness" and urged younger historians to focus on class conflict, environmental exploitation, and the abuses of "concentrated power." He celebrated the coming of the New Western History, an advent prompted by historians "shaken" by the Vietnam War and by "poverty, racism, and environmental degradation." He thought historians should take a "hard look at the violent imperialistic" West.[98] The goal of the leaders of the New Western History, according to Kerwin Lee Klein, was to "escape the evil priestcraft of the Turnerian dark ages."[99]

Despite the claims to newness by the New Western historians, however, Lamar's *Dakota Territory* is another reminder that topics such as class conflict have long been a subject of historical inquiry. Some historians have taken the New Western historians to task for inflated claims to originality. Gerald Thompson calls it an "intellectual cheapshot" to not recognize the books written in western history before 1980.[100] John Mack Faragher, who now holds Lamar's former position at Yale, notes that the "publications first articulating the themes now identified with the 'new western history' were in fact written by historians of previous generations," including Lamar's *Dakota Territory*, which placed class conflict at its center. "By failing to give full recognition to these pathbreaking studies," Faragher argues, "the generational thesis violates one of the cardinal rules of history: close attention to antecedents."[101] Instead of "killing the fathers," Donald J. Pisani says that the New Western historians "should spend some time studying our family tree so that we understand what we have inherited and from whom."[102]

The New Western historians, according to Gerald Nash, were "products of the 1960s" who applied the "New Left perspectives of that era to the history of the American West" and thus wrote "ideological history."[103] The result was a series of "one-sided indictments," Nash lamented, that did "a disservice to the profession."[104] Although Donald Worster sees historians of the first half of the twentieth century as "prisoners of ideology," *Dakota Territory* indicates that progressive social thought and the historians influenced by the ideological turn of the New Deal era have long had a strong influence on historical scholarship.[105] Similar to early-twentieth-century reformers who sought a "usable past," the New Western historians looked for a way "to use history as a way of altering society" and thus "return to the fundamentalism of Progressive history."[106] They often repeated the critiques of earlier historians such as Lamar, though he was more moderate. Lamar could deliver a strong indictment without losing his perspective. "Progressive History was not," Peter Novick notes, "all that radical," especially when compared with the scholarly turn of the 1960s, which helped launch the New Western history.[107]

In recent decades, Lamar has "largely stayed out" of the rancorous debates in western history, according to Richard White, "because he had students on both sides," but his talent for discerning interpretation and fairness, especially in the decades after the publication of *Dakota Territory*, should be remembered by all sides.[108] Despite his dismissal of Turner's interpretation in *Dakota Territory,* Ray Allen Billington asked Lamar early in his career, "You don't hate Turner do you?"[109] Even a Turner devotee such as Billington could see that Lamar's capacity for measured but bold judgments trumped ideological inclinations, but Billington's question anticipated the coming storm. The criticism of the settlement of the American West advanced by critics of Turner starting in the 1930s would reach a much higher level of intensity and negativity in the writings of the New Western historians, who were more aggressive in their attempts to transcend the "useless past" of the American West.

Due in part to Lamar's scholarly progeny, who inherited some of Lamar's interpretative openness, the work of the New Western historians does not dominate the stage of western history. While their work currently represents a powerful strand in western history, their influence is diluted by new works, many of them produced by students of Lamar (who directed sixty dissertations), that do not place conflict and power at the center of the story and that display greater respect for Turner. Lamar's students William Cronon, George Miles, and Jay Gitlin, for example, recognize Turner's insights.[110] Lamar's successor as the western historian at Yale, John Mack Faragher, purposely placed the "F-word" back at center stage in western history in his and Robert V. Hine's 2007 synthesis, *Frontiers: A Short History of the American West*.[111] One of the leaders of the New Western history, also trained by Lamar, has even relinquished some of her hopes of reconfiguring western history and transcending Turner. Patricia Limerick now says she did not intend her "Frontier Antithesis, *The Legacy of Conquest*, to stand for the ages" and only hoped it would serve as "provocation" for more study.[112] Perhaps this new sentiment of evenhandedness and modesty serves as one more example of Lamar's continuing influence on his students and the field of western history in general.

This influence is readily evident in the work of the latest generation of western historians—the post–New Western historians—who write from a diversity of perspectives and have also benefitted from Lamar's tutelage. Lamar and his student William Cronon, for example, codirected the Yale dissertation of Susan Lee Johnson, who added several layers of complexity to the story of the California Gold Rush.[113] Karl Jacoby, who also worked with Cronon and Lamar at Yale, similarly benefitted from Lamar's insights into the American West and his scholarly openness when writing his study of early conservation efforts in the West.[114] Lamar's emphasis on the important role of the federal government has been taken up by Louis Warren, a Lamar student who also studied western conservation.[115] Gunther Peck, another Lamar student, followed Lamar's work on the differing labor patterns in the West in his study of padrones and their control of immigrant workers.[116] The flowering of American Indian history can also be traced through the works of Lamar's student Philip J. Deloria, whose ancestors hailed from Lamar's first subject of study, the Dakotas.[117] Lamar's students have similarly noted the important role of his book *The Far Southwest* in promoting the study of Hispanic American history in recent years.[118] Sam Truett, Lamar's final dissertation advisee at Yale, again demonstrated the reach and influence of Lamar's scholarship and his anticipation of new areas of historical focus by using *The Far Southwest* as a point of departure for his exploration of the history of the American-Mexican borderlands.[119] Beyond his doctoral students, Lamar's impact on his Yale undergraduates has led ultimately to well-known works about the American West. The popular television producer David Milch credited Lamar's western history course at Yale and *Dakota Territory* for inspiring the HBO series *Deadwood*. Popular writer and Yale alumnus Hampton Sides has also pointed to Lamar's influence on his book about Kit Carson.[120]

While Lamar grew with the development of the discipline of western history in later decades and trained many of its younger and most creative historians, his *Dakota Territory* remains a product of the 1930s and 1940s. The book firmly rejects a Turnerian interpretation of events and sees a clash between classes in Dakota Territory. Lamar later conceded that he perhaps offered an interpretation of Dakota politics that was too harsh.[121] Perhaps he recognized the ideological currents of the age in which he wrote and came to doubt the wisdom of progressive historians' quest for a "usable past." When the New Western historians again emphasized class conflict in the West and renewed the assault on Turner, Lamar was not as enthusiastic about such an interpretation as he had been in the 1940s. He said he had to "part company" with the New Western historians who obsessed over the "dark side of things."[122] In this ongoing historical debate, Lamar now sounds closer to Turner than he was in the 1940s. Perhaps western historians should follow Lamar's lead, as they have often done for fifty years, and ponder his words of caution and his personal history of interpretative flexibility and tolerance. Although *Dakota Territory* remains a product of a particular ideological time and place, Lamar's subsequent career and leadership in western history indicate that he would see the main currents at work in Dakota Territory differently were he writing its history today. His willingness to break through the constraints of an existing interpretative model and consider new methods and evidence, and to encourage his students to do the same, is the greatest testament to his commitment to history.

The story of the origins of *Dakota Territory* and Lamar's long-term intellectual development can help reconceptualize the history of Dakota Territory. The overreliance on progressive history in Lamar's *Dakota*

Territory, an interpretive focus continued by the New Western historians, underscores the importance of considering noneconomic forces in American history. In the case of Dakota Territory, this must include the centrality of republicanism and religion, forces that, though overlooked by progressive historians, have been taken more seriously by historians in the past few years. During the 1880s, Dakota settlers consistently relied on a republican idiom in the public sphere, and Christianity ordered their private lives. Several recent histories have also viewed farmers, whom Lamar viewed as class warriors, in keeping with progressive history, as embracing republicanism and sounding Christian themes. Lamar deserves to be credited for first putting the history of Dakota Territory on the scholarly map and, given his intellectual openness and willingness to consider new perspectives, would probably agree that it is time to rethink the major currents of life in Dakota Territory.

Conclusion

Settlers in those days were happy people, thankful for a land where
they could work and have a good life, and worship God together
at meetings in their homes, which made happy memories for all
of us.

Dakota pioneer, 1880s

Five years after the Civil War ended, settlers had filed claims upon a
mere half-million acres of land in Dakota Territory, a geographic space
equivalent to the size of France or the entirety of the British Isles. By
1883, when the Great Dakota Boom was fully under way, land claims in
the territory totaled 7.5 million acres; by the time of statehood in 1889,
they exceeded 42 million acres. In 1887, twenty-two counties in Dakota
ran out of "free land," and nine others had only some two thousand acres
left, much of which was untillable. During the high point of the boom,
the population of Dakota Territory exploded by 750 percent. During
1883, one of the boom's most active years, the population of the territory
grew by a thousand people per day. That year in Turner County, four
thousand railroad cars passed through the town of Hurley filled with the
personal property of Dakota settlers bound for their new homesteads.[1]

During the boom, the Dakota settlers laid the foundation of social and
political life in the territory. Dakotans embraced and employed a rich
culture of American republican precedent and practice as they organized
homesteads, built schools, established local governments, and battled
to attain statehood. Many Dakota settlers, hailing from the Midwest
and New England, brought with them their home regions' heritage of
republican citizenship, which had its origins in the American Revolution
and the English civil wars. Their republican habits and institutions were

bolstered by an archipelago of Christian churches on the Dakota prairie that deepened community ties, inculcated social virtue, and generally promoted social order. When Dakotans crafted a constitution, that most American of political rituals, they did so by relying on republican ideology and a Christian heritage, both of which taught them to abhor the corruption of the territorial system, celebrate self-government, and prize private virtue. The constitution Dakotans crafted and the social order they created rested on the twin pillars of American republicanism and the Christian tradition.

A Norwegian settler later summarized the Dakotans' achievement:

The Pioneers made the beginnings of everything that we now value. They laid the cornerstone and the foundation. They built the homes, broke the virgin sod, planted the beautiful groves that dot the broad plains. They organized the Township governments, formed the school districts, organized congregations, built churches and formed various business organizations for our mutual benefit. They laid here the foundation of the fundamental institutions of our civilization, the home, the church and the school. Any of these failing, the community, the state and the nation would have suffered. But they builded well, better than they themselves knew.[2]

Dakota Territory was not, of course, a perfect republican utopia. Battles with corrupt territorial officials were sometimes lost, Dakota republicans were divided at times over substance and procedure, and partisanship or personal gain could collide with public-interestedness. Women were also barred from voting in that age of separate spheres, and Protestant, old-stock Americans maintained social advantages over Catholics and European immigrants. Catholics, in particular, were at times seen as a suspect class and a potential threat to republican government. Although the political culture of Dakota Territory during the 1880s would fail to meet contemporary expectations of social tolerance, this place and time in American history does not deserve to be dismissed for its democratic shortcomings. Despite the gender assumptions of the age, many Dakotans supported women's suffrage, and many others may have offered their support if such a position had not jeopardized Dakotans' ultimate goal of statehood. Animosity toward Catholics was also a reflection of deeply held religious beliefs and a genuine fear of Catholic interference with republican governance, and it seldom rose above the level of social ridicule. Protestant opposition to the spending of public money on Catholic schools was miles short of programmatic state-sponsored persecution, although the prejudice underlying such positions surely caused social pain and feelings of exclusion. The Masons' distaste for Catholicism, and Protestant clergymen's' castigation of immigrant Germans or Irishmen for imbibing, cannot be classified as systemic oppression and should be considered in the context of Dakotans' general desire to promote social stability and orderly civic affairs.

Historians since the late 1960s have done well to study the depth of racial or ethnic categorizing and discrimination in the American past, but they have also too readily embraced a narrative in which nineteenth-century Americans focused solely on the preservation of a capitalist and Protestant white man's republic. A complete portrait of the American experience should include the virtuous elements of the republican tradition to be considered alongside the darker aspects of American history. Some proportionality, in other words, is in order. Territorial leader General William Beadle cited the Anglo-Saxon origins of Dakota democracy, it is true, but he did so to emphasize the many democratic precedents and the long chain of historical development that led to the Dakota settlers' founding moment, not to purposely exclude certain groups from the new republican order. Beadle was also quick to praise the immigrant elements of Dakota life, to support women's suffrage, to promote governmental reform, and generally to welcome all comers to Dakota, in addition to acting on his republican principles by participating in civic life, embracing constitutionalism, and aiding public schools. One cannot know what was in Beadle's heart, but his invocations of Anglo-Saxon history seem closer to rhetorical puffery and an honest respect for the Anglo-American heritage of ordered liberty than substantive racial dogma.[3] Beadle sounds much more republican than racist. Many of the Union veterans, including Beadle, who settled Dakota Territory had fought to free the slaves, after all, and to push the American republic closer to its own ideals.[4] These ideals animated their endeavor to craft a new republican polity on the prairie and were manifest in their rush to start five hundred newspapers, raise 1,000 churches, build 3,500 schools, and organize 80,000 farms.

A wide-ranging comparative perspective on the late-nineteenth-century can provide added context that helps to properly place the experience of Dakota Territory in the history of modern democratic development, both in the United States and Europe. During the 1880s, after the North had abandoned its efforts to reconstruct Southern society, racial segregation became systematic in the South, and lynchings and anti-black terror more common. In the Far West, an organized campaign against Chinese immigrants triggered numerous riots and homicides and a complete ban on Chinese immigration. Internationally, at the time Dakota Territory was approaching statehood, the Russian government abetted a brutal anti-Semitic pogrom, and the German government initiated an anti-Catholic Kulturkampf. Thousands of Irish peasants were uprooted from their land, triggering an escalation of anti-British political violence. In the 1880s, King Leopold II of Belgium personally seized the "Congo Free State" in Africa and began a campaign of severing heads and hands that has traumatized the Congo down to the present day.[5] In the broader sweep of global events during the 1880s, then, the republicans of Dakota appear rather impressive. They serve as a reminder of the strengths and distinctiveness of the American democratic heritage and the fact that Americans, at times, did approximate the ideals of pioneer democracy imagined by the much-maligned Frederick Jackson Turner. The experience of the Dakotans described in this study provides another needed perspective on the history of the American West, a region, historians have begun to emphasize, that encompasses a diverse constellation of peoples, moments, and histories.

The genuine attachment to American democratic ideals among Dakotans can best be distilled from their effort to craft a constitution and achieve statehood. Constitutional convention delegates and statehood leaders relied upon the American founders and thoroughly studied other states' constitutional precedents. They deliberately pursued provisions promoting the republican goals of limiting government power and combating corruption. Although they denounced the territorial system and congressional resistance to statehood, they did not pursue revolutionary doctrines or simply assert statehood in contravention of constitutional precedent. Despite claims that the drive for statehood was controlled by an economic elite, a view based on the dated assumptions of early-twentieth-century progressive historiography, the convention delegations shifted throughout the decade and included many farmers, and they generally agreed to include provisions that promoted farmers' interests at the expense of influential economic interests such as the railroads.

To reach some positive conclusions about a particular time and place in the American past is not meant to justify a sanitized worldview that ignores obvious acts of injustice or disgrace. But it does serve to justify Carl N. Degler's warning about certain historians' tendency to overlook the "diversity and complexity of the past" and the "untidiness of human responses to people and events."[6] A recognition of the complex and multifaceted history of the trans-Mississippi West is particularly important at a time when a popular school of history has highlighted the harshness and brutality of the western past and when some have come to view this narrative as a new "orthodoxy."[7] A positive conclusion about the political culture of Dakota Territory, it should be emphasized, is not the end of the matter for those with reformist sympathies. As David Brown notes in his biography of Richard Hofstadter, it is a mistake to assume that the finding of a workable political consensus in the past "is intrinsically a prescriptive one which commits us to this or that particular arrangement."[8] Political progressives can still advance a program to reconstruct the social and political present without relying on a one-sided view of the American past. Some historians who confess sympathies for the political left and social reform have actually concluded that the writings of past conservatives, many of whom have offered penetrating critiques of certain developments in American life, are an effective weapon to use in the battle to transform the existing social order.[9] The story of Dakota Territory could thus end up on either side of the ledger of political usefulness.

Although the Dakota experience can have different meanings to different people, one particular social critic would surely have found reason for hope in the history of Dakota Territory. In the last decade of his life, Christopher Lasch was intensely concerned with the erosion of community life in the United States, the declining sources of republican and religious spirit, rampant consumerism, social elites' neglect of their duties to the commonwealth, and what he saw generally as the declining prospects for American democracy. In his magisterial work *The True and Only Heaven*, Lasch went searching for past sources of strength in American democracy. Dakota Territory would have met his criteria.[10] Its political culture included many of the ingredients Lasch thought necessary to make American democracy function. For this reason alone, the history of Dakota Territory deserves attention. John D. Hicks once argued that such places could provide the hope necessary to bolster the nation's democratic prospects. Hicks thought that perhaps the "western belief that the disorders of the world can yet be righted will help to right them, [that] perhaps even the naïve western assumption that the American experiment in democracy cannot possibly fail will help to keep it from failing."[11]

The presence of republican unity in Dakota Territory can be lost on scholars too wedded to interpretive models that highlight social conflict or that assume American political history to be oppressive and coercive. Wilfred M. McClay notes that one must be careful to distinguish "between agreement and acquiescence, consensus and hegemony, reconciliation and domination."[12] The language of republican ordering was the dominant discourse in Dakota Territory, but there was no substantive dissent from it or resistance to it. Since most Dakotans willingly embraced the tradition of American republicanism, they felt no need to protect its hegemony by violent means or by domination of the intellectual sphere. The political culture of Dakota Territory was not a coercive hegemonic system, in other words, but largely a good-faith social consensus.[13]

The history of Dakota Territory is another reminder that we should take the American republican heritage and its cohesive properties more seriously and consider the implications of their decline. Too many intellectuals have taken the republican tradition for granted. Its slow dissipation is what troubled social critics such as Lasch about the future of the American republic. Lasch thought the "danger to democracy comes . . . from the erosion of its psychological, cultural, and spiritual foundations from within."[14] Even if one generally celebrates the centripetal forces in American history and views them as indices of social liberation, it is important to recognize how greatly they alarmed Americans in the past and how our ancestors sought to contain them, and to at least consider the consequences of their acceleration. After several decades of focusing on what divided the republic, historians should also remember what held it together and dispassionately consider what Josiah Royce called the "conservative forces" in western life.[15] Some historians in the past have detected these tendencies, but they have never congealed into a prominent category of historical analysis. Scholars have, however, noted concerns about disorder or "anomie" and a longing among western settlers for traditional social structures.[16] Local studies increasingly indicate that western settlers were a "conservative people committed to the sanctity of the family and community."[17] These critical insights, along with the experience of settlers in Dakota, could help historians fully open a window on the past that may come closer to revealing the lived experience of people in the American West, but first some of the cobwebs of progressive history need to be cleared away and the heavy interpretive curtain of division and conflict pulled back.

This is not to argue that a darker interpretation of other episodes in the history of the American West is inappropriate, but instead to emphasize the complexity of this history and to warn against sweeping models of historical explanation that privilege coercive domination. The history of Dakota Territory, which conflicts with a now-popular mode of interpreting western history, highlights the frustration of scholars who seek a "grand theory" to explain American history. As Ronald G. Walters once noted, "society and culture in the United States are so pluralistic and localistic that there really is no coherence."[18] In the rush to overturn the "western super narrative" of Turner's democratic frontiersmen moving West, some historians have argued that it should be replaced by a diverse "bundle of visions," not by another metanarrative.[19] This bundle, however, should surely include Turner. And it should be remembered that Turner's democratic model offers discerning insights on particular times and places, including Dakota Territory during the 1880s.

EPILOGUE

In October 2003, as the component parts of this book began to take shape, I enjoyed suppers in two church basements in rural South Dakota. The first was the annual "soup and pie supper" at the Union Presbyterian Church (founded in 1883), perched on a swell of yellow prairie about ten miles from Fedora (population 188) in Miner County. The second was the annual "turkey feed" at the Congregational Community Church (founded in 1884) in Winfred (population 176), which straddles the line dividing Miner from Lake County. The pie and turkey were excellent, but the circumstances felt precarious. These community gatherings, whose roots extend to the territorial era, are passing, and with them a critical ingredient of workable democracy.

"Democracy must begin at home," argued John Dewey, "and its home is the neighborly community."[1] The erosion of long-standing communities, including those centered in South Dakota church basements, threatens America's long-term democratic prospects. The debate over the decline of community activities, associations, and participation—what Robert Putnam collectively refers to as "social capital"—is really a debate about democracy's ability to function. When citizens retreat from civic participation and community affairs, democracy shrivels. Putnam, whose first interest is Italian political culture, fears that the United States will become Sicily, where participation in social and cultural activities is weak. For Sicilians, "public affairs is somebody else's business—that of *i notabili,* 'the bosses,' 'the politicians'—but not theirs."[2] The worry is that as community recedes in places like Miner County, where strong civic and social traditions were planted deep during the territorial years, the broader danger of the Sicilianization of the American republic increases.

Concerns about Miner County should be particularly acute because it is one of the capitals of social capital. Although not disclosed in his book on the subject, Robert Putnam's conclusions about the rich social capital of the northern plains are based in part on his survey work in Miner County. Putnam's research concluded that the Dakotas ranked highest in the nation in social capital. The erosion of community and community institutions in Miner County is particularly alarming to those concerned about our democratic prospects. If this heartland of social capital cannot preserve its democratic character, perhaps no place can.

My close encounter with Miner County and my consideration of its place in the broader debate over democracy's future happened in the midst of my research and discovery of the strong elements of republicanism in territorial Dakota. My parents invited me to the Union Presbyterian Church soup and pie supper, and I accepted because I wanted to show my would-be wife, a city girl from Sioux Falls, the "real South Dakota." My parents were born on farms near Winfred, and my Aunt Thelma, who then lived on a farm in rural Miner County with her son, made several of the pies for the supper. Although my parents later bought a farm in adjacent Lake County, they often return to the old neighborhood and visit with longtime friends, validating Putnam's conclusions about the level of social capital among the Great Depression–World War II generation. I took particular interest in the relationship between social capital and persisting small-scale communal institutions in Miner County began when I asked one of the Union Presbyterian Church volunteers about their membership: "Oh, we have eleven active members."

Miner County deserves its place in the history of republicanism. In the 1960s and early 1970s, before political scientists began speaking of "social capital," historians were studying and writing about the ideology of republicanism, or the social and political ingredients necessary for a republic to function properly.[3] Much of this research has focused on the importance of republican ideas to the American Revolution and was prompted by Gordon S. Wood's magisterial *Creation of the American Republic*. Community, civic obligations, and the "sacrifice of individual interests to the greater good of the whole," according to Wood, "formed the essence of republicanism."[4] Republicanism exalted community and civic virtue and served to restrain individualism and self-interest.

The context of the republican revival of the eighteenth century was the erosion of English social institutions, political corruption, and the "degeneracy" that accompanied the expansion of the British Empire. Social critics turned to Cicero and Tacitus, who had critiqued the collapse of republican Rome and had "contrasted the growing corruption and disorder they saw about them with an imagined earlier republican world of ordered simplicity and Arcadian virtue and sought continually to explain the transformation." For the American revolutionaries, the "nostalgic image of the Roman Republic became a symbol of all their dissatisfactions with the present and their hopes for the future."[5] Greek and Roman republicanism "supplied the material used by the pamphleteers of the American Revolution."[6]

In his study of the artisan political culture of early-nineteenth-century New York, Sean Wilentz found that "artisans sustained a classical republican political language long after what Gordon Wood has described as the death of 'classical politics' in America." In the new United States, Wilentz explained, "versions of republicanism multiplied," but a "singular political language bound Americans together."[7] Just as New York artisans "elaborated their own democratic variant of American republican ideology," the residents of Miner County did the same. New York artisans used the Mechanics' Committee; Miner County people used community picnics. One Swedish immigrant to the county later recorded: "Many picnics have been held, generally sponsored by a church, the school, or Sunday school, when people come together for a big dinner, a program and games. Sometimes it was a last day for a school, a day for Sunday school or a Fourth of July."[8] In Miner County, the pioneer picnic gradually evolved into soup and pie suppers and turkey feeds.

The earliest citizens of Miner County, and the settlers of Dakota Territory in general, would have adhered, in part, to an early, classical form of republicanism, one that emphasized the superior qualities of rural life and the virtues of agriculture. As Wood explained, many early Americans believed that rural culture and its characteristics made republics function: "It was not the force of arms which made the ancient republics great or which ultimately destroyed them. It was rather the character and spirit of their people. Frugality, industry, temperance, and simplicity—the rustic traits of the sturdy yeoman—were the stuff that made society strong. The virile martial qualities—the scorn of ease, the contempt of danger, the love of valor—were what made a nation great."[9]

Farmers from midwestern states and European immigrants began moving into Miner County following the Civil War, especially in the late 1870s and early 1880s. Cooperation was critical for sod-house building, the planting of trees for timber claims, and harvesting. Settlers quickly built schoolhouses, women of the Ladies Library Association established a library in 1884, and editors started newspapers such as *Prairie Home,* the *Howard Farmer,* and the *Howard Advance.* Indirectly linking the development of Miner County to the age of Rome and ancient republicanism, an immigrant named one of the county's villages Carthage (borrowing it from his hometown in New York), whose newspaper was called the *Carthaginian.* In yeoman republican fashion, 90 percent of farmers owned the land they worked in Miner County and enjoyed a high degree of economic independence, addressing a core concern of republican theorists, who thought the wage system degraded republican virtue and citizenship.[10]

Since so many Miner County settlers were Civil War veterans, in 1883 the George R. Stevens Post of the Grand Army of the Republic was mustered in with one hundred members as part of the "GAR's fraternal revival in the 1880s."[11] George R. Stevens was a member of the 2nd Wisconsin Infantry Volunteer Regiment, part of what General Joseph Hooker deemed the "Iron Brigade," and was killed at Gettysburg, a battle whose remembrance was steeped in classicism and was fought during a time when the United States was thought of as a "second Athens."[12] The 2nd Wisconsin was the first three-year regiment to arrive after Lincoln's call for troops to defend the capital. The naming of the GAR post may also have been influenced by the fact that many South Dakota settlers were from Wisconsin. In neighboring Lake County, the county seat of Madison was named by immigrants from Wisconsin who thought the area reminiscent of Madison, Wisconsin.

A Wisconsin link also applies to politics. The Republican Party, whose opposition to slavery precipitated the Civil War in which so many Miner County GAR members had fought, was founded in Rippon, Wisconsin, during the 1850s. Wisconsin immigrants to Miner County brought with them their attachment to the Republican Party. In the 1890 race for governor, the Republican candidate outpolled the Democrat in Miner County by more than two-to-one.[13] When Dakota was first settled in the 1860s, 80 percent of new residents registered as Republicans.[14] The GAR lodge reinforced the settlers' Republican proclivities. But the GAR was no "bloody-shirt Republican club," as Stuart McConnell has pointed out. It also bolstered community by wearing "several masks: fraternal lodge, charitable society, special-interest lobby, patriotic group, political club."[15] In short, the GAR spawned social capital.

The settlers were also well aware that their new farms had been earned as a result of the Republican Party's "free soil" platforms of the 1850s and 1860s, which helped produce the Homestead Act of 1862, a bill that congressional Republicans could not pass until the defection of Southern Democrats during the Civil War.[16] According to Leif Fjellestad's study, "most early settlers in Miner County made use of [the act] to secure for themselves a quarter section of land."[17] If measured in terms of free-holding agrarian settlement, which some theorists believed critical for republican institutions, Miner County in the 1880s represented a great Jeffersonian achievement.

The immigrant farmers of Miner County were also a particular source of republicanism. Roughly one-third of Miner County residents in 1890 were foreign-born. Of the 1,230 foreign-born, 330 were from Norway, 300 from Germany, 125 from Sweden, 100 from Denmark, and 70 from Ireland.[18] Rowland Berthoff has emphasized how such immigrants adhered to the ideals of classical republicanism and embraced its focus on community. The smallholding European peasant who later made his way to places like Miner County in the 1880s was intimately familiar with classical republicanism. Berthoff notes that the "character of the thrifty plowman or herdsman was explicitly described, in fourteenth-century poems and morality plays, in terms of traits like those attributed to the virtuous citizen by republican theorists: diligence, care, prudence, frugality." The late-nineteenth-century emphasis on republican community "must have been due in no small part to the renewed immigration, between 1815 and 1914, of still more peasants."[19] European immigrants held an "image of America as the land of democracy," and pro-immigration literature emphasized "Americans' success in blotting out slavery—the final vestige of European feudalism."[20] The elements of republicanism embraced by the immigrant and American farmers of Miner County showed up later, in Putnam's research, in the form of social capital.

In addition to organizing their farms, Miner County settlers also quickly began building churches. The Methodist Episcopal Church was organized in 1881 with the proceeds from the minister's sale of his Timber Act tree claim. In 1882, a Catholic priest said the first mass in Howard, and St. John's Evangelical Lutheran Church was organized. The Union Presbyterian Church, whose later soup and pie suppers prompted this epilogue, was built in 1883. The Winfred Congregational Church, now home of the annual turkey feed, was built in 1884. In the northeast corner of the county, where many Norwegian immigrants settled, the Belleview Lutheran Church was completed in 1886. Other churches would quickly follow.[21]

Starting in 1881, Miner County residents also mounted elaborate Fourth of July celebrations. In 1883, four or five *thousand* settlers flocked to the celebration in the county seat of Howard, which included a band, a parade, speeches, and the county's first fireworks display. One of the main speeches was given by D. D. Holdridge, the commander of the GAR post.[22] One memoir recalled that on the Fourth of July in 1905, in Green Valley Township, "a group of neighbors numbering thirty-four held a picnic in the nice grove of trees by the ruins of the old Moses Martin sod buildings."[23] The presence of Civil War veterans, the GAR lodge, and the Fourth of July celebrations all reinforced and entrenched a tradition of intense patriotic fervor. During World War I, the small Miner County village of St. Mary's even renamed itself Argonne to honor the heroism of American soldiers during the bloody Muesse-Argonne offensive in France in 1918.[24] Respect for military service also explains the county's name, which originated with Captain Nelson Miner, who served in Dakota during the Civil War.[25] Underscoring the connections among Dakota settlement, republicanism, social capital, and civic participation, Captain Miner built a school, joined the Masons, and served several terms in the territorial legislature.[26]

The early parades and picnics, GAR lodge formation, church building, and political participation laid the groundwork for Miner County's later strength in social capital surveys. This heritage was bolstered by the fact that Miner County was settled in the golden age of fraternal organizations—of the 568 fraternal orders in the nation in 1901, 490 had been formed after 1880.[27] In the 1960s the county's fraternal organizations (one of Putnam's favorite measures of social capital) included the American Legion and the VFW (essentially successors to the GAR), the Masonic Lodge, L.O.O.F. (Odd Fellows), Rebekahs, Royal Neighbors, and the P.E.O. Other organizations included the Community Club, the Howard Service Club, the Homemakers Extension Club, the Civic League, the Miner County Young Men and Women, the Athletic Association, the Sportsman's club, a golf club, and a snowmobile club. In 1965 the mayor of Howard, in yeoman republican fashion, made the case for Miner County community and rural life:

> Our big city neighbors may sneer; but we that live here can perhaps feel a little smug, knowing something they do not—most here are on a first name basis; we can breathe fresh air and sleep secure; most of our lives and work are tailored to the needs of our rural friends; lives depend on God, Earth, Mother Nature, and hopefully, us—to complete the circle of our lives. Good schools, churches, clean homes, and parks are other reasons to make us proud of Howard and to say 'I like it here!'"[28]

In a review of the data that Robert Putnam collected from Miner County for his book *Bowling Alone,* Wendy Rahn noted the persistence of critical indicators of social capital. The indicia of "civic engagement," according to Rahn, put Miner County "in a class by itself."[29] Community is also stronger where individuals trust one another, and Rahn concluded that "general social trust as well as many specific forms of trust are much higher in Miner County than the rest of the nation." This includes levels of trust in local government and in "collective efficacy," or the effectiveness of people coming together to solve a problem, levels that "are considerably higher in Miner County than in the nation as a whole."[30] According to the data, 96 percent of county residents believed it "very likely" or "likely" that people would cooperate to save water or electricity in the event of an emergency. Eighty percent voted in the 1996 presidential election, 52 percent had worked on a community project in the previous year, 34 percent had been involved in a charity or social welfare organization in the previous year, 81 percent were members of a church, and 64 percent had taken part in church activities in the previous year. Ninety-eight percent of county residents said they were "happy" or "very happy."[31]

Miner County's republican roots and its persistently strong manifestations of social capital are, some fear, becoming the exception. The current imbalance in American life between agrarian and republican influences on the one hand and liberal individualism on the other is what obsessed the social critic Christopher Lasch in his final years. He would have worried about the slow erosion of Miner County's community institutions and the chiseling away of the rich layers of social capital Putnam found there. The mounting social and economic problems of the late-twentieth-century United States, according to Lasch, "reopened the historic debate about democracy." Lasch criticized advocates of individualism who "have always taken the position that democracy can dispense with civic virtue." He believed it was critical to promote a "heightened respect for hitherto neglected traditions of thought, deriving from classical republicanism and early Protestant theology, that never had any illusions about the unimportance of civic virtue." Instead of mere tolerance of one another, according to Lasch, workable democracy requires "loyalties," "fortitude," "workmanship," "moral courage," "honesty," "self-respect," and "citizenship." "Unless we are prepared to make demands on one another," Lasch says, "we can enjoy only the most rudimentary kind of common life." Democracy, according to Lasch, requires the community, social capital, and the "character-forming discipline of the family, the neighborhood, the school, and the church," community pillars that places like Miner County provide and that were widely evident during the settlement of Dakota Territory.[32]

For those worried about community and social capital, the trends in Miner County are unmistakable. In 1940, the county was home to 7,400 people—now it has 2,700. In the 1950s, the county seat of Howard had four car dealerships and four grocery stores. Now it has one grocery store. The local priest told me that the present funeral-to-baptism ratio in his church is two-to-one. In the weeks prior to my 2003 visit, the Nazarene Church in Carthage closed. The Union Presbyterian Church, for which my aunt Thelma made five of the pies for the soup and pie supper, almost lost one of its eleven members in 2004. Thelma, then eighty-one, was trampled as she was helping round up the cattle on her and her son's farm. Without her pies and her church, the social capital of Miner County will suffer. Those cattle were trampling on our democratic prospects. In 2009 hope finally began to fade for her church. On January 11, 2009, after the Sunday service, the members of the Union Presbyterian Church held a meeting to decide their future. They voted to continue church services until the propane tank ran dry. They figured that would take about a month. By summer, Thelma had moved into a nursing home, and the Union Presbyterian Church had closed and another vestige of Dakota Territory's republican heritage had faded. But the republican flame has hardly been extinguished, as evidenced by the continued and widely recognized efforts toward economic development and the preservation of community in Miner County.[33] These efforts stem in fundamental ways from the social and political legacy left by the county's founding generation.

NOTES

ABBREVIATIONS

CWS   Center for Western Studies, Augustana College, Sioux Falls, S.Dak.
DB   document box
FF   file folder
SDSHS   South Dakota State Historical Society

Book epigraph: Turner, "Middle Western Pioneer Democracy" (1918), in John Mack Faragher, *Rereading Frederick Jackson Turner: "The Significance of the Frontier in American History" and Other Essays* (New Haven, Conn.: Yale University Press, 1994), 167–69, 171, 176.

PREFACE

1. I. F. Stone, *The Trial of Socrates* (New York: Doubleday, 1988), ix.

2. While editing a new edition of Theodore Roosevelt's *The Winning of the West*, Christopher Lasch simply dropped the section on the Northwest Territory in favor of a focus on Kentucky and Tennessee because these two states "taxed the strength and courage of the settlers in a way that migration to the Northwest did not." Christopher Lasch, "Editor's Introduction," in Theodore Roosevelt, *The Winning of the West* (New York: Fawcett, 1963 [1899]), xv.

3. Nathaniel Hawthorne, *The Marble Faun* (Cambridge, Mass.: Houghton Mifflin, 1901 [1860]), 15.

4. Peter Novick, *That Noble Dream: The "Objectivity Question" and the American Historical Profession* (New York: Cambridge University Press, 1988), 440.

5. Lawrence Stone, "The Revival of Narrative: Reflections on a New Old History," *Past and Present,* no. 85 (November 1979), 4; J. H. Hexter, *On Historians: Reappraisals of Some of the Makers of Modern History* (Cambridge, Mass.: Harvard University Press, 1979), 4.

6. Richard White, "What Are We Afraid Of?" *OAH Newsletter,* 34 (August 2006); Patricia Nelson Limerick, *Something in the Soil: Legacies and Reckonings in the New West* (New York: W. W. Norton, 2001), 337–38.

7. Sean Wilentz, *The Rise of American Democracy: Jefferson to Lincoln* (New York: W. W. Norton, 2005), xxii–xxiii.

8. "Biography of Mrs. A. P. Dragseth," FF GFWC, Lake County A–, DB 6830, SDSHS; "Minnie Hanneman Schultz," FF GFWC, Lake County A–, DB 6830, SDSHS.

9. "Biography of Mary Agnes Kessler-Sullivan," FF GFWC, Lake County A–, DB 6830, SDSHS. Fires seem to have been an incessant problem. One pioneer remembered that "fires that destroyed houses were frequent." Jean Saville, FF GFWC, Aurora County M–W, Pioneer Daughters Collection, DB 6828, SDSHS.

10. *Sodbusters: Tales of Southeastern South Dakota* (Mitchell, S.Dak.: South Dakota Writers' League, 1938), 23. For the history of a Dakota blizzard in 1888 that killed hundreds of settlers, including many children returning home from school, see David Laskin, *The Children's Blizzard* (New York: Harper Perennial, 2005). Letters recounting the hardships of Great Plains pioneers are compiled in Steven R. Kinsella, *900 Miles from Nowhere: Voices from the Homestead Frontier* (St. Paul: Minnesota Historical Society Press, 2006).

11. Hettie Elsie Ferguson, FF Beadle County A-C, Pioneer Daughters Collection, DB 6828, SDSHS. One observer deemed prairie fires "The Terror of the Settlers." H. B. Reese, *Some Pioneers and Pilgrims on the Prairies of Dakota* (Mitchell, S.Dak.: John B. Reese, 1920), 61.

1. Time, Place, Method

1. Oscar Handlin, *Chance or Destiny: Turning Points in American History* (Boston: Little, Brown, 1954), 47–48; David J. Weber, *The Spanish Frontier in North America* (New Haven, Conn.: Yale University Press, 1992), 290–91; Ray Allen Billington, *Westward Expansion: A History of the American Frontier,* 4th ed. (New York: Macmillan, 1974 [1949]), 236–37. For a new history of New France, see David Hackett Fischer, *Champlain's Dream* (New York: Simon and Schuster, 2008).

2. Drew R. McCoy, *The Elusive Republic: Political Economy in Jeffersonian America* (New York: W. W. Norton, 1980), 202–203. Oscar Handlin noted that the French foreign minister, Charles Maurice de Talleyrand, feared that "American democracy was a danger to the society of the Old World, and that the manners and customs of the American people would inevitably make them allies of the English." Handlin, *Chance or Destiny,* 34.

3. Peter S. Onuf, *Jefferson's Empire: The Language of American Nationhood* (Charlottesville: University of Virginia Press, 2000), 1–17; Jeffrey Ostler, "Empire and Liberty: Contradictions and Conflicts in Nineteenth-Century Western Political History," in William Deverell (ed.), *A Companion to the American West* (Malden, Mass.: Blackwell, 2004), 200. On the obstacles to Jefferson's plan, see Roger G. Kennedy, *Mr. Jefferson's Lost Cause: Land, Farmers, Slavery, and the Louisiana Purchase* (New York: Oxford University Press, 2003).

4. "Fifteenth Annual Report of the Superintendent of Public Instruction of the Territory of Dakota, 1882–3–4," p. 23, no FF, DB 7254-B, SDSHS.

5. Joseph Ward, "The Territorial System of the United States," *Andover Review* (July 1888), 52–62; and "Admission of Dakota," U.S. Senate Report, January 11, 1886, 49th Cong., 1st sess., Report no. 15, 6, FF "Dakota" and Dakota Territory, DB 5602, SDSHS (both citing the treaty with France). See Jon Kukla, *A Wilderness So Immense: The Louisiana Purchase and the Destiny of America* (New York: Knopf, 2003), 350–53, which reprints the Treaty between the United States of America and the French Republic, April 30, 1803. Article III of the treaty declared that the "inhabitants of the ceded territory shall be incorporated in the Union of United States and admitted as soon as possible according to the principles of the federal Constitution to the enjoyment of all the rights, advantages and immunities of citizens of the United States, and in the mean time they shall be maintained and protected in the free enjoyment of their liberty, property and the Religion which they profess."

6. Donald Worster, "Beyond the Agrarian Myth," in Clyde A. Milner II, Patricia Nelson Limerick, and Charles E. Rankin (eds.), *Trails: Toward a New Western History* (Lawrence: University Press of Kansas, 1991), 10, 13, 15–16.

7. Gene Gressley (ed.), *Old West/New West* (Norman: University of Oklahoma Press, 1997), 12.

8. T. J. Jackson Lears, *No Place of Grace: Antimodernism and the Transformation of American Culture, 1880–1920* (Chicago: University of Chicago Press, 1981), 26–27.

9. Wallace Stegner, *Beyond the 100th Meridian: John Wesley Powell and the Second Opening of the West* (New York: Penguin, 1954), 31; Earl S. Pomeroy, *The Territories and the United States, 1861–1890: Studies in Colonial Administration* (Philadelphia: University of Pennsylvania Press, 1947), 2.

10. Schurz quoted in Howard Wayne Morgan, *From Hayes to McKinley: National Party Politics, 1877–1896* (Syracuse: Syracuse University Press, 1969), 69; John G. Sprout, *"The Best Men": Liberal Reformers in the Gilded Age* (Chicago: University of Chicago Press, 1968), 4–10. On reform in general, see Steven L. Piott, *American Reformers, 1870–1920: Progressives in Word and Deed* (Lanham, Md.: Rowman and Littlefield, 2006); Michael McGerr, *A Fierce Discontent: The Rise and Fall of the Progressive Movement in America, 1870–1920* (New York: Free Press, 2003); and Ari Hoogenboom, *Outlawing the Spoils: A History of the Civil Service Reform Movement, 1865–1883* (Urbana: University of Illinois Press, 1961).

11. Worth Robert Miller, "The Lost World of Gilded Age Politics," *Journal of the Gilded Age and Progressive Era* vol. 1, no. 1 (January 2002), 54; Henry Clyde Hubbart, *The Older Middle West, 1840–1880* (New York: D. Appleton-Century, 1936), 249–52.

12. S. M. Cullom, "The Six New States," *Forum* (November 1890).

13. Ibid.

14. A. B. Smart to D. T. Elmer, June 30, 1883, FF H92-125, DB 3327B, SDSHS.

15. Chas. G. Brown to Brother, August 11, 1883, FF H92-125, DB 3327B, SDSHS.

16. "Are You Coming West?" *Dakota Outlook*, vol. 1, no. 4 (April 1884), Beinecke Library, Yale University.

17. "The Public Domain," *Aberdeen Daily News*, October 2, 1885. In 1884–85, for example, 4.5 million acres of land were distributed in Dakota Territory, while 3.7 million acres were disbursed in Nebraska, 3 million in Kansas, 3 million in Washington, 1.3 million in California, 1.1 million in Montana, and 800,000 in Oregon. Ibid.

18. E. P. Wilson, "Preface," in *Voices from Dakota: Actual Experiences of Actual Residents* (Chicago: Rand, McNally & Company, Printers, 1889), 2, Beinecke Library, Yale University.

19. Louis B. Wright, *Culture on the Moving Frontier* (Bloomington: Indiana University Press, 1955), 127.

20. Julie Roy Jeffrey, *Frontier Women: The Trans-Mississippi West, 1840–1880* (New York: Hill and Wang, 1979), xi.

21. Bernard Bailyn, *The Peopling of British North America: An Introduction* (New York: Knopf, 1986), 18.

22. Ibid., 9.

23. Bernard Bailyn, *Atlantic History: Concept and Contours* (New York: Knopf, 1986), 93. Bailyn also estimates the total Spanish immigration to the Atlantic colonies to be 688,000 and the immigration to French Canada to be 70,000.

24. Ray Allen Billington, Introduction, in Gilbert C. Fite, *The Farmers' Frontier, 1865–1900* (New York: Holt, Rinehart & Winston, 1966), vi. Frederick C. Luebke similarly noted that during the latter part of the 19th century the United States was the "beneficiary of the largest mass movement of peoples in the history of the world." Luebke, *Immigrants and Politics: The Germans of Nebraska, 1880–1900* (Lincoln: University of Nebraska Press, 1969), vii.

25. "The Public Domain."

26. Fite, *The Farmers' Frontier*, 98 (41 million figure).

27. Ibid.

28. W. H. Ware, "Dakota! The Justly Famed," *Aberdeen Daily News*, February 13, 1885.

29. Fite, *The Farmers' Frontier,* 100.

30. "Report of the Governor of Dakota to the Secretary of the Interior, 1885," FF Report of Governor of Dakota Territory to Secretary of Interior, 1878–1889, DB 7254A, SDSHS (report from Gilbert Pierce to L. Q. C. Lamar). See generally Gary Olson, "The Historical Background of Land Settlement in Eastern Dakota," in Arthur Huseboe (ed.), *Big Sioux Pioneers* (Sioux Falls: Nordland Heritage Foundation, 1980), 25–28.

31. Harold E. Briggs, *Frontiers of the Northwest: A History of the Upper Missouri Valley* (New York: D. Appleton-Century, 1940), 421.

32. Ibid., 422.

33. Reverend A. M. Pilcher, "Dakota," *Western Christian Advocate*, January 13, 1883.

34. Thomas Bender, *A Nation among Nations: America's Place in World History* (New York: Hill and Wang, 2006), 134; Bailyn, *Atlantic History*, 107–109; Merle Curti, "Impact of the Revolutions of 1848 on American Thought," *Proceedings of the American Philosophical Society,* vol. 93 (June 1949), 209–15. William Cronon, George Miles, and Jay Gitlin also stress links to European developments in "Becoming West: Toward a New Meaning for Western History," in William Cronon, George Miles, and Jay Gitlin (eds.), *Under an Open Sky: Rethinking America's Western Past* (New York: W. W. Norton, 1992), 9.

35. Hattie Plum Williams, *The Czar's Germans* (Lincoln, Nebr.: American Historical Society of Germans from Russia, 1975), 175–204.

36. Weston Arthur Goodspeed, *The Province and the States* (Madison, Wisc.: Western Historical Association, 1904), 6: 291–92.

37. Between 1871 and 1885, 3.5 percent of the German population emigrated. Ninety-five percent of these Germans migrated to the United States. This migration peaked in 1881–82, the early years of the Great Dakota Boom. Mack Walker, *Germany and the Emigration, 1816–1885* (Cambridge, Mass.: Harvard University Press, 1964), 181.

38. John Edward Pfeiffer, "The German-Russians and Their Immigration to South Dakota," *South Dakota Historical Collections,* vol. 35 (1970), 303–21; Rowland Berthoff, *An Unsettled People: Social Order and Disorder in American History* (New York: Harper & Row, 1971), 305; La Vern J. Rippley, "Germans," in Richard Sisson, Christian Zacher, and Andrew Cayton (eds.), *The American Midwest: An Interpretive Encyclopedia* (Bloomington: Indiana University Press, 2007), 208; George P. Aberle, *From the Steppes to the Prairies* (Bismarck: Bismarck Tribune Company, 1963), 102–104.

39. Berthoff, *An Unsettled People*, 306; John P. Johansen, "Immigrant Settlements and Social Organization in South Dakota," Department of Rural Sociology Bulletin 313, South Dakota State University (June 1937), 9. On Norwegian emigration, see John B. Reese, *Some Pioneers and Pilgrims on the Prairies of Dakota* (Mitchell, S.Dak: n.p., 1920), 26–34; J. Olson Anders, *From Selbu to the Dakota Prairie: Recollections of Frontier Life on the Middle Border* (CWS, n.d.); and Jon Gjerde, *From Peasants to Farmers: The Migration from Balestrand, Norway to the Upper Middle West* (New York: Cambridge University Press, 1989).

40. In 1890, 32 percent of South Dakotans were foreign born. Out of a population of 329,000, 36,000 were Norwegians, 39,000 were Germans, and 18,000 were "Russians" who were almost exclusively Germans from Russia. Briggs, *Frontiers of the Northwest*, 429. The German-Russians in South Dakota were predominantly from the Black Sea region. Their largest settlements were in Hutchinson, McPherson, Edmunds, Walworth, and Campbell counties. Pfeiffer, "The German-Russians and Their Immigration to South Dakota," 311. See also Adolph Schock, *In Quest of Free Land* (San Jose, Calif.: San Jose State College, 1965), 106–13.

41. This book uses the popular term "Midwest" primarily when referring to Ohio, Indiana, Michigan, Wisconsin, Illinois, Minnesota, and Iowa, the primary states of origin for Dakota settlers. Some primary sources, however, include several of these states within the designation "Old Northwest," which refers to states such as Illinois, Indiana, Michigan, Ohio, and Wisconsin, all of which emerged under the auspices of the Northwest Ordinance. For much of the nineteenth century, "the West" also referred to the states of what is now popularly known as the Midwest. In the nineteenth century, "the Middle West" often referred to Kansas and Nebraska. By the early twentieth century, "the Middle West" or "Midwest" generally came to mean the states of the Old Northwest and Iowa, Minnesota, Missouri, Kansas, Nebraska, and the Dakotas. On the shifting meaning of these terms, see James R. Shortridge, *The Middle West: Its Meaning in American Culture* (Lawrence: University Press of Kansas, 1989), and John C. Hudson, *Making the Corn Belt: A Geographical History of Middle-Western Agriculture* (Bloomington: Indiana University Press, 1994).

42. Robert W. Cherny, *American Politics in the Gilded Age, 1868–1900* (Wheeling, Ill.: Harlan Davidson, 1997), 45; Miller, "The Lost World of Gilded Age Politics," 52.

43. Mark Walgren Summers, *Rum, Romanism, and Rebellion: The Making of a President, 1884* (Chapel Hill: University of North Carolina Press, 2000), 309.

44. Cherny, *American Politics in the Gilded Age*, 93.

45. John Higham, *Strangers in the Land: Patterns of American Nativism, 1860–1925* (New Brunswick, N.J.: Rutgers University Press, 1955), 42; Richard Hofstadter, *The Progressive Historians: Turner, Beard, Parrington* (New York: Knopf, 1968), 56–61; Henry Nash Smith, *Virgin Land: The American West as Symbol and Myth* (Cambridge, Mass.: Harvard University Press, 1950), 206; Howard Lamar, "Frederick Jackson Turner," in Marcus Cunliffe and Robin W. Winks (eds.), *Pastmasters: Some Essays on American Historians* (New York: Harper & Row, 1969), 84, 88; David M. Wrobel, *The End of American Exceptionalism: Frontier Anxiety from the Old West to the New Deal* (Lawrence: University Press of Kansas, 1993), 5; William Cronon, "Landscapes of Abundance and Scarcity," in Clyde A. Milner II, Carol A. O'Connor, and Martha A. Sandweiss (eds.), *The Oxford History of the American West* (New York: Oxford University Press, 1994), 605–606.

46. Ralph Henry Gabriel, *The Course of American Democratic Thought* (New York: Ronald Press, 1940), 320; Allan G. Bogue, "Frederick Jackson Turner Reconsidered," *History Teacher,* vol. 27, no. 2 (February 1994), 202.

47. Gail Bederman, *Manliness and Civilization: A Cultural History of Gender and Race in the United States, 1880–1917* (Chicago: University of Chicago Press, 1996), 43.

48. Christopher Lasch, "Editor's Introduction," in Theodore Roosevelt, *The Winning of the West* (New York, Fawcett, 1963 [1899]), viii; G. Edward White, *The Eastern Establishment and the Western Experience: The West of Frederic Remington, Theodore Roosevelt, and Owen Wister* (New Haven: Yale University Press, 1968), 91–93.

49. Stephen Aron has described the difference between Kentucky and the Far West as follows: "The former lies amidst the wettest, densest woodlands in North America, while the latter presents a semiarid, treeless terrain." Stephen Aron, "Lessons in Conquest: Toward a Greater Western History," *Pacific Historical Review,* vol. 63, no. 2 (May 1994), 135. See generally, Stephen Aron, *How the West Was Lost: The Transformation of Kentucky from Daniel Boone to Henry Clay* (Baltimore: Johns Hopkins University Press, 1999).

50. Wallace Stegner noted that "the lands beyond the 100th meridian received less than twenty inches of annual rainfall, and twenty inches was the minimum for unaided agriculture." Stegner, *Beyond the 100th Meridian,* 214; John David Unruh, "South Dakota in 1889" (Ph.D. dissertation, University of Texas, 1939), 79.

51. After the 1858 Yankton Treaty, the Sioux essentially cleared out of the area from the Big Sioux River to the Missouri River; as early as 1859 the area was opened to settlement. James Frederic Hamburg, *The Influence of Railroads upon the Processes and Patterns of Settlement in South Dakota* (New York: Arno Press, 1981), 42. "East of the Missouri River, by 1867, the Indians had relinquished all territorial claims with the exception of what was retained in the Yankton reservation along the Missouri in the southeastern part of the state, the Lake Traverse or Sisseton reserve in the northeastern corner of the state, and a strip along the Missouri in the central part of the state." Unruh, "South Dakota in 1889," 9–10.

52. L. E. Q., "New Empires in the Northwest," *Library of Tribune Extras* (August 1889), 6, Beinecke Library, Yale University.

53. "Fifteenth Annual Report of the Superintendent of Public Instruction of the Territory of Dakota, 1882–3–4," 23–24, no FF, DB 7254-B, SDSHS. See also Richard White, "The Winning of the West: The Expansion of the Teton Sioux during the Eighteenth and Nineteenth Centuries," *Journal of American History,* vol. 55, no. 2 (September 1978), 319–43.

54. The Sioux have been a frequent topic of historical research, as recorded by Herbert T. Hoover and Karen P. Zimmerman (comps.), *The Sioux and Other Native American Cultures of the Dakotas: An Annotated Bibliography* (Westport, Conn.: Greenwood Press, 1993). Jeffrey Ostler notes the "vast literature on the western Sioux" in *The Plains Sioux and U.S. Colonialism from Lewis and Clark to Wounded Knee* (New York: Cambridge University Press, 2004), 2. Although not examined here, American Indian history has been an active field of study in recent years. See George Miles, "To Hear an Old Voice: Rediscovering Native Americans in American History," in Cronon, Miles, and Gitlin, *Under an Open Sky,* 52–70; David Rich Lewis, "Still Native: The Significance of Native Americans in the History of the Twentieth-Century American West," in Clyde A. Milner II (ed.), *A New Significance: Re-envisioning the History of the American West* (New York: Oxford University Press, 1996), 213–32, David Rich Lewis, "Native Americans in the Nineteenth-Century West," in William Deverell (ed.), *A Companion to the Native American West* (Malden, Mass.: Blackwell, 2004),

143–61; R. David Edmunds, "Native Americans, New Voices: American Indian History, 1895–1995," *American Historical Review,* vol. 100, no. 3 (June 1995), 717–40; and Donald L. Parman and Catherine Price, "A 'Work in Progress': The Emergence of Indian History as a Professional Field," *Western Historical Quarterly,* vol. 20, no. 2 (May 1989), 185–96.

55. General William Beadle noted that the Black Hills and northern Dakota tended to "combine with one another and against the south." "Personal Memoirs of William H. H. Beadle," *South Dakota Historical Collections,* vol. 3 (1906), 149; Unruh, "South Dakota in 1889," 179; John D. Hicks, "The Constitutions of the Northwest States," *University Studies,* vol. 23, nos. 1–2 (1923), 13–14; Frederic Logan Paxson, "The Admission of the 'Omnibus' States, 1889–90," *Proceedings of the State Historical Society of Wisconsin,* October 26, 1911, 82–83. Unless specifically referring to the entirety of the territory, for the sake of verbal economy references to Dakota Territory in this study will generally refer to the southern half of the territory east of the Missouri River.

56. One study asserted that "South Dakota is essentially one of the great agricultural States of the Mississippi Valley." It added, "When we speak of South Dakota as a commonwealth at the present time, we simply speak of the half of the State which lies east of the Missouri River. As such it is almost the counterpart of the other great agricultural States: Indiana, Ohio, Michigan, Wisconsin, and Iowa. Perhaps it resembles Iowa more than any other one of these." *North Dakota, South Dakota, Montana & Washington: The New States* (New York and Chicago: Ivison, Blakeman & Co., 1889), 53, Beinecke Library, Yale University.

57. Ray Allen Billington, *The Genesis of the Frontier Thesis: A Study in Historical Creativity* (San Marino, Calif.: Huntington Library Press, 1971), 42.

58. Ray Allen Billington, *America's Frontier Heritage* (New York, Holt, Rinehart & Winston, 1966), 17.

59. Stegner, *Beyond the 100th Meridian,* xviii.

60. Quoted in Andrew R. L. Clayton and Susan E. Gray, "The Story of the Midwest: An Introduction," in Andrew R. L. Clayton and Susan E. Gray (eds.), *The Identity of the American Midwest: Essays on Regional History* (Bloomington: Indiana University Press, 2001), 10.

61. C. Vann Woodward, *Tom Watson: Agrarian Rebel* (New York: Macmillan, 1938), 133.

62. Ibid., 106.

63. C. Vann Woodward, *The Burden of Southern History,* rev. ed. (Baton Rouge: Louisiana State University Press, 1968 [1960]), xi, 8, 12, 22.

64. David J. Weber, "Turner, the Boltonians, and the Borderlands," *American Historical Review,* vol. 91, no. 1 (February 1986), 69. On Spanish influence in the United States, see generally Weber, *The Spanish Frontier in North America.*

65. Howard R. Lamar, *The Far Southwest, 1846–1912: A Territorial History* (New Haven, Conn.: Yale University Press, 1966), 2.

66. Ibid., 3.

67. Ibid., 25–26, 36.

68. Ibid., 44, 46, 56, 60, 88; Sydney E. Ahlstrom, *A Religious History of the American People* (New Haven, Conn.: Yale University Press, 1972), 42–43, 46–49.

69. *Chicago Inter Ocean*, excerpted in *Yankton Press and Dakotaian*, September 2, 1885.

70. Andrew R. L. Cayton, "The Anti-Region: Place and Identity in the History of the American Midwest," in Cayton and Gray, *The Identity of the American Midwest*, 142.

71. Cayton and Gray, "The Story of the Midwest: An Introduction," 1, 252. Cayton also argues that "politically constructed spatial organizations" such as the Midwest are considered the products of European men and thus less interesting. One of the reasons for the popularity of western history since the 1960s is the field's attention to race, class, gender, and environmental concerns that transcend regions. The New Western historians, Cayton notes, "align themselves directly with other scholars whose purpose is to deconstruct and delegitimize the supposed national hegemony of white males." Cayton, "The Anti-Region," 152.

72. Susan E. Gray, *The Yankee West: Community Life on the Michigan Frontier* (Chapel Hill: University of North Carolina Press, 1996), 9. These laments are not new. In the 1940s, Thomas Wertenbaker similarly concluded that the "transplanting of our eastern civilizations to the West, certainly one of the most important movements in our history, is also one of the most neglected." Thomas J. Wertenbaker, "The Molding of the Middle West," *American Historical Review,* vol. 52, no. 2 (January 1948), 225.

73. John D. Hicks, "The Development of Civilization in the Middle West, 1860–1900," in Dixon Ryan Fox (ed.), *Sources of Culture in the Middle West: Backgrounds versus Frontier* (New York: Russell & Russell, 1964 [1934]), 77.

74. Marilynne Robinson, *The Death of Adam: Essays on Modern Thought* (New York: Picador, 2005), 132.

75. Patricia Nelson Limerick, *The Legacy of Conquest: The Unbroken Past of the American West* (New York: W. W. Norton, 1987), 21.

76. Ibid.

77. Howard Lamar, "Frederick Jackson Turner," in Cunliffe and Winks, *Pastmasters,* 89, 104. Lamar's students also note that "Turner's critics ultimately went too far in their attacks on his work." Cronon, Miles, and Gitlin, "Becoming West," 6.

78. Gerald Thompson, "The New Western History: A Critical Analysis," in Gressley, *Old West/New West,* 63; Benjamin F. Wright, Jr., "Political Institutions and the Frontier," in Fox, *Sources of Culture in the Middle West,* 33; Jane Marie Pederson, *Between Memory and Reality: Family and Community in Rural Wisconsin, 1870–1970* (Madison: University of Wisconsin Press, 1992), 6.

79. Frederick Jackson Turner, quoted in Earl Pomeroy, "Comments on 'Space, Time, Culture and the New Frontier,'" *Agricultural History,* vol. 38, no. 1 (January 1964), 31.

80. Donald K. Pickens, "The Turner Thesis and Republicanism: A Historiographical Commentary," *Pacific Historical Review,* vol. 61, no. 3 (May 1992), 337.

81. David Allen Johnson, *Founding the Far West: California, Oregon, and Nevada, 1840–1890* (Berkeley: University of California Press, 1992), ix–x.

82. Ibid., 3, 6.

83. Ibid., 8. Many of the "old Californios" became the founders of Nevada. Ibid., 10.

84. Historians have frequently noted Turner's failure to study ethnic minorities. See, for example, William Cronon, "Revisiting the Vanishing Frontier: The Legacy of Frederick Jackson Turner," *Western Historical Quarterly,* vol. 18, no. 2 (April 1987), 159; Richard White, "Race Relations in the American West," *American Quarterly,* vol. 38, no. 3 (1986), 396. Limerick noted that "Turner was, to put it mildly, ethnocentric and nationalistic. English-speaking white men were the stars of his story; Indians, Hispanics, French Canadians, and Asians were at best supporting actors and at worst invisible." *Legacy of Conquest,* 21.

85. David G. Gutiérrez, "Significant to Whom? Mexican Americans and the History of the American West," in Milner, *A New Significance,* 70.

86. Gail M. Nomura, "Significant Lives: Asia and Asian Americans in the U.S. West," in Milner, *A New Significance*, 149. For a general review of this history, see Jean Pfaelzer, *Driven Out: The Forgotten War against Chinese Americans* (New York: Random House, 2007). On the effort to assimilate Mexicans and Asians in the West, see Frank Van Nuys, *Americanizing the West: Race, Immigrants, and Citizenship, 1890–1930* (Lawrence: University Press of Kansas, 2002). On the Chinese immigrants in the Black Hills, see Liping Zhu and Rose Estep Fosha, *Ethnic Oasis: The Chinese in the Black Hills* (Pierre: South Dakota State Historical Society Press, 2004). The peak year of Chinese population was 1880. That year, 221 of the 230 Chinese in Dakota Territory were in Deadwood. Zhu and Fosha, *Ethnic Oasis,* 9.

87. Quintard Taylor, "Through the Prism of Race: The Meaning of African-American History in the West," in Milner, *A New Significance,* 289–90. For a recent survey, see Quintard Taylor, *In Search of the Racial Frontier: African Americans in the American West, 1528–1990* (New York: W. W. Norton, 1998). On African Americans in Dakota, see Betti Van Epps-Taylor, *Forgotten Lives: African-Americans in South Dakota* (Pierre: South Dakota State Historical Society Press, 2008).

88. According to the state census of 1905, only 166 blacks were then living in South Dakota's organized counties (some counties west of the Missouri River that included Sioux reservation lands were considered "unorganized"). The 1905 census also listed 3,912 "others," including Indians, Chinese, and Japanese, who were counted in state totals as "white." *Second Census of the State of South Dakota, 1905* (Aberdeen, S.Dak.: News Printing Company, 1905), 88. Stephen Aron notes the absence in general of Hispanics in South Dakota and of Asians on the Great Plains in his discussion of the difficulties of defining the West. Aron,

"Lessons in Conquest," 131. Mark R. Ellis notes that "Hispanics, African Americans, and Asians largely ignored the northern and central Great Plains during the nineteenth century." Ellis, *Law and Order in Buffalo Bill's Country: Legal Culture and Community on the Great Plains, 1867–1910* (Lincoln: University of Nebraska Press, 2007), 28. Also see Michael C. Steiner and David M. Wrobel, "Many Wests: Discovering a Dynamic Western Regionalism," in David M. Wrobel and Michael C. Steiner (eds.), *Many Wests: Place, Culture, and Regional Identity* (Lawrence: University Press of Kansas, 1997), 11.

89. Elliott West, "Strangeness and Work, History and Memory," in Clyde Milner II (ed.), "A Historian Who Has Changed Our Thinking: A Roundtable on the Work of Richard White," *Western Historical Quarterly,* vol. 33 (Summer 2002), 143.

90. Cronon, Miles, and Gitlin, "Becoming West," 7, 11; Clyde A. Milner II, "The View from Wisdom: Four Layers of History and Regional Identity," in Cronon, Miles, and Gitlin, *Under an Open Sky,* 222. On Turner's focus on the importance of particular regions, see Michael C. Steiner, "The Significance of Turner's Sectional Thesis," *Western Historical Quarterly,* vol. 10, no. 4 (October 1979), 437–66.

91. Robert Johnston, "Beyond 'The West': Regionalism, Liberalism and the Evasion of Politics in the New Western History," *Rethinking History,* vol. 2, no. 2 (1998), 259. Stephen Aron emphasizes that "there were, and still are, many Wests." Aron, "Lessons in Conquest," 132. Don Flores also notes that "no set of generalized definitions, regardless of how inclusive, accurately explains the loose cluster of subregions comprising the huge swath of continental topography and ecology that is the Western United States." Dan Flores, "Place: An Argument for Bioregional History," *Environmental History Review,* vol. 18, no. 4 (Winter 1994), 4. Steiner and Wrobel argue that the "New Western History, in its efforts to replace the frontier framework with a geographically bounded, regional West has given less attention to another important area of western diversity: regional diversity." "Many Wests," 11. See also Steven L. Danver, "A Sense of Place: The Diversity of Localities in the West," *Journal of the West,* vol. 45, no. 3 (Summer 2006), 8; and Dean L. May, *Three Frontiers: Family, Land, and Society in the American West, 1850–1900* (New York: Cambridge University Press, 1994).

92. Dakota Territory was also larger than France and the entire United Kingdom (Ireland, Wales, Scotland, and England). J. G. Towles, "History of Dakota," *Lake County Leader,* January 1, 1885, FF Dakota Territory, DB 5602, SDSHS.

93. Frederick Jackson Turner, quoted in Pomeroy, "Comments on 'Space, Time, Culture and the New Frontier,'" 33.

94. Jeffrey Ostler has called on western historians to give greater attention to the political sphere. Ostler, "Empire and Liberty," 202. Also see Johnston, "Beyond 'The West,'" 239–77.

95. David Hackett Fischer, *Historians' Fallacies: Toward a Logic of Historical Thought* (New York: Harper & Row, 1970), 7.

96. Robert Shalhope, "Toward a Republican Synthesis: The Emergence of an Understanding of Republicanism in Early American Historiography," *William and Mary Quarterly,* vol. 29 (January 1972), 49–80; Daniel T. Rodgers, "Republicanism: The Career of a Concept," *Journal of American History,* vol. 79, no. 1 (June 1992), 17.

97. Rodgers, "Republicanism," 28. The debate between historians of republicanism and those who believe that classical liberalism was a more powerful tradition has been deemed a "historiographical inferno" by James T. Kloppenberg in *The Virtues of Liberalism* (New York: Oxford University Press, 1998), 21.

98. Lawrence Levine, "The Revival of Narrative: Reflections on a New Old History," *Past and Present,* no. 85 (November 1979), 5.

99. Kloppenberg, *Virtues of Liberalism,* 21; Mark A. Noll, *America's God: From Jonathan Edwards to Abraham Lincoln* (Oxford: Oxford University Press, 2002), 53–92.

100. Henry F. May, *The Divided Heart: Essays on Protestantism and the Enlightenment in America* (New York: Oxford University Press, 1991), 18.

101. In western history, "one broad area is even more neglected than most: religion." Elliott West, "Thinking West," in William Deverell (ed.), *A Companion to the American West* (Malden, Mass.: Blackwell, 2004), 38. Howard Lamar has also noted that western historians "totally left religion out of their work on the frontier except for revivals." Lamar, interview with the author, June 5, 2006. Robert Johnston has criticized the New Western historians for their "evasion of the messy realm of the political." "Beyond 'The West,'" 240.

102. William G. Robbins, "Laying Siege to Western History: The Emergence of New Paradigms," *Reviews in American History,* vol. 19, no. 3 (September 1991), 326; Cayton, "The Anti-Region," 152; Robert V. Remini, "American Political Biography," John F. Marszalek and Wilson D. Miscamble (eds.), *American Political History: Essays on the State of the Discipline* (Notre Dame, Ind.: University of Notre Dame Press, 1997), 147. By the beginning of the 1990s the focus of the New Western historians was, according to Patricia Limerick, "becoming orthodoxy." Patricia Nelson Limerick, *Something in the Soil: Legacies and Reckonings in the New West* (New York: W. W. Norton, 2000), 23.

103. Peter Burke, *History and Social Theory,* 2nd ed. (Ithaca, N.Y.: Cornell University Press, 2005), 63.

104. Carl N. Degler, "Remaking American History," *Journal of American History,* vol. 67, no. 1 (June 1980), 16.

105. Hofstadter, *The Progressive Historians,* xv–xvi (emphasis added).

106. Sean Wilentz, *The Rise of American Democracy: Jefferson to Lincoln* (New York: W. W. Norton, 2005); Richard Kluger, *Seizing Destiny: How America Grew from Sea to Shining Sea* (New York: Knopf, 2007); Morton Keller, *America's Three Regimes: A New Political History* (New York: Oxford University Press, 2007); David S. Reynolds, *Waking Giant: America in the Age of Jackson* (New York: Harper, 2008); Jon Meacham, *American Lion: Andrew Jackson in the White House* (New York: Random House, 2008).

107. James Bryce, *The American Commonwealth* (New York: Common-wealth Publishing Company, 1908 [1888]), 789.

108. George Wilson Pierson, *Tocqueville in America* (Baltimore: Johns Hopkins University Press, 1996), 776.

2. A MACHIAVELLIAN MOMENT ON THE MIDDLE BORDER

Epigraph: W. H. Ware, "Dakota! The Justly Famed," *Aberdeen Daily News*, February 13, 1885.

1. J. G. A. Pocock, *The Machiavellian Moment: Florentine Political Thought and the Atlantic Republican Tradition* (Princeton: Princeton University Press, 1975). On the revival of republicanism in Italy, see Maurizio Viroli, *Republicanism* (New York: Hill & Wang, 2002), 22–23; and Frederic C. Lane, "At the Roots of Republicanism," *American Historical Review,* vol. 71, no. 2 (January 1966), 404. Lane notes that "Machiavelli is best known for advising princes to be unscrupulous . . . but his standard of health [for the polis] was republican." Lane, "At the Roots of Republicanism," 415. Quentin P. Taylor sees Machiavelli as the "father of modern republicanism" and "the unrecognized 'grandfather' of the American republic." Taylor, *The Other Machiavelli: Republican Writings by the Author of "The Prince"* (Lanham, Md.: University Press of America, 1998), ix, xi. On Machiavelli and republicanism, also see Iseult Honohan, *Civic Republicanism* (London: Routledge, 2002), 44–63. On the revival of the study of republicanism in general, see Rodgers, "Republicanism," and Bernard Bailyn, *Atlantic History,* 52–53.

2. Paul A. Rahe, "Introduction," in Paul A. Rahe (ed.), *Machiavelli's Liberal Republican Legacy* (New York: Cambridge University Press, 2006), xix–xxx; Robert A. Kocis, *Machiavelli Redeemed: Retrieving His Humanist Perspectives on Equality, Power, and Glory* (London: Associated University Presses, 1998), 198–208.

3. Robert E. Shalhope, *The Roots of Democracy: American Thought and Culture, 1760–1800* (Lanham, Md.: Rowman & Littlefield, 1990), 44–46. According to Daniel T. Rodgers, the main "themes" of republicanism expressed during the American Revolution included "the Americans' fear of British corruption, fear of the grasping, fatal effects of luxury, fear of their own inability to sustain the self-denying virtues on which a republic depended." Rodgers, "Republicanism," 15.

4. Pickens, "The Turner Thesis and Republicanism," 327 (polis quote); John Patrick Diggins, *The Lost Soul of American Politics: Virtue, Self-Interest, and the Foundations of Liberalism* (Chicago: University of Chicago Press, 1984), 122 (moment quote). Describing the settlement of Dakota Territory as a "Machiavellian moment" should not be taken to mean an act of ruthlessness or extreme political realism or cynicism, which is the context in which Machiavelli is sometimes invoked, but instead as an instance of republican vigor. For an explanation, see Kocis, *Machiavelli Redeemed.*

5. Jean Baker, "From Belief into Culture: Republicanism in the Antebellum North," *American Quarterly,* vol. 37, no. 4 (Autumn 1985), 538.

6. Rowland Berthoff, *Republic of the Dispossessed: The Exceptional Old-European Consensus in America* (Columbia: University of Missouri Press, 1997), 6.

7. Ibid., 146, 149.

8. Ibid., 151.

9. Ibid., 153.

10. Ibid.

11. Pickens, "The Turner Thesis and Republicanism," 331.

12. Ibid., 327.

13. Joseph Ward, "The Territorial System of the United States," *Andover Review* (July 1888), 57.

14. George W. Kingsbury, *History of Dakota Territory* (Chicago: S. J. Clarke Publishing Company, 1915), 1670.

15. Ibid., 1732.

16. "Personal Memoirs of William H. H. Beadle," 216.

17. Doane Robinson, "Sketch of South Dakota's History," *New York Evangelist*, October 10, 1901.

18. "Admission of Dakota," Report of the Senate Committee on Territories, 50th Cong., 1st Session, January 23, 1888, 42, Beinecke Library, Yale University.

19. Louis B. Wright, *Culture on the Moving Frontier* (Bloomington: Indiana University Press, 1955), 88; Thomas J. Wertenbaker, "The Molding of the Middle West," *American Historical Review,* vol. 52, no. 2 (January 1948), 227; John D. Barnhart, *Valley of Democracy: The Frontier vs. the Plantation in the Ohio Valley, 1775–1818* (Bloomington: Indiana University Press, 1953), 122; Susan Sessions Rugh, "Nineteenth-Century Americans," in Sisson, Zacher, and Cayton, *The American Midwest,* 190; Graham Hutton, *Midwest at Noon* (Chicago: University of Chicago Press, 1946), 33.

20. Gray, *Yankee West,* 2–6; George McKenna, *The Puritan Origins of American Patriotism* (New Haven, Conn.: Yale University Press, 2007), 3. See generally John C. Hudson, "Yankeeland in the Middle West," *Journal of Geography,* vol. 85 (1986), 195–200; Hudson, "North American Origins of Middlewestern Frontier Populations," *Annals of the Association of American Geographers,* vol. 78, no. 3 (September 1988), 395–413; and Hudson, "Who Was 'Forest Man'? Sources of Immigration to the Plains," *Great Plains Quarterly,* vol. 6, no. 2 (Spring 1986), 72–75.

21. Nicole Etcheson, *The Emerging Midwest: Upland Southerners and the Political Culture of the Old Northwest, 1787–1861* (Bloomington: Indiana University Press, 1996), xi, 13. On midwestern regionalism, see David Herbert Donald, *Lincoln Reconsidered: Essays on the Civil War Era* (New York: Vintage, 1961), 167–72.

22. See generally Virginia Driving Hawk Sneve (ed.), *South Dakota Geographic Names* (Sioux Falls, S.Dak.: Brevet Press, 1973). On the transference of

New England place-names to the Midwest, see Thomas J. Schlereth, "The New England Presence on the Midwest Landscape," *The Old Northwest,* vol. 9, no. 2 (Summer 1983), 126–28.

23. *Laws Passed at the First Session of the Legislature of the State of South Dakota* (Pierre, S.Dak.: State Bindery Co., Printers, 1890), 254; Bernard Floyd Hyatt, "A Legal Legacy for Statehood: The Development of the Territorial Judicial System in Dakota Territory, 1861–1889" (Ph.D. dissertation, Texas Tech University, 1987), 591, 599; Gordon Morris Bakken, *The Development of Law on the Rocky Mountain Frontier: Civil Law and Society, 1850–1912* (Westport, Conn.: Greenwood Press, 1983), 130, 67. Of the nineteen justices appointed to Dakota Territorial Supreme Court from 1882 to 1889, six were from the East, four were from the Midwest, and eight were from Dakota Territory. Hyatt, "A Legal Legacy for Statehood," 439. In 1877 the territory adopted much of the Field uniform statutory code, and "Dakota did not change the Field draft provisions concerning the relationship between the Code and the Anglo-American common law, and this left the reconciliation of what might seem to be inconsistent commands to the courts." Hyatt, "A Legal Legacy for Statehood," 171–72. Judicial officials in the West generally "strove to impose legal uniformity, rather than to differentiate themselves from the East." Sarah Barringer Gordon, "Law and the Contact of Cultures," in Deverell, *A Companion to the American West,* 134.

24. Wright, *Culture on the Moving Frontier,* 221; Keith Newlin, *Hamlin Garland: A Life* (Lincoln: University of Nebraska Press, 2008), 7.

25. Wright, *Culture on the Moving Frontier,* 119, 209. The town of Waverly was named for Sir Walter Scott's *Waverly Novels,* and the town of Montrose may also have been named for Scott's *Legend of Montrose.* Driving Hawk Sneve, *South Dakota Geographic Names,* 80, 99. On Scott, see Arthur Herman, *How the Scots Invented the Modern World: The True Story of How Western Europe's Poorest Nation Created Our World and Everything in It* (New York: Three Rivers Press, 2001), 291–319.

26. "The School and Endowment Lands," n.d., Beadle Papers, FF 1, DB 3536A, SDSHS.

27. Norma C. Wilson and Charles Woodward (eds.), *One-Room Country School* (Brookings: South Dakota Humanities Foundation, 1999), xiii; Lydia M. Swift to Emma, November 1883, FF H92-125, DB 3327B, SDSHS.

28. Ella S. to Dill, July 16, 1880, FF H92-125, DB 3327B, SDSHS.

29. William Henry Harrison Beadle, "Address Delivered at the Laying of the Corner Stone of the Capitol Building of South Dakota," FF 1, DB 3563A, Beadle Papers, SDSHS. Beadle's sense of history comported with a common understanding of the origins of American liberty. Bernard Bailyn, *The Ideological Origins of the American Revolution* (Cambridge, Mass.: Harvard University Press, 1967), 66–67, 79–83; H. Trevor Colbourn, *The Lamp of Experience: Whig History and the Intellectual Origins of the American Revolution* (New York: W. W. Norton, 1974 [1965]), 7–8, 26–36; Forrest McDonald, *Novus Ordo Seclorum:*

The Intellectual Origins of the Constitution (Lawrence: University Press of Kansas, 1985), 76–77.

30. Wright, *Culture on the Moving Frontier*, 8.

31. Unruh, "South Dakota in 1889," 52.

32. Ibid., 52. On the influence of the Midwest on the settlement of the Sacramento Valley, see David Vaught, "After the Gold Rush: Replicating the Rural Midwest in the Sacramento Valley," *Western Historical Quarterly,* vol. 34 (Winter 2003), 447–67.

33. *North Dakota, South Dakota, Montana & Washington: The New States* (New York: Ivison, Blakeman & Co., 1889), 28, Beinecke Library, Yale University; L. E. Q., "New Empires in the Northwest," *Library of Tribune Extras* (August 1889), 13, Beinecke Library, Yale University.

34. Herbert S. Schell, *History of Clay County South Dakota* (Vermillion, S.Dak.: Clay County Historical Society, 1976), 105.

35. John Hudson, "Two Dakota Homestead Frontiers," *Annals of the Association of American Geographers,* vol. 63, no. 4 (December 1973), 462.

36. *Press and Dakotaian*, September 7, 1883; *Grant County Review*, March 14, 1889; Merle Curti, *The Making of an American Community: A Case Study of Democracy in a Frontier County* (Stanford: Stanford University Press, 1959), 66. "Wisconsin, heavily settled by Vermont and Massachusetts natives, provided the largest number of immigrants (11,685) to the Dakota Territory in 1880." Gregory Rose, "Yankees/Yorkers," in Sisson, Zacher, and Cayton, *The American Midwest*, 194.

37. Unruh, "South Dakota in 1889," 46.

38. Frederick Jackson Turner, "The Problem of the West" (1896), in Raymond J. Cunningham (ed.), *The Populists in Historical Perspective* (Boston: D. C. Heath, 1968), 7. Turner cited the example of Senator Allen of Nebraska, who was born in Ohio, moved to Iowa, and then moved to Nebraska after serving in the Civil War.

39. Andrew R. L. Cayton and Peter S. Onuf, *The Midwest and the Nation: Rethinking the History of an American Region* (Bloomington: Indiana University Press, 1990), 3.

40. Ibid., xvii.

41. Ibid., 1; Barnhart, *Valley of Democracy*, 134–35; Orville Vernon Burton, *The Age of Lincoln* (New York: Hill & Wang, 2007), 16; Robert P. Swierenga, "The Settlement of the Old Northwest: Ethnic Pluralism in a Featureless Plain," *Journal of the Early Republic,* vol. 9 (Spring 1989), 73–74.

42. Cayton and Onuf, *The Midwest and the Nation*, 8; Barnhart, *Valley of Democracy*, 122–23; Robert F. Berkhofer, Jr., "The Northwest Ordinance and the Principle of Territorial Evolution," in John Porter Bloom (ed.), *The American Territorial System* (Athens: Ohio University Press, 1973), 45.

43. Cayton and Onuf, *The Midwest and the Nation*, 19.

44. Ibid., 70.

45. Barnhart, *Valley of Democracy*, 121.

46. Etcheson, *The Emerging Midwest*, 142–43.

47. William Beadle to Editor, *New York Tribune*, January 21, 1878, Beadle Papers, FF 1, DB 3536A, SDSHS. This is not to argue that the Midwest did not include a variety of ethnic groups. Swierenga, "The Settlement of the Old Northwest," 73–105.

48. Malcolm J. Rohrbaugh, "The Continuing Search for the American West: Historians Past, Present, Future," in Gressley, *Old West/New West,* 136. See also, Stephen Aron, "Lessons in Conquest," 136–40.

49. Howard Wayne Morgan, *From Hayes to McKinley: National Party Politics, 1877–1896* (Syracuse: Syracuse University Press, 1969), 372.

50. Fite, *Farmers' Frontier,* 25; Herbert S. Schell, "Official Immigration Activities of Dakota Territory," *North Dakota Historical Quarterly,* vol. 7 (October 1932), 5–24.

51. Lamar, *Dakota Territory,* 190; L. E. Q., "New Empires in the Northwest," 13.

52. Charles N. Herreid, "The Pioneers of Dakota," *South Dakota Historical Collections,* vol. 13 (1926), 18–19.

53. Ward, "The Territorial System of the United States," 53.

54. Ibid., 55.

55. Kingsbury, *History of Dakota Territory*, 1442.

56. Quoted in ibid., 1444–45.

57. Ibid., 1528.

58. Ibid., 1517.

59. Ibid., 1570.

60. Billington, *America's Frontier Heritage,* 64.

61. Ralph Henry Gabriel, *The Course of American Democratic Thought: An Intellectual History since 1815* (New York: Ronald Press, 1940), 316–17; Kermit L. Hall, "Mostly Anchor and Little Sail: The Evolution of American State Constitutions," in Paul Finkelman and Stephen E. Gottlieb (eds.), *Toward a Usable Past: Liberty under State Constitutions* (Athens: University of Georgia Press, 1991), 389. Michael Kammen notes that "throughout the eighties other books about the Constitution, aimed at a general audience, appeared at an accelerating pace." Kammen, *A Machine That Would Go of Itself: The Constitution in American Culture* (New York: Knopf, 1986), 127–28. Kammen also notes that the "half century following 1880 involved the emergence of constitutional history as a major field of scholarship in the United States." Ibid., 176.

62. Gabriel, *The Course of American Democratic Thought*, 315. On the development of the early-nineteenth-century consensus of support for the American Constitution, see Jurgen Gebhardt, *Americanism: Revolutionary Order and Societal Self-Interpretation in the American Republic* (Baton Rouge: Louisiana State University Press, 1993), 168–69.

63. "July 13, 1787–July 13, 1886, Dakota State League," FF H75.54, DB 3538A, SDSHS.

64. "Admission of Dakota," Report of the Senate Committee on Territories, 50th Cong., 1st Session, January 23, 1888, 4, Beinecke Library, Yale University.

65. Robert Dollard, *Recollections of the Civil War and Going West to Grow Up with the Country* (Scotland, S.Dak.: privately printed, 1906), 268. See also "Personal Memoirs of William H. H. Beadle," 121.

66. Kingsbury, *History of Dakota Territory*, 1757; Doane Robinson, *South Dakota, Sui Generis* (Chicago: American Historical Society, 1930), 488–89.

67. Review of territorial governor applications, March 8, 1889, FF Data Governor, DB 149, RG 48, Records of the Department of the Interior, Records of the Appointments Division, Field Office Appointment Papers, 1849–1907, Dakota Territory Appointment Papers, National Archives.

68. Frank Bloodgood, "Homesteading in Custer Township, Beadle County, South Dakota," 17–18, FF H75.36, DB 3538A, SDSHS. The "stronghold" of the GAR was the Midwest, which sent many settlers to Dakota. Wallace Evan Davies, *Patriotism on Parade: The Story of Veterans' and Hereditary Organizations in America, 1783–1900* (Cambridge, Mass.: Harvard University Press, 1955), 36. On the Dakota GAR, see Stephen T. Morgan, "Fellow Comrades: The Grand Army of the Republic in South Dakota," *South Dakota History*, vol. 36, no. 3 (Fall 2006), 229–259.

69. R. Hal Williams, "The Politics of the Gilded Age," in John F. Marszalek and Wilson D. Miscamble (eds.), *American Political History: Essays on the State of the Discipline* (Notre Dame, Ind.: University of Notre Dame Press, 1997), 111 (Holmes quote). On how the soldiers viewed the high stakes of the Civil War, see Earl J. Hess, *Liberty, Virtue, and Progress: Northerners and Their War for the Union* (New York: New York University Press, 1988), 26–27. See also James M. McPherson, *For Cause and Comrades: Why Men Fought the Civil War* (New York: Oxford University Press, 1998). On the impact of the Civil War in Wisconsin, see Curti, *The Making of an American Community*, 131–36.

70. Williams, "Politics of the Gilded Age," 111.

71. *The Wi-Iyohi*, vol. 5, no. 2 (May 1, 1951); Herbert Schell, *History of South Dakota* (Lincoln: University of Nebraska Press, 1975), 169; Winifred Fawcett and Thelma Hepper, *Veterans of the Civil War Who Settled in Potter County, Dakota Territory* (Gettysburg, S.Dak.: privately printed, 1993), CWS.

72. Herbert T. Hoover, "Territorial Politics and Politicians," in Harry Thompson (ed.), *A New South Dakota History* (Sioux Falls, S.Dak.: CWS, 2004), 103, 113, 114.

73. Albert Allen (ed.), *Dakota Imprints, 1858–1889* (New York: R. R. Bowker, 1947), 102.

74. Kingsbury, *History of Dakota Territory*, 1525.

75. Ibid., 1761.

76. Ibid., 1444–45.

77. Ibid., 1741.

78. Ibid., 1466.

79. Carrol Gardner Green, "The Struggle of South Dakota to Become a State," *South Dakota Historical Collections*, vol. 12 (1924), 528.

80. Lewis E. Bloodgood to Father, Pine Bluff, Arkansas, November 12, 1864, FF H75.36, DB 3538A, SDSHS.

81. Lewis E. Bloodgood to Mother and Father, Marine Hospital, New Orleans, May 9, 1865, FF H75.36, DB 3538A, SDSHS.

82. Frank Bloodgood, "Homesteading in Custer Township, Beadle County, South Dakota," pp. 5–6, FF H75.36, DB 3538A, SDSHS.

83. Weston Arthur Goodspeed, *The Province and the States* (Madison, Wis.: Western Historical Association, 1904), 2: 470; John E. Miller, "The State of South Dakota," in Benjamin F. Shearer (ed.), *The Uniting States: The Story of Statehood for the Fifty United States,* vol. 3: *Oklahoma to Wyoming* (Westport, Conn.: Greenwood Press, 2004), 1106, 1109.

84. Waldo Potter to Augustine Davis, January 4, 1888, FF Letters, January–February 1888, DB 3544B, Augustine Davis Collection, SDSHS; Kingsbury, *History of Dakota Territory*, 1898.

85. *Laws Passed at the Seventeenth Session of the Legislative Assembly of the Territory of Dakota* (Bismarck, N.Dak.: Tribune, Printers and Binders, 1887), 343; Drew Gilpin Faust, *This Republic of Suffering: Death and the American Civil War* (New York: Vintage, 2008), 62, 100.

86. *Laws Passed at the Seventeenth Session of the Legislative Assembly of the Territory of Dakota,* 399. By 1889 the territorial legislature had passed a Soldier's Burial Act and a Soldier's Preference Act and had funded a Soldier's Home and the National Guard. "Veterans," *The Wi-Iyohi*, vol. 9, no. 1 (April 1, 1955).

87. Hicks, *Populist Revolt*, 10.

88. "Growth of the Grand Army Republic," *Aberdeen Daily News*, April 24, 1885; Kingsbury, *History of Dakota Territory*, 1385, 1757; Lamar, *Dakota Territory*, 246; Morgan, "Fellow Comrades," 229–59. John Higham called the GAR the "most powerful patriotic society of the day." Higham, *Strangers in the Land,* 57.

89. "The G.A.R. Reunion," *Bismarck Tribune*, September 17, 1885.

90. *Laws Passed at the Eighteenth Session of the Legislative Assembly of the Territory of Dakota* (Bismarck, N.Dak.: Tribune, Printers and Binders, 1889), 157; "Veterans," *The Wi-Iyohi*, vol. 9, no. 1 (April 1, 1955).

91. Kingsbury, *History of Dakota Territory*, 1447, 1465.

92. Cayton and Gray, "The Story of the Midwest," 16–17.

93. Ibid., 15.

94. Marc W. Kruman, "The Second American Party System and the Transformation of Revolutionary Republicanism," *Journal of the Early Republic,* vol. 12, no. 4 (Winter 1992), 536.

95. David W. Noble, *Historians Against History: The Frontier Thesis and the National Covenant in American Historical Writing* (Minneapolis: University of Minnesota Press, 1965), 49.

96. Ward, "Territorial System of the United States," 52; Miller, "The State of South Dakota," 1105.

97. Quoted in Pomeroy, *The Territories and the United States,* 104.

98. Unruh, "South Dakota in 1889," 123.

99. Ward, "Territorial System of the United States," 52–62.

100. Ibid., 62. The territorial system that Dakotans protested against was, at least, more democratic than earlier iterations, especially prior to the 1830s. Pomeroy, *The Territories and the United States*, 97.

101. "Personal Memoirs of William H. H. Beadle," 199.

102. Pickens, "Turner Thesis and Republicanism," 335–36.

103. Christopher Lasch, *The True and Only Heaven: Progress and Its Critics* (New York: W. W. Norton, 1991), 274.

104. Ward, "Territorial System of the United States," 54–55.

105. Review of governor applications, March 8, 1889, FF Data Governor, DB 149, RG 48, Records of the Department of the Interior, Records of the Appointments Division, Field Office Appointment Papers, 1849–1907, Dakota Territory Appointment Papers, National Archives.

106. John O. Strand to Arthur Mellette, August 10, 1889, FF H74.188 Correspondence S, DB 3525A, Mellette Papers, SDSHS.

107. Fite, *Farmers' Frontier*, 13.

108. William Maxwell Blackburn, "A History of Dakota," *South Dakota Historical Collections*, vol. 1 (1902), 80.

109. Song quoted in Thomas H. McKee, "A Boy in Bismarck, When Both Were Very Young," March 1953, Thomas McKee Collection, State Historical Society of North Dakota (hereinafter SHSND).

110. Pickens, "Turner Thesis and Republicanism," 324; David M. Emmons, *Garden in the Grasslands: Boomer Literature of the Central Great Plains* (Lincoln: University of Nebraska Press, 1971), 34.

111. Lears, *No Place of Grace,* 18 (industrious quote); John E. Miller, *Laura Ingalls Wilder's Little Town: Where History and Literature Meet* (Lawrence: University Press of Kansas, 1994), 45. Hamlin Garland emphasized the hard work of prairie settlers in his book of short stories. *Main-Travelled Roads* (New York: Fawcett, 1961 [1891]). See also Hamlin Garland, "Dakota" (1885), *South Dakota Historical Review,* vol. 1, no. 3 (April 1936), 132.

112. Vinnie Hannaman to Arthur Mellette, February 4, 1883, FF Correspondence Pre-1889, DB 3524B, Mellette Papers, SDSHS (plainly quote); Frank Parsons to Arthur Mellette, January 6, 1886, FF Correspondence Pre-1889, DB 3524B, Mellette Papers, SDSHS (negligent quote); Catherine McNicol Stock, *Main Street in Crisis: The Great Depression and the Old Middle Class on the Northern Plains* (Chapel Hill: University of North Carolina Press, 1992), 48. Lewis Bloodgood, who migrated to Dakota Territory after the war, criticized those who said "they will never work for a living after the war." Lewis Bloodgood to Father, Marine Hospital, New Orleans, April 18, 1865. Observers of the American West have noted Americans' "belief in the universal obligation of

all persons to work endlessly in their eternal pursuit of material gain" and their scorn of luxury, "frivolity," and "esthetic and intellectual pursuits." Billington, *America's Frontier Heritage*, 64.

113. Thomas Sterling, "Biennial Address," *South Dakota Historical Collections,* vol. 4 (1908), 94. On the origins of Yankee industriousness, see Stephen Innes, *Creating the Commonwealth: The Economic Culture of New England* (New York: W. W. Norton, 1995).

114. *North Dakota, South Dakota, Montana & Washington,* 46.

115. Unruh, "South Dakota in 1889," 77. On tenancy and inequality of land-ownership as causes of political conflict, see Reeve Huston, *Land and Freedom: Rural Society, Popular Protest, and Party Politics in Antebellum New York* (New York: Oxford University Press, 2000); and Alan Taylor, *Liberty Men and Great Proprietors: The Revolutionary Settlement on the Maine Frontier, 1760–1820* (Chapel Hill: University of North Carolina Press, 1990). For another view of the disputes caused by the "maldistribution" of frontier land, see Aron, *How the West Was Lost,* 83–85. On agrarian concerns over concentrated landholdings in the late twentieth century, see Jon Lauck, "The Corporate Farming Debate in the Post–World War II Midwest," *Great Plains Quarterly,* vol. 18, no. 2 (Spring 1998), 139–53.

116. Harold E. Briggs, "The Development of Agriculture in Territorial Dakota," *Culver-Stockton Quarterly,* vol. 7, no. 1 (1931), 33.

117. Fite, *The Farmers' Frontier*, 23. On the increasingly positive reviews of government land distribution, see Robert P. Swierenga, "Land Speculation and Its Impact on American Economic Growth and Welfare: A Historiographical Review," *Western Historical Quarterly,* vol. 8, no. 3 (July 1977), 292–302.

118. Gilbert C. Fite, "Agricultural Pioneering in Dakota: A Case Study," *Great Plains Quarterly,* vol. 1, no. 3 (Summer 1981), 169–79. See also Gilbert C. Fite, "'The Only Thing Worth Working For': Land and Its Meaning for Pioneer Dakotans," *South Dakota History,* vol. 15, nos. 1–2 (Spring–Summer 1985), 2–25; and L. E. Q., "New Empires in the Northwest," 13. On the growing "reverence for the land" itself in the late nineteenth century, see Steiner, "The Significance of Turner's Sectional Thesis," 452–66.

119. Rowland Berthoff, "Writing a History of Things Left Out," *Reviews in American History,* vol. 14, no. 1 (March 1986), 2–5.

120. L. E. Q., "New Empires in the Northwest," 15.

121. Ware, "Dakota! The Justly Famed."

122. Reverend A. M. Pilcher, "Dakota," *Western Christian Advocate*, January 13, 1883.

123. Selmer Hatlestad, "The Ethnic Consciousness Era, 1889–1920," in Donald J. Sneen (ed.), *Prairie Faith, Pioneering People: A History of the Lutheran Church in South Dakota* (Garretson, S.Dak.: American Lutheran Church, 1981), 62.

124. Lears, *No Place of Grace,* 28; Lamar, "Frederick Jackson Turner," 84; Merle Curti, *The Roots of American Loyalty* (New York: Columbia University Press, 1946), 36–40; Jon Lauck, *American Agriculture and the Problem of*

Monopoly: The Political Economy of Grain Belt Farming, 1953–1980 (Lincoln: University of Nebraska Press, 2000), 167.

125. Kingsbury, *History of Dakota Territory*, 672; Emmons, *Garden in the Grasslands*, 101.

126. Kloppenberg, *Virtues of Liberalism*, 24; Daria Frezza, *The Leader and the Crowd: Democracy in American Public Discourse, 1880–1941* (Athens: University of Georgia Press, 2007), 26; Matthew Frye Jacobson, *Barbarian Virtues: The United States Encounters Foreign Peoples at Home and Abroad, 1876–1917* (New York: Hill & Wang, 2000), 65.

127. Stock, *Main Street in Crisis*, 10.

128. On the market orientation of western settlers and midwestern farmers, see John Phillip Reid, *Law for the Elephant: Property and Social Behavior on the Overland Trail* (San Marino, Calif.: Huntington Library, 1980), 18; and Cayton and Onuf, *The Midwest and the Nation*, 32. A group of historians has argued that during the early nineteenth century some farmers resisted market forces. The historiography of the "new rural history" includes a "heated debate between historians who argue that preindustrial farmers stood in opposition to the values of an emerging industrial society and limited their participation in the market, and historians who claim that northern farmers were motivated by the same capitalist spirit of liberal individualism and acquisitiveness as the rest of society—the so-called social and market perspectives." Hal S. Barron, *Mixed Harvest: The Second Great Transformation in the Rural North, 1870–1930* (Chapel Hill: University of North Carolina Press, 1997), 12. Even historians who believe that early-nineteenth-century farmers resisted capitalism, however, concede that the market "clearly came to dominate the rural sector during the second half of the nineteenth century." Steven Hahn, "The 'Unmaking' of the Southern Yeomanry: The Transformation of the Georgia Upcountry, 1860–1890," in Steven Hahn and Jonathan Prude (eds.), *The Countryside in the Age of Capitalist Transformation* (Chapel Hill: University of North Carolina Press, 1985), 180. See also Lauck, *American Agriculture and the Problem of Monopoly*, 167–70.

129. Fite, *Farmers' Frontier*, 19–20, 22. On the frontier land market, see Allan G. Bogue and Margaret Beattie Bogue, "'Profits' and the Frontier Land Speculator," *Journal of Economic History*, vol. 17, no. 1 (March 1957), 1–24. On the land market in Dakota in later years, see Allan G. Bogue, "Foreclosure Tenancy on the Northern Plains," *Agricultural History*, vol. 39, no. 1 (January 1965), 3–16.

130. Cayton and Onuf, *The Midwest and the Nation*, 25.

131. Wright, *Culture on the Moving Frontier*, 239. In *The Bourgeois Virtues: Ethics for an Age of Commerce* (Chicago: University of Chicago Press, 2006), xiv. Deirdre N. McCloskey promises a book (to be published by the University of Chicago Press) entitled *Bourgeois Towns: How a Capitalist Ethic Grew in the Dutch and English Lands, 1600–1800*.

132. Cayton and Onuf, *The Midwest and the Nation*, 15, 31; Stock, *Main Street in Crisis*, 10.

133. On social cooperation in the form of such activities as house and barn raising, threshing, and the sharing of farm equipment, see Robert V. Hine, *Community on the American Frontier: Separate but Not Alone* (Norman: University of Oklahoma Press, 1980), 104–105; Scott G. McNall and Sally Allen McNall, *Plains Families: Exploring Sociology through Social History* (New York: St. Martin's Press, 1983), 71; Fite, *Farmers' Frontier*, 221; and Curti, *Making of an American Community*, 115, 123. Robert Johnston has emphasized the republican and moral constraints on the operation of the market in "Beyond 'The West': Regionalism, Liberalism and the Evasion of Politics in the New Western History," *Rethinking History*, vol. 2, no. 2 (1998), 246; and *The Radical Middle Class: Populist Democracy and the Question of Capitalism in Progressive Era Portland, Oregon* (Princeton: Princeton University Press, 2003), 74–75. On legislative limitations on mortgage interest rates in Dakota Territory, for example, see Herbert S. Schell, "The Grange and the Credit Problem in Dakota Territory," *Agricultural History*, vol. 10, no. 2 (April 1936), 59–83.

134. Scott McNall, in his study of Kansas Populism, similarly notes that it "was not capitalism, per se, that infuriated the farmers, but monopoly relations." Members of the Farmers' Alliance were "not socialists," but "Jeffersonian democrats," and "farmers often went out of their way to explain that they meant no harm to capitalism." Scott G. McNall, *The Road to Rebellion: Class Formation and Kansas Populism, 1865–1900* (Chicago: University of Chicago Press, 1988), 46, 145.

135. Chester McArthur Destler, "Western Radicalism, 1865–1901: Concepts and Origins," *Mississippi Valley Historical Review*, vol. 31, no. 3 (December 1944), 356. See, generally, Lauck, *American Agriculture and the Problem of Monopoly*.

136. Unruh, "South Dakota in 1889," 128.

137. Ibid., 133–34.

138. Kingsbury, *History of Dakota Territory*, 1855.

139. Ibid., 1334. Dakota "surpassed probably every state in its common school facilities," Kingsbury concluded. The territorial legislature and religious groups also established several colleges during the 1880s.

140. Unruh, "South Dakota in 1889," 133–34.

141. Ibid., 148–49.

142. Ibid., 135.

143. Shalhope, *Roots of Democracy*, 114.

144. Baker, "From Belief into Culture," 540; Carl F. Kaestle, *Pillars of the Republic: Common Schools and American Society, 1780–1860* (New York: Hill & Wang, 1983), x.

145. S.Dak. Constitution, Article VIII, §1.

146. Baker, "From Belief into Culture," 541–42.

147. Unruh, "South Dakota in 1889," 138–142.

148. R. W. Kraushaar, "Brief Chronological History of School Legislation and Growth," *South Dakota Historical Collections*, vol. 18 (1936), 17; Cayton and Onuf, *The Midwest and the Nation*, 60; Wright, *Culture on the Moving*

Frontier, 217; Lewis Atherton, *Main Street on the Middle Border* (Bloomington: Indiana University Press, 1984), 65–72, 77–86. In McGuffey's books, the "full measure of censure is . . . reserved for the mortal sin of laziness." D. A. Saunders, "Social Ideas in McGuffey Readers," *Public Opinion Quarterly,* vol. 5, no. 4 (Winter 1941), 585. Sales of McGuffey schoolbooks were strongest from 1870 to 1890, and the books had their largest circulation in the Midwest. Forty percent of the 1879 edition of the McGuffey Reader emphasized moral teachings. John A. Nietz, "Why the Longevity of the McGuffey Readers," *History of Education Quarterly*, vol. 4, no. 2 (June 1964), 119–23. "McGuffey's influence was primarily on children on the moving frontier." Laurence M. Hauptman, "Mythologizing Westward Expansion: Schoolbooks and the Image of the American Frontier before Turner," *Western Historical Quarterly,* vol. 8, no. 3 (July 1977), 275 n. 25.

149. G. O. Sandro, "Charter Schools of Dakota Territory," *South Dakota Historical Collections,* vol. 18 (1936), 102–103.

150. Walter Ludeman, "Studies in the History of Public Education in South Dakota," *South Dakota Historical Collections,* vol. 12 (1924), 462, 464–65, 468–69; Unruh, "South Dakota in 1889," 138–42; *Glimpse of a Marvelous City: Watertown in 1889* (published by the City Council), 23, Beinecke Library, Yale University.

151. Gerald D. Nash, *Creating the West: Historical Interpretations, 1890–1990* (Albuquerque: University of New Mexico Press, 1991), 64. See also Carl J. Richard, *The Founders and the Classics: Greece, Rome, and the American Enlightenment* (Cambridge, Mass.: Harvard University Press, 1995); and Caroline Winterer, *The Culture of Classicism: Ancient Greece and Rome in American Intellectual Life, 1780–1910* (Baltimore: Johns Hopkins University Press, 2002). On the American founders and Greece and Rome, see Gordon S. Wood, *The Creation of the American Republic, 1776–1787* (New York: W. W. Norton, 1969), 48–53; Bailyn, *Ideological Origins of the American Revolution*, 21–26; Colbourn, *The Lamp of Experience*, 21–25; McDonald, *Novus Ordo Seclorum*, 67.

152. On the Founders' familiarity with Seneca and Virgil, see Bailyn, *Ideological Origins of the American Revolution*, 24.

153. "Report of the Board of Education, Territory of Dakota, 1888," 257, 258–60, no FF, DB 7254B, SDSHS.

154. Viroli, *Republicanism,* 79.

155. Stock, *Main Street in Crisis*, 61.

156. Schell, *History of Clay County South Dakota,* 157.

157. Ibid., 156.

158. Faye C. Lewis, *Nothing to Make a Shadow* (Ames: Iowa State University Press, 1971), 48; Edna LaMoore Waldo, *Dakota: An Informal Study of Territorial Days* (Caldwell, Idaho: Caxton Printers, 1936), 365; William H. Pease, "Tales of Pioneering," FF "Wm. M. Pease Manuscript," DB 3543A, SDSHS; Hine, *Community on the American Frontier*, 114; Dick, *Sod-House Frontier*, 74; Miller, *Laura Ingalls Wilder's Little Town*, 48; Curti, *Making of an American Community*, 123–24, 131–36.

159. "Personal Memoirs of William H. H. Beadle," 167.

160. Patriotic societies also "influenced the selection of school textbooks and the teaching of national history." Merle Curti, review, Wallace Evan Davies, *Patriotism on Parade: The Story of Veterans' and Hereditary Organizations in America, 1783–1900* (Cambridge, Mass.: Harvard University Press, 1955), *Mississippi Valley Historical Review,* vol. 43, no. 2 (September 1956), 328.

161. Hicks, "Constitutions of the Northwest States," 148, 150; Billington, *Genesis of the Frontier Thesis,* 125.

162. Saunders, "Social Ideas in McGuffey Readers," 586; Stuart McConnell, "Reading the Flag: A Reconsideration of the Patriotic Cults of the 1890s," in John Bodnar (ed.), *Bonds of Affection: Americans Define Their Patriotism* (Princeton: Princeton University Press, 1996), 102; Higham, *Strangers in the Land,* 75; Berthoff, *An Unsettled People,* 431–32.

163. Bederman, *Manliness and Civilization,* 11–12.

164. "The Passing of Maj. Robt. Dollard," *Daily Argus-Leader,* May 15, 1912; "Major Dollard as a Soldier Candidate for Congress" (clipping), FF H20-001, DB 3649A, SDSHS.

165. "The Passing of Major Robert Dollard," (clipping), FF H20-001, DB 3649A, SDSHS.

166. "Oration by Dr. Franklin B. Gault," *South Dakota Historical Collections,* vol. 6 (1912), 67.

167. "Personal Memoirs of William H. H. Beadle," 216–17.

168. *North Dakota, South Dakota, Montana & Washington,* 28.

169. Pomeroy, *The Territories and the United States,* 103.

170. Bederman, *Manliness and Civilization,* 185, 192; Jacobson, *Barbarian Virtues,* 3. In the post–Civil War years, "Anglo-Saxon doctrine" remained popular with the "cultivated classes," especially New Englanders. Higham, *Strangers in the Land,* 32. A mid-nineteenth-century preoccupation with Anglo-Saxon liberty helped justify westward expansion to places like Dakota. Ibid., 10. See also Frezza, *The Leader and the Crowd,* 41–48.

171. Etcheson, *Emerging Midwest,* 37; Stock, *Main Street in Crisis,* 53.

172. Deborah Fink, *Agrarian Women: Wives and Mothers in Rural Nebraska, 1880–1940* (Chapel Hill: University of North Carolina Press, 1992), 7. Fink finds that most pioneer women did "not appear to have questioned the broad contours of their lives." Fink, *Agrarian Women,* xiv–xv. The records of pioneer women, according to Julie Roy Jeffrey, "show wide acceptance of domestic ideology." Jeffrey says she started her book as a feminist hoping to "find that pioneer women used the frontier as a means of liberating themselves from stereotypes and behaviors which I found constricting and sexist. I discovered that they did not." Julie Roy Jeffrey, *Frontier Women: The Trans-Mississippi West, 1840–1880* (New York, Hill & Wang, 1979), xiv–xvi.

173. Glenda Riley, *The Female Frontier: A Comparative View of Women on the Prairie and the Plains* (Lawrence: University Press of Kansas, 1988), 197. Women often helped with farmwork. Mary Neth, *Preserving the Family*

Farm: Women, Community, and the Foundations of Agribusiness in the Midwest, 1900–1940 (Baltimore: Johns Hopkins University Press, 1995), 18–19; Joanna L. Stratton, *Pioneer Women: Voices from the Kansas Frontier* (New York: Simon & Schuster, 1981), 57. Sandra Myres also noted, based on her research in women's diaries and reminiscences, that men often helped with household duties too: "Most women suggested that men frequently helped with heavier household chores and could and did take over child care and cooking duties when women were indisposed." Sandra L. Myres, *Westering Women and the Frontier Experience, 1800–1915* (Albuquerque: University of New Mexico Press, 1982), 164.

174. The lives of pioneer women have often been portrayed as grim. See Ann F. Hyde, "Cultural Filters: The Significance of Perception," in Milner, *A New Significance,* 183; Mary W. M. Hargreaves, "Women in the Agricultural Settlement of the Northern Plains," *Agricultural History,* vol. 50, no. 1 (January 1976), 182–83; *Sodbusters: Tales of Southeastern South Dakota* (Mitchell, S.Dak.: South Dakota Writers' League, 1938), 22; Christine Stansell, "Women on the Great Plains, 1865–1890," *Women's Studies,* vol. 4 (1976), 87. A story counter to that of unhappy frontier women, according to Glenda Riley, revealed "that many unhappy prairie women were negative only during the early stages of their lives on the frontier and that their outlooks often brightened as time passed." Riley, *The Female Frontier,* 71.

175. Baker, "From Belief into Culture," 540; Linda Kerber, "The Republican Mother," *American Quarterly,* vol. 28 (Summer 1976), 187–205; John B. Reese, *Some Pioneers and Pilgrims on the Prairies of Dakota* (Mitchell, S.Dak., privately printed, 1920), 44–47; H. C. Halvorson, *The First Fifty Years in Lake Sinai Township* (Brookings, S.Dak.: privately printed, 1956), 15. Julie Roy Jeffrey also notes, "Nineteenth-century society sharply distinguished between the world of men and the world of women, and defined women as agents of civilization and keepers of morals." Jeffrey, *Frontier Women,* xiii.

176. "Personal Memoirs of William H. H. Beadle," 216; Thomas Sterling, "Otto C. Berg," *South Dakota Historical Collections,* vol. 3 (1906), 82.

177. Women were often seen as the primary victims of alcohol abuse. "There was nothing more devilish for a woman on an isolated western farm than to have her man come home drunk. Every farmer's wife was a temperance advocate—a more or less vociferous one—and when in their right minds the erring farmers themselves sensed the utter depravity of their acts." Seth K. Humphrey, *Following the Prairie Frontier* (Minneapolis: University of Minnesota Press, 1931), 144; Robert T. Handy, *A Christian America: Protestant Hopes and Historical Realities* (New York: Oxford University Press, 1971), 92; McNall, *Road to Rebellion,* 156.

178. "Prohibition Fight in South Dakota," *Christian Advocate,* August 8, 1889; C. H. Smith, "Letter from Dakota," *Zion's Herald,* July 31, 1889; "Dakota and the Brewers," *The Independent,* January 28, 1886; Berthoff, *An Unsettled People,* 428; Luebke, *Immigrants and Politics,* 129–30.

179. All songs from "South Dakota Equal Suffrage Song Book," Coe Collection, Beinecke Library, Yale University.

180. Miller, "The State of South Dakota," 1124; Riley, *Female Frontier*, 191. During the 1880s, opponents of women's suffrage also pointed to Utah, where women had been given the vote in 1870, and argued that women voters made poor political choices, such as supporting Mormon polygamy. Sarah Barringer Gordon, "'The Liberty of Self-Degradation': Polygamy, Woman Suffrage, and Consent in Nineteenth-Century America," *Journal of American History,* vol. 83, no. 3 (December 1996), 823.

181. Kruman, "Second American Party System," 511; Joel H. Silbey, *The American Political Nation, 1838–1893* (Stanford, Calif.: Stanford University Press, 1991), 125–40. Worth Robert Miller notes that, contrary to earlier stereotypes, late-nineteenth-century "politicians and parties truly engaged the American public on fundamental issues concerning the direction of the nation and the role government should play in national life." Miller, "The Lost World of Gilded Age Politics," *Journal of the Gilded Age and Progressive Era*, vol. 1, no. 1 (January 2002), 50. Charles W. Calhoun also notes that historians in the late 1980s and early 1990s "concluded that political leaders of the late nineteenth century were generally hard-working public servants, serious about issues and governance." Calhoun, "The Political Culture: Public Life and the Conduct of Politics," in Charles W. Calhoun (ed.), *The Gilded Age: Essays on the Origins of Modern America* (Wilmington, Del.: Scholarly Resources, 1996), 186. Earlier, John Garraty warned about embracing the excessively negative critiques of party politics advanced in the late-nineteenth century by progressive historians. Garraty, *The New Commonwealth, 1877–1890* (New York: Harper & Row, 1968), 3–4. For the prominence of political ceremonies, see Jean H. Baker, "The Ceremonies of Politics: Nineteenth-Century Rituals of National Affirmation," in William J. Cooper, Jr., Michael F. Holt, and John McCardell (eds.), *A Master's Due: Essays in Honor of David Herbert Donald* (Baton Rouge: Louisiana State University, 1985), 161–78. On the nineteenth-century democratization of language, see Kenneth Cmiel, *Democratic Eloquence: The Fight over Popular Speech in Nineteenth-Century America* (New York: William Morrow, 1990).

182. Jean Baker, *Affairs of Party: The Political Culture of Northern Democrats in the Mid-Nineteenth Century* (Ithaca, N.Y.: Cornell University Press, 1983; repr., New York: Fordham University Press, 1998), 9.

183. Cherny, *American Politics in the Gilded Age,* 45, 93; Silbey, *American Political Nation*, 218–19.

184. Cherny, *American Politics in the Gilded Age*, 13; Miller, "The Lost World of Gilded Age Politics," 49–67; Silbey, *American Political Nation*, 141–58.

185. The population of the territory in 1886 was 480,610. If we subtract half of this total (since women could not vote), the 103,384 children of school age, and an additional tenth to account for unregistered or otherwise ineligible voters, we are left with 169,751 voters, 114,130 of which voted in the 1888 election, or 67 percent. This number is a rough approximation since the Secretary of State's office does not possess territorial voting records. For the raw numbers used in this approximation, see Kingsbury, *History of Dakota Territory*, 1451, 1463, 1541. A

territorial governor's report noted that 100,000 voters were eligible to vote during the 1884 election and that 86,703 did so, making voter turnout 87 percent.

186. Jon Lauck, John E. Miller, and Edward Hogan, "The Contours of South Dakota Political Culture," *South Dakota History,* vol. 34, no. 2 (Summer 2004), 158–59.

187. Alan L. Clem, *South Dakota Political Almanac: A Presentation and Analysis of Election Statistics, 1889–1960,* Report no. 47 (Vermillion, S.Dak.: Government Research Bureau, 1962), 25.

188. Kingsbury, *History of Dakota Territory,* 1664.

189. Ibid., 1726.

190. Ella S. to Dill, July 16, 1880, FF H92-125, DB 3327B, SDSHS.

191. Newspapers were seen as a sign of "civilization" by one pioneer, who noted that one town that had had virtually no population a few years before came to have eight weekly newspapers. A. P. Miller, *Tom's Experience in Dakota* (Minneapolis, Minn.: Miller, Hale & Co. Publishers, 1883), 88.

192. Arthur C. Mellette, "Report of the Governor of Dakota to the Secretary of the Interior, 1889," 25, FF "Dakota Territory Report of Governor to Secretary of Interior, 1878–1889," DB 7254A SDSHS; Robert F. Karolevitz, *With a Shirt Tail Full of Type: The Story of Newspapering in South Dakota* (n.p.: privately printed for the South Dakota Press Association, 1982), 17–24. The number of newspapers published during the territorial period was 558. Ruth Elizabeth Bergman, "Printing in South Dakota during the Territorial Period" (master's thesis, University of Illinois, 1936), 157.

193. Kingsbury, *History of Dakota Territory,* 1855.

194. Unruh, "South Dakota in 1889," 73–74.

195. Augustine Davis to Dakota Press Association, December 7, 1886, FF H75.54, DB 3538A, SDSHS.

196. Pease, "Tales of Pioneering."

197. Lewis, *Nothing to Make a Shadow,* 146; FF 3 "The Chautauqua Hand-Books," FF 4 "Circulars, Broadsides," and FF 5 "The Chautauquan," DB 3539A, SDSHS; Andrew Chamberlin Rieser, "Secularization Reconsidered: Chautauqua and the De-Christianization of Middle-Class Authority, 1880–1920," in Burton J. Bledstein and Robert D. Johnston (eds.), *The Middling Sorts: Explorations in the History of the American Middle Class* (New York: Routledge, 2001), 140–44.

198. Wright, *Culture on the Moving Frontier,* 229.

199. In 1887, the territorial assembly passed a law promoting the "establishment of free libraries in cities, villages and townships." *Laws Passed at the Seventeenth Session of the Legislative Assembly of the Territory of Dakota,* 160; Bill establishing Free Library Commission, FF H75.294 Fd 1, DB 3548A, SDSHS.

200. Curti, *Making of an American Community,* 382, 409–15.

201. Cayton and Gray, "Story of the Midwest," 10.

202. Unruh, "South Dakota in 1889," 73–74; George H. Phillips, *Post Offices and Postmarks of Dakota Territory* (Crete, Nebr.: J-B Publishing Company, 1973); Richard D. Brown, *The Strength of a People: The Idea of an Informed*

Citizenry in America, 1650–1870 (Chapel Hill: University of North Carolina Press, 1996), 91.

203. Earl S. Pomeroy, "Toward a Reorientation of Western History," *Mississippi Valley Historical Review,* vol. 41, no. 4 (March 1955), 594 (appetite quote); Frederick Jackson Turner, "The Significance of History" (1891), in John Mack Faragher, *Rereading Frederick Jackson Turner: "The Significance of the Frontier in American History" and Other Essays* (New Haven: Yale University Press, 1998), 174–75; Wright, *Culture on the Moving Frontier,* 227; McNall and McNall, *Plains Families,* 70; Howard R. Lamar, "Much to Celebrate: The Western History Association's Twenty-Fifth Birthday," *Western Historical Quarterly,* vol. 17, no. 4 (October 1986), 409; Dick, *Sod-House Frontier,* 70–74; Waldo, *Dakota,* 357. See also Sidney Ditzion, *Arsenals of Democratic Culture: A Social History of the American Public Library Movement in New England and the Middle States from 1859 to 1900* (Chicago: American Library Association, 1947); Carl Bode, *The American Lyceum: Town Meeting of the Mind* (New York: Oxford University Press, 1950); James R. Schultz, *The Romance of Small-Town Chautauquas* (Columbia: University of Missouri Press, 2002); Andrew C. Rieser, *The Chautauqua Moment: Protestants, Progressives, and the Culture of Modern Liberalism* (New York: Columbia University Press, 2003); Angela G. Ray, *The Lyceum and Public Culture in the Nineteenth-Century United States* (East Lansing: Michigan State University Press, 2005).

204. Thomas Bender, *Community and Social Change in America* (Baltimore: Johns Hopkins University Press, 1978), 98. Another indication of civic energy in Dakota Territory was the battle between communities over who would host the county seat. Leslie W. Moser, *History of South Dakota Highlights* (n.p.: privately printed, 1981), 32–33, CWS; Herbert S. Schell, *South Dakota: Its Beginnings and Growth* (New York: American Book Company, 1942), 128–30.

205. Jean Saville, FF Aurora County M–W, Pioneer Daughters Collection, DB 6828, SDSHS; Unruh, "South Dakota in 1889," 171–73; Bloodgood, "Homesteading in Custer Township, Beadle County, South Dakota," 18–20; Waldo, *Dakota,* 348; Hine, *Community on the American Frontier,* 112; Fite, *Farmers' Frontier,* 219; Stock, *Main Street in Crisis,* 42–43. The first agricultural fair was held in Huron in 1884. Goodspeed, *The Province and the States,* 298; Kingsbury, *History of Dakota Territory,* 1331–32.

206. Bloodgood, "Homesteading in Custer Township, Beadle County, South Dakota," 5. On "good neighborship" in pioneer communities, see John Mack Faragher, *Sugar Creek: Life on the Illinois Prairie* (New Haven, Conn.: Yale University Press, 1986), 130–36; John Mack Faragher, "Americans, Mexicans, and Métis: A Community Approach to the Comparative Study of North American Frontiers," in Cronon, Miles, and Gitlin, *Under an Open Sky,* 96–99. One settler told a later chronicler that "when you pulled your team outside a house, you didn't wonder if you could stay here—you KNEW you could. The houses were open to the traveler as the medieval monasteries had been open to the pilgrim." Another settler recalled that when he was not home, he placed a sign on the door

that read: "Make yourself at home but be sure to wash the dishes." J. L. Carr, *The Old Timers* (1957), 54, CWS.

207. Bloodgood, "Homesteading in Custer Township, Beadle County, South Dakota," 14–15. See also Iola M. Anderson, *The Singing Hills: A Story of Life on the Prairies of South Dakota* (Stickney, S.Dak.: Argus, 1977), 53–54.

208. Carr, *The Old Timers*, 54.

209. Dora to Brother and Sister, June 30, 1883, FF H92-125, DB 3327B, SDSHS.

210. Riley, *The Female Frontier*, 174. On the promotion of book sharing and access to books, see Lisa Lindell, "Bringing Books to a 'Book-Hungry Land': Print Culture on the Dakota Prairie," *Book History*, vol. 7 (2004), 215–38. One woman was noted as "an avid reader and had several hundred books of her own, besides having access to her father's extensive library." "A Biographical Sketch of Edith Katherine Zimmerman," FF GFWC, Lake County A–, DB 6830, SDSHS.

211. Schell, *History of South Dakota*, 184; "Personal Memoirs of William H. H. Beadle," 147; Berthoff, *An Unsettled People*, 273; Hine, *Community on the American Frontier*, 139–40; Stock, *Main Street in Crisis*, 60. See, generally, David T. Beito, *From Mutual Aid to the Welfare State: Fraternal Societies and Social Services, 1890–1967* (Chapel Hill: University of North Carolina Press), 7–16.

212. "Knights Templar Proceedings," 1888, FF Knights Templar Proceedings, 1884–1894, DB 3711, SDSHS. The Knights were considered an "outgrowth of the days of chivalry and the crusades, when in the twelfth century the Christians of Europe arose to wrest Palestine and the Holy City from infidel Saracens." Kingsbury, *History of Dakota Territory*, 1349. "International Order Odd Fellows, Proceedings, Grand Encampment of Dakota," 1889, no FF, DB 3712B, SDSHS; "Proceedings of the Convention of Chapters, Order of the Eastern Star," 1889, p. 21, FF Proceedings, 1889–1898, DB 3721, SDSHS. On the organization of Sons of Norway lodges and membership in the Norwegian Singers' Association, see John P. Johansen, "Immigrant Settlements and Social Organization in South Dakota," Department of Rural Sociology Bulletin 313 (June 1937), South Dakota State University, 14–16.

213. "Proceedings of the Fourteenth Annual Communication, Most Worshipful Grand Lodge, Ancient Free and Accepted Masons of Dakota," 1888, FF Proceedings 1885–, DB 3705A, SDSHS.

214. "Proceedings of the Sixth Annual Communication, Grand Lodge, Ancient Free and Accepted Masons of Dakota," 1880, FF Proceedings 1875–84, DB 3705A, SDSHS.

215. "The School and Endowment Lands," FF 1, DB 3536A, SDSHS.

216. Robert Benton, "Masonry in the Constitutions of the State of South Dakota," FF Masonic Lodge, DB 5619, SDSHS. On the American tendency to join organizations such as fraternal lodges, see Arthur Schlesinger, Sr., "Biography of a Nation of Joiners," *American Historical Review*, vol. 50, no. 1 (October 1944), 1–25.

217. Cayton and Onuf, *The Midwest and the Nation*, 57.

218. Hildegard Binder Johnson, *Order upon the Land: The U.S. Rectangular Survey and the Upper Mississippi Country* (New York: Oxford University Press, 1976), 3. On the organization of towns, see Miller, *Laura Ingalls Wilder's Little Town*, 23–26; and John C. Hudson, *Plains Country Towns* (Minneapolis: University of Minnesota Press, 1985), 8–9. The design of small towns in Dakota was based on the medieval bastide, which "revived earlier Greek and Roman ideas about grid-pattern towns." Hudson, *Plains Country Towns*, 7.

219. W. H. Droze, "Changing the Plains Environment: The Afforestation of the Trans-Mississippi West," *Agricultural History*, vol. 51, no. 1 (January 1977), 12; Peter R. Schaefer, Sheridan Dronen, and David Erickson, "Windbreaks: A Plains Legacy in Decline," *Journal of Soil and Water Conservation*, vol. 42, no. 2 (July–August 1987), 266; *Tom's Experience in Dakota*, 20.

220. Ward, "Territorial System of the United States," 51; Hine, *Community on the American Frontier*, 121. In his study of the overland trail, John Phillip Reid noted that of "all the forces that shaped emigrant values—community, church, country, education, profession—none was more pronounced than family." Reid, *Law for the Elephant*, 25.

221. Lears, *No Place of Grace*, 15.

222. "On average, Russian-German couples raised seven or eight children, Norwegians six or seven, and those of American parentage about four." Walter Nugent, *Into the West: The Story of Its People* (New York: Vintage, 1999), 72.

223. Bloodgood, "Homesteading in Custer Township, Beadle County, South Dakota," 9.

224. Riley, *Female Frontier*, 173, 179. On the importance of family ties in frontier Minnesota, see Kathleen Neils Conzen, "Peasant Pioneers: Generational Succession among German Farmers in Frontier Minnesota," in Hahn and Prude, *The Countryside in the Age of Capitalist Transformation*, 259–92.

225. *Laws Passed at the Fifteenth Session of the Legislative Assembly of the Territory of Dakota* (Yankton, Dak. Terr.: Bowen & Kingsbury, 1883), 202. On the preservation of moral standards during the late nineteenth century, see Rochelle Gurstein, *The Repeal of Reticence: America's Cultural and Legal Struggles over Free Speech, Obscenity, Sexual Liberation, and Modern Art* (New York: Hill & Wang, 1996), 32–33.

226. Stratton, *Pioneer Women*, 253 (destroyer quote); Kingsbury, *History of Dakota Territory*, 1467–68, 1532; Handy, *A Christian America*, 89–90. Seth Humphrey, who lived in Dakota Territory during the 1880s, noted that "in the small-town West the saloon represented all that was bad in the community, and its keeper was down mighty close to the social level of the red-light pimp on the outskirts." Humphrey, *Following the Prairie Frontier*, 144.

227. Hicks, *Populist Revolt*, 118.

228. Kingsbury, *History of Dakota Territory*, 682. On moral legislation in late-nineteenth-century America, see Gaines M. Foster, *Moral Reconstruction: Christian Lobbyists and the Federal Legislation of Morality, 1865–1920* (Chapel Hill: University of North Carolina Press, 2002).

229. Ware, "Dakota! The Justly Famed.".

230. McNall and McNall, *Plains Families*, 41 (source of quotation); Don Harrison Doyle, *The Social Order of a Frontier Community: Jacksonville, Illinois* (Urbana: University of Illinois Press, 1978), 14.

231. Bernard Floyd Hyatt, "A Legal Legacy for Statehood: The Development of the Territorial Judicial System in Dakota Territory, 1861–1889" (Ph.D. dissertation, Texas Tech University, 1987), 168–72, 357, 379, 593–94; "Personal Memoirs of William H. H. Beadle," 129–31; Goodspeed, *The Province and the States*, 281–82. On the popularity of the Anglo-American common law tradition in the 1880s, see Kammen, *A Machine That Would Go of Itself*, 166; and Richard A. Cosgrove, *Our Lady the Common Law: An Anglo-American Legal Community, 1870–1930* (New York: New York University Press, 1987), 59–94.

232. L. E. Q., "New Empires in the Northwest," 15, Beinecke Library, Yale University. In his study of the overland trail, John Phillip Reid noted that "lawful behavior was the expected as well as the normal pattern." Reid, *Law for the Elephant*, 7. Western violence was "no higher on average than in the contemporary urban East or the South." Michael A. Bellesiles, "Western Violence," in Deverell, *A Companion to the American West*, 162. A recent study by Mark R. Ellis found that "nineteenth-century plains settlers created an environment where law and order rather than lawlessness prevailed." Ellis, *Law and Order in Buffalo Bill's Country: Legal Culture and Community on the Great Plains, 1867–1910* (Lincoln: University of Nebraska Press, 2007), 217.

233. *Glimpse of a Marvelous City,* 25.

234. Unruh, "South Dakota in 1889," 156.

235. One source notes that four public executions were held in all of Dakota Territory for the entire twenty-eight-year territorial period (1861–89): two for murders committed West River (Jack McCall's assassination of Wild Bill Hickock and Crow Dog's assassination of Spotted Tail); one for a settler who killed an Indian named Brave Bear near Fort Sully on the Missouri River; and one for a homesteader named Thomas Egan who allegedly murdered his wife near Sioux Falls but was exonerated years later. The Egan trial stands out for its careful deliberation and attention to procedure, despite the apparently erroneous verdict. The thorough preparation for the trial and the publicity it received are reviewed in C. John Egan, *Drop Him Till He Dies: The Twisted Tragedy of Immigrant Homesteader Thomas Egan* (Sioux Falls, S.Dak.: Ex Machina, 1994). The bungled hanging of Egan, which was the first public execution performed in Dakota Territory, is reviewed in "A Horrible Affair," *Chicago Daily Tribune*, July 14, 1882. The *Daily Tribune* noted that "every effort was made by [Egan's] attorneys to save him." Cases of vigilante violence were seldom mentioned in the newspapers of eastern Dakota Territory. For the entirety of Dakota Territory from 1882 to 1889, Bernard Floyd Hyatt found seven cases of lynching, most of which occurred West River or in the north. From 1878 to 1846 in Louisiana, by comparison, Michael Pfeifer counted 422 cases of lynching. Hyatt, "A Legal Legacy for Statehood," 345, 550; Michael J. Pfeifer, *Rough Justice: Lynching*

and American Society, 1874–1847 (Urbana: University of Illinois Press, 2004), 24. A rare case of lynching occurred near Pierre in 1885 over a legal dispute. The person lynched, a white man, was on trial for killing a minister's son. A Pierre newspaper noted "a strong feeling of indignation that the mob should step in and cast a stain upon the fair name of our city and county." "Judge Lynch Holds a Night Session in Pierre," *Weekly Free Press*, April 16, 1885. See also Frank E. Vyzralek, "Murder in Masquerade: A Commentary on Lynching and Mob Violence in North Dakota's Past, 1882–1931," *North Dakota History*, vol. 57, no. 1 (Winter 1990), 20–29; and W. Eugene Hollon, *Frontier Violence: Another Look* (New York: Oxford University Press, 1974), 200–201.

236. Pfeifer, *Rough Justice*, 26–27. Pfeifer, citing David Hackett Fischer's famous study, notes that the folkways of the Puritans who settled New England "emphasized consensus, public order, individual rights, and a disinclination toward violence." Pfeifer, *Rough Justice*, 186 n. 5. The descendents of the New England Puritans were an important political and social force in Dakota Territory.

237. Earl Pomeroy, introduction to Josiah Royce, *California: From the Conquest in 1846 to the Second Vigilance Committee in San Francisco* (Santa Barbara: Peregrine, 1970 [1886]), vii–ix.

238. Gabriel, *Course of American Democratic Thought*, 306.

239. Ibid., 306.

240. Royce, *California*, 295; Michel Steiner, "From Frontier to Region: Frederick Jackson Turner and the New Western History," *Pacific Historical Review*, vol. 64, no. 4 (November 1995), 488–89.

241. Royce quoted in Hine, "Josiah Royce," 23; Crerar Douglas, "The Gold Rush and the Kingdom of God: The Rev. James Woods' Cure of Souls," in William M. Kramer (ed.), *The American West and the Religious Experience* (Los Angeles: Will Kramer, 1974), 2–3; E. Bradford Burns, *Kinship with the Land: Regionalist Thought in Iowa, 1894–1942* (Iowa City: University of Iowa Press, 1996), 25–26.

242. Royce quoted in Robert V. Hine, "Josiah Royce: The West as Community," in Richard W. Etulain (ed.), *Writing Western History: Essays on Major Western Historians* (Albuquerque: University of New Mexico Press, 1991), 23.

243. Hine, "Josiah Royce," 32.

3. GOD'S COUNTRY

Epigraph: Martha [in Carthage, Miner County] to Husband, September 11, 1885, FF H92-125, DB 3327B, SDSHS.

1. Quoted in Ann Goetz, "History of Yankton County to 1886" (master's thesis, University of South Dakota, 1927), 41; Robert C. Ostergren, "European Settlement and Ethnicity Patterns on the Agricultural Frontiers of South Dakota," *South Dakota History*, vol. 13, nos. 1–2 (Spring–Summer 1983), 74–78; Stock, *Main Street in Crisis*, 58.

2. Blackburn, "A History of Dakota," 78.

3. *Glimpse of a Marvelous City,* 25.

4. "Personal Memoirs of William H. H. Beadle," 101. John P. Johansen found an "unusually active religious life" on the Dakota frontier. Johansen, "Immigrant Settlements and Social Organization," 53.

5. Kingsbury, *History of Dakota Territory,* 1855.

6. "Choice Farm Land, Miner County, South Dakota," n.d., Beinecke Library, Yale University.

7. "Biography of Mrs. A. P. Dragseth," FF GFWC, Lake County A–, DB 6830, SDSHS; J. G. Morrison, *Other Days: Boyhood Reminiscences of Frontier Hardships* (Kansas City: Nazarene Publishing House, [1930s]), 10–14.

8. Cayton and Onuf, *The Midwest and the Nation,* 49.

9. George Steinkamp, "The German Experience, 1874–1899," in Sneen, *Prairie Faith, Pioneering People,* 47 (Lutheran quote); Unruh, "South Dakota in 1889," 169; Stratton, *Pioneer Women,* 171–72; Ferenc Morton Szasz, *The Protestant Clergy in the Great Plains and Mountain West, 1865–1915* (Albuquerque: University of New Mexico Press, 1988), 46.

10. Diary of Elizabeth Meadville Farrell Hall, January 1, 1884, and September 19, 1883, FF H99-137, DB 7015A, SDSHS.

11. Doris Stensland, Robert Lundgren, and Donald J. Sneen, "Life in the New Land, 1859–1880: The Scandinavian Experience," in Sneen, *Prairie Faith, Pioneering People*, 32.

12. Sidney Hewitt to Children, May 21, 1882, FF H92-125, DB 3327B, SDSHS. See also Anderson, *Singing Hills,* 50.

13. Lewis, *Nothing to Make a Shadow,* 80. On respect for the Sabbath on the overland trail, see Reid, *Law for the Elephant,* 20–21.

14. Pease, "Tales of Pioneering."

15. Robert P. Swierenga, "The Little White Church: Religion in Rural America," *Agricultural History,* vol. 71, no. 4 (Fall 1997), 416–17.

16. Quoted in Sneen, *Prairie Faith, Pioneering People*, iii.

17. H. B. Reese, *Some Pioneers and Pilgrims on the Prairies of Dakota* (Mitchell, S.Dak.: privately printed, 1920), 73.

18. "Personal Memoirs of William H. H. Beadle," 147.

19. Unruh, "South Dakota in 1889," 170; Tarrel R. Miller, *The Dakotans* (Stickney, S.Dak.: Argus, 1964), 76.

20. "Personal Memoirs of William H. H. Beadle," 210.

21. Kingsbury, *History of Dakota Territory*, 1726.

22. Herreid, "The Pioneers of Dakota," 15; Robert Ostergren, "The Immigrant Church as a Symbol of Community and Place in the Upper Midwest," *Great Plains Quarterly,* vol. 1, no. 4 (1981), 225–26.

23. Howard R. Lamar, "Persistent Frontier: The West in the Twentieth Century," *Western Historical Quarterly,* vol. 4, no. 1 (January 1973), 7; David Noble, *Death of a Nation: American Culture and the End of Exceptionalism* (Minneapolis: University of Minnesota Press, 2002), 252; Rudolph J. Vecoli, "Ethnicity: A Neglected Dimension of American History," in Herbert Bass (ed.), *The State of American*

History (Chicago: Quadrangle, 1970), 71; Anne C. Loveland, "Later Stages of the Recovery of American Religious History," in Harry S. Stout and D. G. Hart (eds.), *New Directions in American Religious History* (New York: Oxford University Press, 1997), 489–91; Paul Kleppner, *The Cross of Culture: A Social Analysis of Midwestern Politics, 1850–1900* (New York: Free Press, 1970), 37 n. 2; Jon Butler, *Awash in a Sea of Faith: Christianizing the American People* (Cambridge: Harvard University Press, 1992); Laurie F. Miffly-Kipp, *Religion and Society in Frontier California* (New Haven, Conn.: Yale University Press, 1994).

24. Kleppner, *Cross of Culture*, 35; Robert Cook, "The Political Culture of Antebellum Iowa: An Overview," in Marvin Bergman (ed.), *Iowa History Reader* (Ames: Iowa State University Press, 1996), 87.

25. Richard J. Jensen, *The Winning of the Midwest: Social and Political Conflict, 1888–1896* (Chicago: University of Chicago Press, 1971), 58; Gaines M. Foster, "A Christian Nation: Signs of a Covenant," in Bodnar, *Bonds of Affection*, 124.

26. Frederick C. Luebke, "Ethnic Group Settlement on the Great Plains," *Western Historical Quarterly,* vol. 8, no. 4 (October 1977), 429.

27. Jon Gjerde, *The Minds of the West: Ethnocultural Evolution in the Rural Midwest, 1830–1917* (Chapel Hill: University of North Carolina Press, 1997), 7–8, 285–88. Robert Hine and Lewis Atherton have also noted Catholic-Protestant tension in small towns. Hine, *Community on the American Frontier,* 145, 147; Atherton, *Main Street on the Middle Border,* 74–75.

28. Robert Kelley, "Ideology and Political Culture from Jefferson to Nixon," *American Historical Review,* vol. 82, no. 3 (June 1977), 532. Richard Hofstadter's work in the 1950s helped historians move past a simple focus on clashing economic interests. See Daniel Joseph Singal, "Beyond Consensus: Richard Hofstadter and American Historiography," *American Historical Review,* vol. 89, no. 4 (October 1984), 976–78.

29. David Hackett Fischer, *Albion's Seed: Four British Folkways in America* (New York: Oxford University Press, 1989), 795; J. C. D. Clark, *The Language of Liberty, 1660–1832: Political Discourse and Social Dynamics in the Anglo-American World* (New York: Cambridge University Press, 1994), 22–24, 29; Gordon S. Wood, "Religion and the American Revolution," in Stout and Hart, *New Directions in American Religious History*, 176–79; Peter S. Onuf, "State Politics and Republican Virtue: Religion, Education, and Morality in Early American Federalism," in Finkelman and Gottlieb, *Toward a Usable Past,* 92; Szasz, *Protestant Clergy*, 12–14.

30. Kloppenberg, *Virtues of Liberalism,* 21; Handy, *A Christian America,* 3; Nathan O. Hatch, *The Sacred Cause of Liberty: Republican Thought and the Millennium in Revolutionary New England* (New Haven, Conn.: Yale University Press, 1977), 104–105; Mark A. Noll, *America's God: From Jonathan Edwards to Abraham Lincoln* (Oxford: Oxford University Press, 2002), 53–92; Hugh Heclo, *Christianity and American Democracy* (Cambridge, Mass.: Harvard University Press, 2007), 32–36.

31. Kloppenberg, *The Virtues of Liberalism*, 46.

32. Ibid., 48; Wilfred M. McClay, *The Masterless: Self and Society in Modern America* (Chapel Hill: University of North Carolina Press, 1994), 20; Butler, *Awash in a Sea of Faith*, 293–95. Mark Y. Hanley notes Lincoln's use of religious imagery and the interrelationship between American Protestantism and republicanism, but also asserts that some Protestant thinkers believed that religion was becoming too devoted to promoting the civic order. Hanley, *Beyond a Christian Commonwealth: The Protestant Quarrel with the American Republic, 1830–1860* (Chapel Hill: University of North Carolina Press, 1994), 32–35.

33. Cayton and Onuf, *The Midwest and the Nation,* 47–48.

34. Ostergren, "The Immigrant Church as a Symbol of Community and Place in the Upper Midwest," 225, 230; Daniel Walker Howe, "Protestantism, Volunteerism, and Personal Identity in Antebellum America," in Stout and Hart, *New Directions in American Religious History*, 213.

35. Faragher, *Sugar Creek,* 168; Szasz, *Protestant Clergy,* 8.

36. T. Scott Miyakawa, *Protestants and Pioneers: Individualism and Conformity on the American Frontier* (Chicago: University of Chicago Press, 1964), 17.

37. J. H. Baldwin, "Reminiscences of Home Mission Work in Dakota," Benjamin Stites Terry Collection, SHSND.

38. Swierenga, "The Little White Church," 419–20; Szasz, *Protestant Clergy,* 73.

39. Frederick C. Luebke, "Regionalism and the Great Plains: Problems of Concept and Method," *Western Historical Quarterly,* vol. 15, no. 1 (January 1984), 33–34.

40. Wright, *Culture on the Moving Frontier*, 97, 196, 197.

41. Avery O. Craven, "The Advance of Civilization into the Middle West in the Period of Settlement," in Fox, *Sources of Culture in the Middle West,* 61, 65–66. Robert Ostergren similarly concluded that the "central role of the church as a conservative force that defended cultural continuity with the past cannot be overestimated." Ostergren, "European Settlement and Ethnicity Patterns," 78.

42. Clipping, FF 128 J. N. McCloney, DB 19 Ministers, First Congregational Church, Sioux Falls.

43. Anthony H. Richter, "A Heritage of Faith: Religion and the German Settlers of South Dakota," *South Dakota History,* vol. 21, no. 2 (Summer 1991), 161; Eugene L. Fevold, "The Norwegian Immigrant and His Church," *Norwegian-American Studies,* vol. 23 (1967), 7–9; Berthoff, *An Unsettled People*, 251. On denominational divisions in the West, see Szasz, *Protestant Clergy,* 87–92; Johansen, "Immigrant Settlements and Social Organization," 57.

44. Fischer, *Albion's Seed*, 16, 212, 233.

45. Lynwood Oyos, "The Protestants," in Thompson, *A New South Dakota History,* 335.

46. Hoover, "Territorial Politics and Politicians," 113.

47. Fischer, *Albion's Seed.* The New England Puritans, according to Perry Miller's famous interpretation, went to America to "work out that complete reformation which was not yet accomplished in England and Europe, but which

would quickly be accomplished if only the saints back there had a working model to guide them." Perry Miller, "Errand into the Wilderness," *William and Mary Quarterly*, vol. 10, no. 4 (January 1953), 14. One sociologist noted that the "American pioneers, though of all kinds, were predominantly Reformation settlers." Adolph Berle quoted in Seymour Martin Lipset, "History and Sociology: Some Methodological Considerations," in Seymour Martin Lipset and Richard Hofstadter (eds.), *Sociology and History: Methods* (New York: Basic Books, 1968), 39. The Reformation settlers of the United States created a culture distinct from that in places such as Brazil, which was shaped by the influences of conquistadores. Nash, *Creating the West,* 140.

48. Szasz, *Protestant Clergy,* 22–23. When describing the early days of Dell Rapids, Dakota Territory, one account took particular notice of the arrival of "pioneers of New England background" after the Civil War. Gertrude Stickney Young, *Dakota Again* (Brookings, S.Dak.: privately printed, 1950), 19.

49. Kingsbury, *History of Dakota Territory*, 1855. See issues of *The Pilgrim Herald* in FF H82.23, DB 3591A, SDSHS.

50. K. Brent Woodruff, "The Episcopal Mission to the Dakotas, 1860–1898," *South Dakota Historical Collections,* vol. 17 (1934), 557.

51. Howard R. Lamar, "Public Values and Private Dreams: South Dakota's Search for Identity, 1850–1900," *South Dakota History,* vol. 8, no. 2 (Spring 1978), 125.

52. Thomas J. Gasque, "Church, School, and State Affairs in Dakota Territory: Joseph Ward, Congregational Church Leader," in Herbert T. Hoover and Larry J. Zimmerman (eds.), *South Dakota Leaders: From Pierre Chouteau, Jr., to Oscar Howe* (Vermillion: University of South Dakota Press, 1989), 144–45.

53. Gasque, "Church, School, and State Affairs in Dakota Territory," 149.

54. E. F. L., "From South Dakota," *Congregationalist and Christian World*, December 20, 1902.

55. "Dakota Images: James H. Kyle," *South Dakota History,* vol. 3, no. 4 (Fall 1973), 469.

56. Henry K. Warren, "Hon. Bartlett Tripp," *South Dakota Historical Collections,* vol. 6 (1912), 69.

57. Oyos, "Protestants," 334.

58. Dorothy Westhorpe Pederson, "The Reverend Melancthon Hoyt, D.D. and His Family," March 5, 1939, FF H41-001, DB 3649A, SDSHS.

59. Hoover, "Territorial Politics and Politicians," 103.

60. Lamar, *Dakota Territory,* 180.

61. Hoover, "Territorial Politics and Politicians," 108.

62. Schell, *History of South Dakota,* 199; Hoover, "Territorial Politics and Politicians," 111–12.

63. Hoover, "Territorial Politics and Politicians," 112.

64. L. E. Q., "New Empires in the Northwest," 3. The source for the cross information is the historical marker in front of Calvary Cathedral in Sioux Falls.

65. Stensland, Lundgren, and Sneen, "Life in the New Land, 1859–1880," 35.

66. Gary Olson, "European Settlement in Dakota," in Thompson, *A New South Dakota History*, 124–29; Ole. E. Rolvaag, *Concerning Our Heritage* (Northfield, S.Dak.: Norwegian-American Historical Association, 1998 [1922]), 116. Frederick Luebke notes that Norwegians "adhered strongly to Lutheranism." Luebke, "Ethnic Group Settlement on the Great Plains," 417.

67. Eugene L. Fevold, "The Norwegian Immigrant and His Church," *Norwegian-American Studies,* vol. 23 (1967), 5, 10; Orm Overland, "Religion and Church in Early Immigrant Letters: A Preliminary Investigation," in Todd W. Nichol (ed.), *Crossings: Norwegian-American Lutheranism as a Transatlantic Tradition* (Northfield, Minn.: Norwegian-American Historical Association, 2003), 32–33. An account of one Norwegian settlement can be found in Gustav O. Sandro, *The Immigrants' Trek* (n.p., 1929), CWS.

68. Stensland, Lundgren, and Sneen, "Life in the New Land, 1859–1880," 27.

69. Herreid, "The Pioneers of Dakota," 17.

70. Lynwood Oyos, "Lutherans Discover Each Other and American Values," in Sneen, *Prairie Faith, Pioneering People*, 99.

71. Kleppner, *Cross of Culture*, 87.

72. Gudrun Hovde Gvale, "A Biographical Note," in O. E. Rolvaag, *Peder Victorious* (Lincoln: University of Nebraska Press, 1982 [1929]), 322 (stern quote); Dag Thorkildsen, "Scandinavia: Lutheranism and National Identity," *The Cambridge History of Christianity,* vol. 8 (Cambridge: Cambridge University Press, 2006), 343; J. C. K. Preus, "From Norwegian State Church to American Free Church," *Norwegian-American Studies,* vol. 25 (1972), 186–87. Some Norwegian immigrants to Dakota sought to reform the State Church and resented harassment from church officials in Norway. Reese, *Some Pioneers and Pilgrims,* 30–31.

73. Selmer Hatlestad, "The Ethnic Consciousness Era, 1889–1920," in Sneen, *Prairie Faith, Pioneering People*, 58; Fevold, "The Norwegian Immigrant and His Church," 7–9. On theological divisions and the issue of maintaining the authority of the Lutheran church, see Jon Gjerde, "The Perils of 'Freedom' in the American Immigrant Church," in Nichol, *Crossings*, 19–20.

74. Hatlestad, "The Ethnic Consciousness Era," 58; Pederson, *Between Memory and Reality,* 116.

75. Hatlestad, "The Ethnic Consciousness Era," 62, 67, 68, 82. In 1930, the Iowa, Ohio, and Buffalo Synods merged to form the American Lutheran Church.

76. George Steinkamp, "The German Experience, 1874–1899," in Sneen, *Prairie Faith, Pioneering People*, 47; Reese, *Some Pioneers and Pilgrims,* 72.

77. Gabriel Tweet, "Early History of Scandinavian Church in the Dakota Territory," April 2, 1938, p. 2, FF H41-001, DB 3649A, SDSHS.

78. Oyos, "Lutherans Discover Each Other and American Values," 99; Johansen, "Immigrant Settlements and Social Organization," 54.

79. Tweet, "Early History of Scandinavian Church in the Dakota Territory," 6–7. Lutheran hymns also focused on the afterlife. Stensland, Lundgren, and Sneen, "Life in the New Land, 1859–1880," 32.

80. Simon Johnson, "An Immigrant Boy on the Frontier," translated by Nora O. Solum, *Norwegian-American Studies,* vol. 23 (1967), 59.

81. Lamar, "Public Values and Private Dreams," 128; Richter, "A Heritage of Faith," 155.

82. Richter, "A Heritage of Faith," 156 n. 1; Luebke, *Immigrants and Politics,* 23–24; Emmons, *Garden in the Grasslands,* 103.

83. Richter, "A Heritage of Faith," 161; Johansen, "Immigrant Settlements and Social Organization," 42.

84. Richter, "A Heritage of Faith," 169.

85. Ward McAfee, *Religion, Race, and Reconstruction: The Public School in the Politics of the 1870s* (New York: State University of New York Press, 1998), 18, 64 (enemy quote); Leo Ribuffo, *Right Center Left: Essays in American History* (New Brunswick, N.J.: Rutgers University Press, 1992), 46; McKenna, *Puritan Origins of American Patriotism,* 11, 174.

86. John T. McGreevy, *Catholicism and American Freedom: A History* (New York: W. W. Norton, 2003), 98. Some blamed the assassination of Lincoln on a "Romanist plot." Donald L. Kinzer, *An Episode in Anti-Catholicism: The American Protective Association* (Seattle: University of Washington Press, 1964), 96, 140, 235.

87. Foster, "A Christian Nation," 122.

88. McKenna, *Puritan Origins of American Patriotism,* 355; Burton, *Age of Lincoln,* 139–40. See, generally, Steven E. Woodworth, *While God Is Marching On: The Religious World of Civil War Soldiers* (Lawrence: University Press of Kansas, 2001).

89. Philip Hamburger, *Separation of Church and State* (Cambridge, Mass.: Harvard University Press, 2002), 322; McGreevy, *Catholicism and American Freedom,* 91; Kinzer, *An Episode in Anti-Catholicism,* 7.

90. McGreevy, *Catholicism and American Freedom,* 107. On Bismarck's Kulturkampf, see Marjule Anne Drury, "Anti-Catholicism in Germany, Britain, and the United States: A Review and Critique of Recent Scholarship," *Church History,* vol. 70, no. 1 (March 2001), 110–20.

91. McAfee, *Religion, Race, and Reconstruction,* 6, 41, 55; Hamburger, *Separation of Church and State,* 325; Kinzer, *An Episode in Anti-Catholicism,* 10.

92. Hamburger, *Separation of Church and State,* 287.

93. Higham, *Strangers in the Land,* 59.

94. Ray Allen Billington, *The Protestant Crusade, 1800–1860* (Chicago: Quadrangle Books, 1938), 4; Robert T. Handy, *Undermined Establishment: Church-State Relations in America, 1880–1920* (Princeton: Princeton University Press, 1991), 15–16.

95. Lynn Dumenil, "The Tribal Twenties: 'Assimilated' Catholics' Response to Anti-Catholicism in the 1920s," *Journal of American Ethnic History,* vol. 11, no. 1 (Fall 1991), 22; Morton Keller, *Affairs of State: Public Life in Late Nineteenth Century America* (Cambridge: Harvard University Press, 1977), 137–42.

96. Kinzer, *An Episode in Anti-Catholicism,* 17.

97. McAfee, *Religion, Race, and Reconstruction*, 41; McGreevy, *Catholicism and American Freedom*, 104–107; Kathleen Neils Conzen, *Germans in Minnesota* (St. Paul: Minnesota Historical Society, 2003), 9.

98. Robert Karolevitz, *Bishop Martin Marty: "The Black Robe Lean Chief"* (n.p.: privately printed, 1980), 12–18.

99. After the events in Switzerland, the Catholic Jesuits were also driven out of Italy, Spain, Germany, and France between 1859 and 1880. According to John McGreevy, the "most immediate consequence of the European revolutions was to thrust European conflicts into American politics." McGreevy, *Catholicism and American Freedom*, 19–20, 22.

100. Higham, *Strangers in the Land*, 85.

101. Ibid., 80–84; Merle Curti, *Growth of American Thought* (New York: Harper & Brothers, 1943), 493; Kinzer, *An Episode in Anti-Catholicism*, 61–64, 71–73. Donald Kinzer also notes the APA's focus on the Middle West, where many Dakota settlers originated. He found "no organizational records of the APA in existence," which inhibits the search for information about possible Dakota affiliates of the APA. Kinzer, however, does cite *The Cyclopedia of Fraternities*, which indicates there were 3,000 APA members in South Dakota in 1897. Ibid., v, 58, 178.

102. Kinzer, *An Episode in Anti-Catholicism*, 97.

103. Higham, *Strangers in the Land*, 85.

104. Ibid., 78; McGreevy, *Catholicism and American Freedom*, 125.

105. Higham, *Strangers in the Land*, 60.

106. Peter H. Argersinger, "Organizing the Farmers' Movement," *Reviews in American History,* vol. 4, no. 4 (December 1976), 566. See, generally, Michael Kazin, *A Godly Hero: The Life of William Jennings Bryan* (New York: Knopf, 2006).

107. Gjerde, *Minds of the West*, 294–95; Odd S. Lovoll, *Norwegians on the Prairie: Ethnicity and the Development of the Country Town* (St. Paul: Minnesota Historical Society Press, 2006), 158–61, 172, 176, 193.

108. Martin Marty, "Das apostolische Vikariat Dakota," March 19, 1885, FF 1879–1894 History, DB Bishop Martin Marty, Diocesan Archives, Sioux Falls.

109. Higham, *Strangers in the Land*, 83.

110. "Fenians in Dakota," *South Dakota Historical Collections,* vol. 6 (1912), 117–30; Robinson, *South Dakota, Sui Generis,* 522; McAfee, *Religion, Race, and Reconstruction*, 21. On the Irish immigrants to Dakota, see Michael F. Funchion, "South Dakota," in Michael Glazier (ed.), *The Encyclopedia of the Irish in America* (Notre Dame, Ind.: University of Notre Dame Press, 1999), 869–72.

111. *Sioux Falls Press*, November 3, 1894.

112. McGreevy, *Catholicism and American Freedom*, 103.

113. Billington, *Protestant Crusade,* 3.

114. Rolvaag, *Peder Victorious*, 104, 175, 235–36.

115. Martin Marty to Father Rosen, February 17, 1885, no FF, DB Bishop Martin Marty, Diocesan Archives, Sioux Falls (legion quote); Sister M. Stanislaus Van Well, *Bishop Martin Marty, O.S.B., 1834–1896: Apostle of the Sioux*

(Yankton, S.Dak.: Sacred Heart Convent, 1979) (translation and adaptation of Ildefons Betschant, *Der Apostel der Siouxindianer, 1834–1896* [1934]), 55.

116. Sister Claudia Duratschek, *Builders of God's Kingdom: The History of the Catholic Church in South Dakota* (Yankton, S.Dak.: Diocese of Sioux Falls, 1979), 87.

117. Lamar, *Dakota Territory*, 246.

118. Olson, "European Settlement in Dakota," 119. For a discussion of the transplantation of New England Yankee culture to the frontier, see Gray, *Yankee West*, 1–16; and John C. Hudson, "North American Origins of Middlewestern Frontier Populations," *Annals of the Association of American Geographers*, vol. 78, no. 3 (September 1988), 395–413.

119. Oyos, "Protestants," 334. W. H. H. Beadle noted that many prominent leaders in Dakota Territory were Congregationalists. Beadle, "Congregationalism and Civic Growth," FF 1, DB 3536A, Beadle Papers, SDSHS. For the impact of Congregationalism in Kansas, see Nathan Wilson, "Congregationalist Richard Cordley and the Impact of New England Cultural Imperialism in Kansas, 1857–1904," *Great Plains Quarterly*, vol. 24 (Summer 2004), 185–200. The famous Congregational minister Josiah Strong, author of the widely read anti-Catholic tract *Our Country* (1885), did missionary work in Wyoming. Dorothea R. Muller, "Church Building and Community Making on the Frontier, A Case Study: Josiah Strong, Home Missionary in Cheyenne, 1871–1873," *Western Historical Quarterly*, vol. 10, no. 2 (April 1979), 191–216; McGreevy, *Catholicism and American Freedom*, 125. Strong worried about Rome "concentrating her strength in the western territories." Kinzer, *An Episode in Anti-Catholicism*, 19.

120. Stock, *Main Street in Crisis*, 13.

121. Jason Kaufman, *For the Common Good? American Civic Life and the Golden Age of Fraternity* (Oxford: Oxford University Press, 2002), 4. For prominent fraternal orders in Dakota Territory, see "Knights Templar Proceedings"; "International Order Odd Fellows, Proceedings, Grand Encampment of Dakota"; "Proceedings of the Convention of Chapters, Order of the Eastern Star." One Catholic priest in Dakota Territory protested when a social group called the Rifles hosted a masquerade ball where attendees dressed as a priest and nuns and were made "objects of ridicule." "Father Haire Takes Exception to Certain Modes of Masquerading," *Aberdeen Daily News*, March 6, 1885.

122. Stock, *Main Street in Crisis*, 171, 178. The Masons were highly organized and rule-oriented, maintained a quasi-religious outlook, and adhered to a "Masonic Code" and a "common law of Masonry," which aided "in the diffusion of Masonic light." "Proceedings of the Twelfth Annual Communication, Most Worshipful Grand Lodge, Ancient Free and Accepted Masons of Dakota," 1886, FF Proceedings 1885–, DB 3705A, SDSHS.

123. *Yankton Press & Dakotan*, April 25, 1875; Pederson, "The Reverend Melancthon Hoyt, D.D. and His Family."

124. Higham, *Strangers in the Land*, 58, 80. The founder of the anti-Catholic American Protective Association was an "enthusiastic Mason" and "considered

the A.P.A. an offspring of Masonry." Kinzer, *An Episode in Anti-Catholicism*, 40–41.

125. Gjerde, *Minds of the West*, 292–93, 301–7, 307.

126. McAfee, *Religion, Race, and Reconstruction*, 73. In his study of a Wisconsin county, Merle Curti noted criticism of the unruly Irish, but also found positive attitudes toward the Irish. Curti, *Making of an American Community*, 94.

127. Kingsbury, *History of Dakota Territory*, 1532.

128. Hicks, "Constitutions of the Northwest States," 118.

129. Edwin Torrey, *Early Days in Dakota* (Minneapolis: Farnham Printing and Stationery Co., 1925), 201–202.

130. Letter to Martin Marty, 1891, FF American Indian Culture Research Center, DB Bishop Martin Marty, Diocesan Archives, Sioux Falls.

131. News clippings, January 1890, FF Prohibition, DB 5, Bishop Hare Papers, CWS.

132. Oyos, "Protestants," 334; Gjerde, *Minds of the West*, 295; Stock, *Main Street in Crisis*, 177.

133. Blackburn, "A History of Dakota," 78.

134. McGreevy, *Catholicism and American Freedom*, 112; Handy, *A Christian America*, 103.

135. McAfee, *Religion, Race, and Reconstruction*, 23.

136. Hamburger, *Separation of Church and State*, 324. The school issue persisted in American politics. In 1960, when attempting to temper anti-Catholic bias among voters, John Kennedy asked Protestants to consider his stand "against unconstitutional aid to parochial schools." Mark S. Massa, *Anti-Catholicism in America: The Last Acceptable Prejudice* (New York: Crossword, 2003), 81.

137. Joseph P. Viteritti, "Blaine's Wake: School Choice, the First Amendment, and State Constitutional Law," *Harvard Journal of Law and Public Policy*, vol. 21 (Summer 1998), 670–71.

138. Ibid., 672.

139. McAfee, *Religion, Race, and Reconstruction*, 178 (Hayes quote); Ahlstrom, *A Religious History of the American People*, 853.

140. Kingsbury, *History of Dakota Territory*, 1354; "The Blaine Boom," *Chicago Daily Tribune*, March 28, 1884.

141. Kingsbury, *History of Dakota Territory*, 1353.

142. Ibid., 1517.

143. Higham, *Strangers in the Land*, 60.

144. Torrey, *Early Days in Dakota*, 213–14.

145. Doane Robinson, "The Roman Catholic Church" (revised by Bishop Thomas O'Gorman), in Donald Dean Parker (ed.), *Denominational Histories of South Dakota* (Brookings: South Dakota State University, 1964), 116.

146. Clipping from *Dakota Journal* (Bridgewater), no FF, DB Bishop Martin Marty, Diocesan Archives, Sioux Falls.

147. O. H. Holt, *Dakota* (Chicago: Rand, McNally & Co., 1885), 25. George Kingsbury noted in his history of Dakota Territory that the "growth of the

Catholic religious and educational institutions in Dakota had been a matter of some discussion in early 1887," but he did not explain why. Kingsbury, *History of Dakota Territory*, 1498.

148. Robinson, "Roman Catholic Church," 117.

149. Ibid., 122–23.

150. Ibid., 123; Parker, *Denominational Histories of South Dakota*, 132.

151. Ludeman, "Studies in the History of Public Education," 377. Richard Jensen has also noted that "education was a New England export." Jensen, "On Modernizing Frederick Jackson Turner: The Historiography of Regionalism," *Western Historical Quarterly*, vol. 11, no. 3 (July 1980), 310. The "dominance of native Protestant culture" underpinned the common school movement. Kaestle, *Pillars of the Republic*, x.

152. Beadle, "Congregationalism and Civic Growth."

153. Cleata B. Thorpe, "Education in South Dakota: Its First Hundred Years, 1861–1961," *South Dakota Historical Collections*, vol. 36 (1972), 232.

154. Ludeman, "Studies in the History of Public Education," 459.

155. Kraushaar, "Brief Chronological History of School Legislation and Growth," 19; *Laws Passed at the Fourteenth Session of the Legislative Assembly of the Territory of Dakota* (Yankton, S.Dak.: Bowen & Kingsbury, 1881), 80–81. On concerns about the loss of the Norwegian language in Dakota, see Johansen, "Immigrant Settlements and Social Organization," 54–57.

156. McGreevy, *Catholicism and American Freedom*, 124.

157. Viteritti, "Blaine's Wake," 677. The Nebraska prohibition on foreign-language instruction, along with similar Iowa and Ohio laws, was found unconstitutional in *Meyer v. Nebraska*, 262 U.S. 390 (1923).

158. For a review of the literature examining expectations of Americanization and a debate over same, see Gary Gerstle, "Liberty, Coercion, and the Making of Americans," *Journal of American History*, vol. 84, no. 2 (September 1997), 524–58; and David A. Hollinger, "National Solidarity at the End of the Twentieth Century: Reflections on the United States and Liberal Nationalism," *Journal of American History*, vol. 84, no. 2 (September 1997), 559–69.

159. Duratschek, *Builders of God's Kingdom*, 87.

160. Hoover, "Catholic Missions, Churches, and Schools," 335; Kinzer, *An Episode in Anti-Catholicism*, 13.

161. Duratschek, *Builders of God's Kingdom*, 87; McGreevy, *Catholicism and American Freedom*, 114.

162. McAfee, *Religion, Race, Reconstruction*, 61.

163. Duratschek, *Builders of God's Kingdom*, 87.

164. Ibid., 87.

165. Martin Marty to Father Rosen, February 9, 1882, no FF, DB Bishop Martin Marty, Diocesan Archives, Sioux Falls.

166. Kraushaar, "Brief Chronological History of School Legislation and Growth," 17; Thorpe, "Education in South Dakota," 215; Oyos, "Protestants," 349.

167. Ruth Miller Elson, *Guardians of Tradition: American Schoolbooks of the Nineteenth Century* (Lincoln: University of Nebraska Press, 1964), 46 (source of quotation); McGreevy, *Catholicism and American Freedom*, 39.

168. McAfee, *Religion, Race, and Reconstruction*, 29.

169. William M. Blackburn, "Pulpit, Pew, and Paper," Scrapbook, no FF, DB 3374A, Blackburn Papers, SDSHS.

170. McAfee, *Religion, Race, Reconstruction*, 57–58; Keller, *Affairs of State*, 484–85.

171. McAfee, *Religion, Race, Reconstruction*, 182.

172. Ibid., 74, 178, 180–82, 190; Higham, *Strangers in the Land*, 86.

173. McAfee, *Religion, Race, Reconstruction*, 220. Joseph P. Viteritti explains that the constitutional convention of Colorado was controlled by supporters of Grant, Blaine, and Henry Blair and that pro-Blaine amendment sentiments were "ingrained in the political culture of the states and territories." Viteritti, "The Inadequacy of Adequacy Guarantees: A Historical Perspective," 21, paper delivered at Kennedy School of Government, Harvard University, October 13–14, 2005. Philip Hamburger notes that "Nativist Protestants . . . because of the strength of anti-Catholic feeling, managed to secure local versions of the Blaine amendment in a vast majority of the states." Hamburger, *Separation of Church and State*, 335.

174. McGreevy, *Catholicism and American Freedom*, 117.

175. McAfee, *Religion, Race, Reconstruction*, 189.

176. Hicks, "The Constitutions of the Northwest States," 23; Howard R. Lamar, "Westering in the Twenty-first Century: Speculations on the Future of the Western Past," in Cronon, Miles, and Gitlin, *Under an Open Sky*, 260.

177. "THE BIBLE: The bible shall not be excluded from any public school, nor deemed a sectarian book. It may be read in school without sectarian comment, not exceeding ten minutes daily, and no pupil shall be required to read it contrary to the wishes of his parent or guardian or other person having him in charge. The highest standard of morals shall be taught, and industry, truthfulness, integrity and self-respect inculcated, obedience to law enjoined, and the aims of an upright and useful life cultivated." § 91, Chapter 44, *Laws Passed at the Fifteenth Session of the Legislative Assembly of the Territory of Dakota*, 102.

178. §§ 1706, 1829, *Compiled Laws of the Territory of Dakota, A.D. 1887* (Bismarck, N.Dak., 1887).

179. Frederick Mark Gedicks, "Reconstructing the Blaine Amendments," *First Amendment Law Review*, vol. 2 (2003), 91. Common school advocates promoted use of the Protestant Bible. Kaestle, *Pillars of the Republic*, 3, 5.

180. Richard Baer, "Perspectives on Religion and Education in American Law and Politics: The Supreme Court's Discriminatory Use of the Term 'Sectarian,'" *Journal of Law and Politics*, vol. 6 (Spring 1990), 457; Hamburger, *Separation of Church and State*, 220; McGreevy, *Catholicism and American Freedom*, 24.

181. Baer, "Perspectives on Religion and Education in American Law and Politics," 456. One study notes that Horace Mann "insisted on Bible reading,

without commentary, as the foundation of moral education." Nondenominational Bible reading and "generalized Protestantism became the common religion of the common school." John C. Jeffries, Jr., and James E. Ryan, "A Political History of the Establishment Clause," *Michigan Law Review,* vol. 100 (November 2001), 298–99.

182. *Dakota Catholic*, August 3, 1889.

183. Marie Louise Lotze, "How South Dakota Became a State," *South Dakota Historical Collections,* vol. XIV (1928), 471; James E. Sefton, "Tribute Pennies and Tribute Clauses: Religion in the First Constitutions of the Trans-Mississippi States, 1812–1912," in Kramer, *The American West and the Religious Experience,* 79.

184. *Congressional Record* 20 (1889), 2100–2101. Senator Blair was named to the American Protective Association's "Roll of Honor." Kinzer, *An Episode in Anti-Catholicism,* 259.

185. Joseph P. Viteritti, "Davey's Plea: Blaine, Blair, Witters, and the Protection of Religious Freedom," *Harvard Journal of Law and Public Policy,* vol. 27 (Fall 2003), 313.

186. Ibid., 313–14. As late as the 1920s, some common schools in South Dakota still required Catholic students to read from the King James version ("KJV") of the Bible in class. One Catholic student's parents brought suit to reverse the expulsion of their son for refusing to read the KJV. In 1929, in a 3–2 decision, the South Dakota Supreme Court ruled in favor of the student, but the arguments are revealing. Noting that the KJV was "acceptable to the Protestants, but not to the Catholics," the court stated: "The King James version is a translation by scholars of the Anglican church bitterly opposed to the Catholics, apparent in the dedication of the translation, where the Pope is referred to as 'that man of sin,' and in which the translators express themselves as expecting to be 'traduced by Popish persons,' who will malign them, because such persons desire to keep the people in 'ignorance and darkness.'" The court rejected the argument that differences between the KJV and the Catholic Bible were insignificant and cited as evidence the "History of the conflicts between Catholics and Protestants." The defendants argued that Bible-based Protestantism had suffered for centuries at the hands of Catholics who favored church-based religious teaching: "There is a determined effort throughout the country to bar the Bible from the public schools. This effort is not being made by atheists, agnostics, and religious bolshevists, but by religionists, who for a thousand years have fought bitterly every effort to give the Bible to the people in the vernacular." Two of the five justices agreed with the school and concluded that use of the KJV of the Bible was not a "sectarian" activity. *State v. Weedman,* 226 N.W. 348, 349–51, 354, 359 (S.Dak. 1929).

187. Kingsbury, *History of Dakota Territory,* 1670–1715.

188. Hicks, "Constitutions of the Northwest States," 128.

189. W. W. Brookings, in *Dakota Constitutional Convention, 1885*, vol. 1 (Huron, S.Dak.: Huronite Printing Company, 1907), 473.

190. Alonzo Edgerton, in *Dakota Constitutional Convention, 1885*, 475.

191. McAfee, *Religion, Race, and Reconstruction*, 195.

192. Hamburger, *Separation of Church and State*, 324; McGreevy, *Catholicism and American Freedom*, 92. In the 1850s some states had also prohibited Catholic bishops from owning property. Ribuffo, *Right Center Left: Essays in American History,* 44.

193. Karolevitz, *Bishop Martin Marty*, 69–70, 94; Joel Rippinger, "Martin Marty: Monk, Abbot, Missionary, Bishop—II," *American Benedictine Review,* vol. 33, no. 4 (December 1982), 376; Bruce David Forbes, "Presbyterian Beginnings in South Dakota: 1840–1900," *South Dakota History,* vol. 7, no. 2 (Spring 1977), 150 (opponents quote); Hans Janssen, "Bishop Marty in the Dakotas," *American-German Review* (June–July 1961), 25; McGreevy, *Catholicism and American Freedom*, 112–13; Kinzer, *An Episode in Anti-Catholicism*, 74–78.

194. Sister Ann Kessler, "First Catholic Bishop of Dakota: Martin Marty, The Blackrobe Lean Chief," in Hoover and Zimmerman, *South Dakota Leaders*, 112.

195. Francis Paul Prucha, *The Great Father: The United States Government and the American Indians* (Lincoln: University of Nebraska Press, 1984), 163.

196. Duratschek, *Builders of God's Kingdom*, 84.

197. Hoover, "Catholic Missions, Churches, and Schools," 319.

198. Ibid., 322. Janssen, "Bishop Marty in the Dakotas," 25. Missionaries did not simply wield spiritual control over the Sioux. Philip Deloria notes a "cohort of Sioux ministers who essentially hijacked their respective denominations (Episcopalian, Congregationist, Presbyterian) to create the cross-denominational Brotherhood of Christian Unity, which effectively organized South Dakota Sioux Christianity—and put the emphasis on the *Sioux* as much as it did on the *Christianity*." Philip J. Deloria, *Indians in Unexpected Places* (Lawrence: University Press of Kansas, 2004), 114.

199. Kinzer, *An Episode in Anti-Catholicism*, 74–78, 205–207.

200. "Das apostolische Vikariat Dakota."

201. Statement of the Agency of the Indian Rights Association, February 4, 1905, FF Indian Rights Association, DB 5, Bishop Hare Papers, CWS; Handy, *Undermined Establishment*, 45–47.

202. *Washington Post*, February 1, 1905.

203. *Catholic Sentinel*, February 6, 1902.

204. Duratschek, *Builders of God's Kingdom*, 158.

205. Martin Marty to Father Rosen, March 11, 1885, no FF, DB Bishop Martin Marty, Diocesan Archives, Sioux Falls.

206. Martin Marty to Bishop, December 19, 1891, FF American Indian Culture Research Center, DB Bishop Martin Marty, Diocesan Archives, Sioux Falls.

207. Newspaper clippings, FF H5/58, DB 5, Bishop Hare Papers, CWS.

208. Letter from Bishop Hare, August 30, 1889, FF 1889, DB 4, Bishop Hare Papers, CWS.

209. Gerald W. Wolff, "First Protestant Episcopal Bishop of South Dakota: William Hobart Hare," in Hoover and Zimmerman, *South Dakota Leaders*, 94.

210. Pamphlets, FF H5/58, DB 5, Bishop Hare Papers, CWS.

211. M. A. DeWolfe Howe, *The Life and Labors of Bishop Hare: Apostle to the Sioux* (New York: Sturgis & Walton, 1913), 5–6, 322, 327, 328.

212. Wolff, "First Protestant Episcopal Bishop," 94.

213. Clipping, FF 36 Notes on Roman Catholic, DB 7, Hare Papers, CWS. William Blackburn, a prominent Presbyterian minister in Dakota Territory, also collected clippings referencing "papal arrogance and bigotry." See "The Reform Movement in Germany," Scrapbook, no FF, DB 3374A, Blackburn Papers, SDSHS.

214. Clipping, FF 24 Regeneration, Conversion, DB 7; clipping, FF 165 Quotes, DB 7, Hare Papers, CWS.

215. McGreevy, *Catholicism and American Freedom*, 99.

216. "Address before the Lake Mohonk Conference of Friends of the Indians, October 9, 1890," FF H5/58, DB 5, Hare Papers, CWS; Higham, *Strangers in the Land*, 60; Handy, *Undermined Establishment*, 42–43.

217. W. H. Hare to Doane Robinson, April 3, 1903, FF 8, DB 3361A, SDSHS. Anti-Catholic attitudes in the years after statehood are reviewed in Lorraine Collins and Scott Stoel, "The Invisible Empire of the Plains," *South Dakota Magazine* (May–June 1995), 34–35; Charles Rambow, "The Ku Klux Klan in the 1920s: A Concentration on the Black Hills," *South Dakota History,* vol. 4, no. 1 (Winter 1973), 63–80; Kenneth R. Stewart, "The Ku Klux Klan in South Dakota," paper presented at the Dakota History Conference, Madison, S.Dak., April 6, 1973; William L. Harwood, "The Ku Klux Klan in Grand Forks, North Dakota," *South Dakota History,* vol. 1, no. 4 (Fall 1971), 301–35; Robert Sam Anson, *McGovern: A Biography* (New York: Holt, Rinehart & Winston, 1972), 95–96; George S. McGovern, *Grassroots: The Autobiography of George McGovern* (New York: Random House, 1977), 83; Dolores Wilson, *From the Wrong Side of the Tracks* (Stickney, S.Dak.: Argus, 1980), 40; David Kranz, "Killing Brought Down Dream," *Argus Leader*, November 20, 1988; Kevin Woster, "Just Being There a Victory in Itself: Catholic Teams Celebrate Inclusion in State Events," *Rapid City Journal*, November 14, 2005. One Dakota Klan organizer, E. C. Haynes, lived in Aberdeen, and the South Dakota Fiery Cross Publishing Company operated out of Spencer. FF 2, DB 1, Clifford N. Taylor Papers, Beinecke Library, Yale University.

218. Oyos, "Lutherans Discover Each Other and American Values," 99.

219. Oyos, "Protestants," 319. Robert Ostergren also notes that ethnic group interaction was difficult due to "cultural values and prejudices." Ostergren, "European Settlement and Ethnicity Patterns," 79.

220. Douglas Chittick, "A Recipe for Nationality Stew," in J. Leonard Jennewein and Jane Boorman (eds.), *Dakota Panorama* (Freeman, S.Dak.: Dakota Territory Centennial Commission, 1961), 102.

221. Luebke, "Ethnic Group Settlement on the Great Plains," 412.

222. *Official Year Book, History and Guide of St. Thomas Catholic Church of DeSmet, South Dakota, and St. John's Catholic Church, Arlington, South Dakota*, FF H74.121, DB 3473B, SDSHS.

223. Kleppner, *Cross of Culture,* 82; McAfee, *Religion, Race, and Reconstruction,* 61; *Official Year Book, History and Guide*; Martin Marty to Father Rosen, November 10, 1883, no FF, DB Bishop Martin Marty, Diocesan Archives, Sioux Falls.

224. John C. Hudson, "Migration to an American Frontier," *Annals of the Association of American Geographers,* vol. 66, no. 2 (June 1976), 57, 65. In a recent memoir, a woman who grew up in a small town in North Dakota noted that a Lutheran marrying a Catholic was "scandal where I came from." Debra Marquart, *The Horizontal World: Growing Up Wild in the Middle of Nowhere: A Memoir* (New York: Counterpoint Press, 2006), 31.

225. "Pastoral Letter of Right Rev. Bishop Marty," April 20, 1889, FF 1879–1894 History, DB Bishop Martin Marty, Diocesan Archives, Sioux Falls.

226. Janssen, "Bishop Marty in the Dakotas," 26.

227. Rippinger, "Martin Marty," 386. Although he participated in the meetings of the German Catholic Katholikentag, Marty avoided "German particularism" and urged the body to "include all other assemblies of Catholic societies in the United States." For his efforts, in 1880 the Irish Catholic Colonization Association appointed him to a committee to promote Irish immigration to the west. He was also the only German-speaking bishop appointed to the committee that organized Catholic University. Marty believed it was important "to preserve the desirable characteristics and culture of the various peoples composing the Catholic Church in America" and avoided association with any single faction. Rippinger, "Martin Marty," 386.

228. McGreevy, *Catholicism and American Freedom*, 120–21. Bishop Ireland supported the Union during the Civil War, opposed postwar racial segregation and legal prohibitions on interracial marriage, and promoted Catholic assimilation and public education. Allen Guttmann, *The Conservative Tradition in America* (New York: Oxford University Press, 1967), 87; Berthoff, *An Unsettled People,* 418–19; Ahlstrom, *A Religious History of the American People,* 829.

229. Rippinger, "Martin Marty," 387.

230. Ribuffo, *Right Center Left*, 27, 43. As late as 1876, when Martin Marty made his first trip to South Dakota, New Hampshire barred Catholics from high office. Ibid., 35.

231. On interdenominational cooperation in the West, see Szasz, *Protestant Clergy,* 92–102. Merle Curti also pointed out that the "older American group welcomed the newcomers." Curti, *Making of an American Community*, 97, 127, 131.

232. "Personal Memoirs of William H. H. Beadle," 102.

233. "Admission of Dakota," Report of the Senate Committee on Territories, 50th Cong., 1st Session, January 23, 1888, 42, Beinecke Library, Yale University.

234. Thomas Sterling, "Biennial Address," *South Dakota Historical Collections,* vol. 4 (1908), 94; Gjerde, *Peasants to Farmers*, 239; Schell, *History of Clay County South Dakota,* 109; Rowland Berthoff, "Peasants and Artisans, Puritans and Republicans: Personal Liberty and Communal Equality in American History," *Journal of American History,* vol. 69, no. 3 (December 1982), 580;

Billington, *America's Frontier Heritage*, 112. According to one recollection, Scandinavians were known for their ability to "liquify at such a low temperature in the melting-pot." Hayden Carruth, "South Dakota: State without End," *The Nation* (January 24, 1923), 89.

235. Robert P. Swierenga, "The New Rural History: Defining the Parameters," *Great Plains Quarterly,* vol. 1, no. 4 (Fall 1981), 216–17; Emmons, *Garden in the Grasslands*, 112; Matthew Frye Jacobson, *Barbarian Virtues: The United States Encounters Foreign Peoples at Home and Abroad, 1876–1917* (New York: Hill & Wang, 2000), 192; Jacobson, *Whiteness of a Different Color: European Immigrants and the Alchemy of Race* (Cambridge, Mass.: Harvard University Press, 1998), 43–52.

236. Kingsbury, *History of Dakota Territory*, 1712.

237. Ibid., 1897.

238. Gudrun Hovde Gvale, introduction to Rolvaag, *Peder Victorious,* xvii.

239. Philip Rieff, *The Triumph of the Therapeutic: Uses of Faith after Freud* (Chicago: University of Chicago Press, 1966), 1–2.

4. "The Organic Law of a Great Commonwealth"

Epigraph: Article II, §26, reprinted in *Dakota Constitutional Convention, 1885*, 12.

1. "Our Birthday," *Daily Argus-Leader*, July 5, 1889 (notes that the weather "opened fair and clear and so continued all day").

2. *Sioux Falls: Metropolis of South Dakota* (Sioux Falls: South Dakota Publishing Company, 1889), 3, FF 1926.4.472, Siouxland Heritage Museum.

3. "The Dakota Pair," *St. Paul Pioneer Press*, July 5, 1889.

4. "Fourth at Sioux Falls," *St. Paul Pioneer Press*, June 29, 1889.

5. "The Dakota Pair."

6. Dana Bailey, *History of Minnehaha County* (Sioux Falls, S.Dak.: Brown & Sanger, 1899), 426–27; "The Convention," *Yankton Press and Dakotaian*, July 11, 1889; *South Dakota Constitutional Convention, 1889*, vol. 2 (Huron, S.Dak.: Huronite Printing Company, 1907), 3. The role of Germania Societies in promoting German settlement in the West—Texas and Wisconsin in particular—is discussed in John A. Hawgood, *The Tragedy of German-America* (New York: G. P. Putnam's Sons, 1940), 99–100, 141, 147, 213. See also Russell A. Kazal, *Becoming Old Stock: The Paradox of German-American Identity* (Princeton: Princeton University Press, 2004), 30–31. The American founders and subsequent political theorists placed great emphasis on the German origins of Anglo-Saxon democracy, a belief traceable to the popularity of Tacitus' book *Germania*. Colbourn, *The Lamp of Experience,* 26.

7. "Our Birthday," *Daily Argus-Leader*, July 5, 1889; "The Third Day," *Daily Argus-Leader*, July 6, 1889; "Fourth at Sioux Falls," *St. Paul Pioneer Press*, June 29, 1889. Edgerton served as a U.S. senator from Minnesota after Senator William Windom was appointed to serve as Secretary of the Treasury.

After Windom sought and won back his Senate seat, Edgerton was appointed to serve as chief justice of the Dakota Territorial Court.

8. *Dakota Constitutional Convention, 1885*, 80. On the uniqueness of the American Constitutional Convention, see R. R. Palmer, *The Age of Democratic Revolution: A Political History of Europe and America, 1760–1800* (Princeton: Princeton University Press, 1959), 214–17.

9. Howard Lamar, *Dakota Territory: A Study in Frontier Politics* (New Haven, Conn.: Yale University Press, 1956), 253.

10. *Dakota Constitutional Convention, 1885*, 658.

11. "An Address by General Hugh J. Campbell," *Yankton Press and Dakotaian*, October 18, 1883.

12. Dollard, *Recollections of the Civil War,* 233–34.

13. "Forming Organic Laws," *St. Paul Pioneer Press*, September 9, 1885.

14. *Chicago Inter Ocean*, excerpted in *Yankton Press and Dakotaian*, September 2, 1885.

15. "Forming Organic Laws," *St. Paul Pioneer Press*, September 9, 1885.

16. Dollard, *Recollections of the Civil War*, 247, 249.

17. "Getting Ready for Important Business," *Yankton Press and Dakotaian*, September 8, 1883.

18. Dollard, *Recollections of the Civil War,* 257.

19. "Judge Moody Speaks," *St. Paul Pioneer Press*, July 6, 1889.

20. *Yankton Press and Dakotaian*, September 11, 1883.

21. Dollard, *Recollections of the Civil War*, 241–42.

22. "An Address by General Hugh J. Campbell."

23. Dollard, *Recollections of the Civil War*, 249.

24. Ibid., 235; Journals of the 9th, 10th, and 11th Annual Convocations, Christ's Church, Protestant Episcopal Church, Beinecke Library, Yale University.

25. Dollard, *Recollections of the Civil War*, 247.

26. "Proceedings from the Convention in Sioux Falls," *Yankton Press and Dakotaian*, September 6, 1883.

27. *Dakota Constitutional Convention, 1885*, 107.

28. "Proceedings from the Convention in Sioux Falls."

29. *Jamestown Alert*, n.d., quoted in *Bismarck Tribune*, September 14, 1883. See, generally, Sefton, "Tribute Pennies and Tribute Clauses," 72.

30. *Church of the Holy Trinity v. United States*, 143 U.S. 226 (1892).

31. "Interesting Resume of the Work of the Constitution Makers," *Yankton Press and Dakotaian*, September 20, 1883.

32. *Spearfish Register*, n.d., excerpted in *Yankton Press and Dakotaian*, September 5, 1883.

33. "An Address by General Hugh J. Campbell."

34. "The Constitutional Convention Pushing Its Labors with Commendable Vim," *St. Paul Pioneer Press*, September 24, 1885.

35. Gordon Morris Bakken, *Rocky Mountain Constitution Making, 1850–1912* (Westport, Conn.: Greenwood Press, 1987), 103.

36. S.Dak. Const., Art. 6, § 27.

37. Hicks, "Constitutions of the Northwest States," 6; Bakken, *Rocky Mountain Constitution Making*, 101. The constitutional law relating to the territorial system is reviewed in Gary Lawson and Guy Seidman, *The Constitution of Empire: Territorial Expansion and American Legal History* (New Haven, Conn.: Yale University Press, 2004). In the South Dakota–based case *National Bank v. County of Yankton*, 101 U.S. 129, 132–33 (1879), the Supreme Court again affirmed that "Congress is supreme" over the territories and that "Congress may not only abrogate laws of the territorial legislatures, but it may itself legislate directly for the local government."

38. *Dakota Constitutional Convention, 1885*, 328.

39. "Not for His Health: Ordway Came Here for an Entirely Different Purpose—How He Proposed to Run the Machine," *Sioux Falls Press*, n.d., excerpted in *Yankton Press and Dakotaian*, September 21, 1883. The editor of the *Sioux Falls Press* in 1883 had been the editor of the *Pantagraph* in 1880. The editor said he refused Ordway's overtures. The editors of the *Press and Dakotaian* and the *Yankton Herald* also reported that Ordway attempted to persuade them to join his combination. "Good for the Soul," *Yankton Herald*, n.d., excerpted in *Yankton Press and Dakotaian*, September 24, 1883. Ruth Elizabeth Bergman acknowledged Ordway's "understanding of the power of the printed word. This understanding caused him, as one of his first acts after he became governor, to begin to build up a press in the territory which he believed could be relied upon to influence public opinion as he desired." Bergman, "Printing in South Dakota during the Territorial Period," 24.

40. Joseph Ward, "The Territorial System of the United States," *Andover Review* (July 1888), 52, 58, 53–55, 60–61, 55, 62, 55, 57.

41. Hicks, "The Constitutions of the Northwest States," 7.

42. Dollard, *Recollections of the Civil War*, 270.

43. *Yankton Press and Dakotaian*, October 4, 1883.

44. Paxson, "Admission of the 'Omnibus' States," 82, 90. *National Bank v. County of Yankton*, 101 U.S. 129 (1879) (holding in favor of the First National Bank of Maine, which held ten railroad bonds issued by Yankton County).

45. "Let Dakota Come In," *Boston Daily Advertiser*, n.d., reprinted in *Bismarck Tribune*, September 8, 1885. John D. Hicks noted that the "Dakotas were overwhelmingly Republican, and would prove an embarrassment to the Democrats whether admitted as one state or two." Hicks, "The Constitutions of the Northwest States," 21. The *Independent* deemed Democratic opposition to Dakota statehood a "disgrace." Clipping from *The Independent*, January 28, 1886.

46. As Earl Pomeroy explained, "Political expediency prompted the admission of Nevada in 1864—not only with fewer inhabitants than a state should have, but also with good prospects of losing those it had—to confirm the Republican Party's control of the Presidency." Pomeroy, *The Pacific Slope: A History of California, Oregon, Washington, Idaho, Utah, and Nevada* (New York: Knopf, 1965), 71; Donald, *Lincoln Reconsidered*, 79.

47. Bakken, *Rocky Mountain Constitution Making*, 6.

48. Hicks, "Constitutions of the Northwest States," 14.

49. *Chicago Inter Ocean,* n.d., excerpted in *Yankton Press and Dakotaian*, September 2, 1885. On politics in the north, see Robert P. Wilkins, "Alexander McKenzie and the Politics of Bossism," in Thomas W. Howard (ed.), *The North Dakota Political Tradition* (Ames: Iowa State University Press, 1981), 3–8.

50. Dollard, *Recollections of the Civil War*, 262.

51. *Yankton Press and Dakotaian*, September 8, 1885; Hicks, "Constitutions of the Northwest States," 14 n. 29; Paxson, "Admission of the 'Omnibus' States," 82–83.

52. "Successful Straddling," *St. Paul Pioneer Press*, September 13, 1883.

53. *St. Paul Pioneer Press*, September 14, 1883; *St. Paul Globe*, n.d., quoted in *Bismarck Tribune*, September 21, 1883; *Fargo Republican*, n.d., excerpted in *Yankton Press and Dakotaian*, September 8, 1883; "Taking a Constitutional," *St. Paul Pioneer Press*, September 8, 1883.

54. *Grand Forks Herald*, n.d., excerpted in *Yankton Press and Dakotaian*, August 29, 1883.

55. *Fargo Republican*, n.d., excerpted in *Yankton Press and Dakotaian*, August 29, 1883.

56. *Fargo Republican*, n.d., excerpted in *Yankton Press and Dakotaian*, September 3, 1883; *Fargo Republican*, n.d., excerpted in *Press and Dakotaian*, September 8, 1883.

57. "Interesting Resume of the Work of the Constitution Makers." On the importance of maintaining consensus in a statehood movement, see Eugene H. Berwanger, *The Rise of the Centennial State: Colorado Territory, 1861–76* (Urbana: University of Illinois Press, 2007), 42.

58. "Interesting Resume of the Work of the Constitution Makers."

59. Ibid.

60. *Leader* (Dickey County), n.d., quoted in "Statehood," *Bismarck Tribune*, September 21, 1883.

61. *Yankton Press and Dakotaian*, September 11, 1883.

62. Bakken, *Rocky Mountain Constitution Making*, 12; Earl S. Pomeroy, "Toward a Reorientation of Western History: Continuity and Environment," *Mississippi Valley Historical Review,* vol. 41 (March 1955), 585; Hicks, "Constitutions of the Northwest States," 33; Christian G. Fritz, "The American Constitutional Tradition Revisited: Preliminary Observations on State Constitution-Making in the Nineteenth-Century West," *Rutgers Law Journal,* vol. 25 (1994), 975–984.

63. "An Address from the State Executive Committee" (Bartlett Tripp, Chair), *Yankton Press & Dakotaian*, October 25, 1883; *North Dakota, South Dakota, Montana & Washington: The New States,* 30.

64. "An Address from the State Executive Committee."

65. L. W. Lansing manuscript, FF Constitutional Conventions, DB 5599, SDSHS.

66. "An Address by General Hugh J. Campbell."

67. *Press and Dakotaian*, September 24, 1883. The year the final Dakota constitution was written, Frederick Jackson Turner argued that the constitutional conventions of the American West had a much longer lineage and compared them to the "warrior-legislatures in the Germanic forests," which became a part of the "English heritage." Turner, of course, is best known for emphasizing the unique characteristics of American frontier democracy: "Too exclusive attention has been paid by institutional students to Germanic origins, too little to the American factors." Turner quoted in Noble, *Historians Against History*, 40.

68. "An Address by General Hugh J. Campbell." Campbell served as U.S. attorney for Dakota Territory and regularly clashed with opponents of statehood such as Ordway. Some Democrats in Congress were critics of Campbell because of his role in persuading the presidential electors from Louisiana to support Rutherford B. Hayes during the 1876 presidential election. Lamar, *Dakota Territory*, 255.

69. Bakken, *Rocky Mountain Constitution Making*, 5–6; Cronon, Miles, and Gitlin, "Becoming West," 17. On congressional enabling legislation, see Henry Z. Johnson, "The Admission of New States," *Central Law Journal*, October 3, 1890, at 269.

70. Pomeroy, *The Territories and the United States*, 100.

71. "Crisis at Sioux Falls: A Disturbing Declaration," *St. Paul Pioneer Press*, September 19, 1885.

72. "Judge Edgerton Argues against Revolution in the Dakota Constitutional Convention," *St. Paul Pioneer Press*, September 20, 1885.

73. "Harmony at Sioux Falls," *St. Paul Pioneer Press*, September 22, 1885. On the increasingly frequent invocation of popular sovereignty in the territories during the mid-nineteenth century, see Berwanger, *Rise of the Centennial State*, 2. On early constitutional debates over popular sovereignty, see Willi Paul Adams, *The First American Constitutions: Republican Ideology and the Making of the State Constitutions in the Revolutionary Era* (Lanham, Md.: Rowman & Littlefield, 2001), 135.

74. "Dakota's Organic Law," *St. Paul Pioneer Press*, September 28, 1885. Echoing Edgerton's conservative counsel, James T. Kloppenberg has noted that the "most radical and profound truth of popular sovereignty—one of the core principles of democracy—is that it puts everything up for grabs." Kloppenberg, "From Hartz to Tocqueville: Shifting the Focus from Liberalism to Democracy in America," in Meg Jacobs, William J. Novak, and Julian E. Zelizer (eds.), *The Democratic Experiment: New Directions in American Political History* (Princeton: Princeton University Press, 2003), 351. On the popular sovereignty debate in the California and Maryland constitutional conventions of 1849–51, see Christian G. Fritz, "Popular Sovereignty, Vigilantism, and the Constitutional Right of Revolution," *Pacific Historical Review*, vol. 63, no. 1 (February 1994), 51–52. More generally, see Edmund S. Morgan, *Inventing the People: The Rise of Popular Sovereignty in England and America* (New York: W. W. Norton, 1988).

75. "An Address by General Hugh J. Campbell."

76. *Chicago Inter Ocean,* n.d., excerpted in *Yankton Press and Dakotaian,* September 11, 1883

77. "Taking a Constitutional."

78. *St. Paul Pioneer Press,* September 6, 1883.

79. "Taking a Constitutional."

80. "The Reports Enrolled, and Two Well under Way," *Yankton Press and Dakotaian,* September 2, 1885.

81. "They Attempt Too Much," *St. Paul Pioneer Press,* September 25, 1885; *Dakota Constitutional Convention, 1885,* 403.

82. Janssen, "Bishop Marty in the Dakotas," 24.

83. Hicks, "Constitutions of the Northwest States," 31.

84. "Interesting Resume of the Work of the Constitution Makers," *Yankton Press and Dakotaian,* September 19, 1883.

85. Bakken, *Rocky Mountain Constitution Making,* 103.

86. Hicks, "The Constitutions of the Northwest States," 57; S.Dak. Const., Article III, §§12, 28.

87. *Yankton Press and Dakotaian,* October 4, 1883.

88. *Yankton Press and Dakotaian,* October 4, 1883.

89. Hicks, "Constitutions of the Northwest States," 34.

90. *Dakota Constitutional Convention, 1885,* 557.

91. "Prohibiting Public Debts," *Bankers' Magazine and Statistical Register* (November 1883), Sterling Memorial Library, Yale University; Hicks, "Constitutions of the Northwest States," 38 (lavish quote). Constitutional limits on state indebtedness became popular in the 1840s and 1850s. Marc W. Kruman, "Second American Party System," 530. Judges also sought to limit activist legislatures. Keller, *Affairs of State,* 345–46, 358–70.

92. Dollard, *Recollections of the Civil War,* 224.

93. *Yankton Press and Dakotaian,* September 15, 1883. On the debate over the location of the capital, see, generally, Marshall Damgaard, *The South Dakota State Capitol: The First Century* (Pierre: South Dakota State Historical Society Press, 2008).

94. Hicks, "Constitutions of the Northwest States," 53, 121; "The Convention," *Bismarck Tribune,* September 14, 1883; "Continuation of the Proceedings of the Constitutional Convention," *Yankton Press and Dakotaian,* September 15, 1883; Kermit L. Hall, "Mostly Anchor and Little Sail," 396. Wisconsin also adopted a constitutional amendment in 1874 limiting local indebtedness to 5 percent of the assessed value of local taxable property. George H. Miller, *Railroads and the Granger Laws* (Madison: University of Wisconsin Press, 1971), 142.

95. Hicks, "Constitutions of the Northwest States," 124; S.Dak. Const., Article XI, §1.

96. "The Sioux Falls Convention," *Bismarck Tribune,* September 21, 1883.

97. Hicks, "Constitutions of the Northwest States," 60–62, 107; S.Dak. Const. Article III, §8, and Article IV, §5.

98. Hicks, "Constitutions of the Northwest States," 78.

99. "Proceedings of the Convention of the Citizens Constitutional Association of Dakota, 1882," in Barrett Lowe, *Twenty Million Acres: The Story of America's First Conservationist, William Henry Harrison Beadle* (Mitchell, S.Dak.: Educator Supply Company, 1937), 451.

100. Hicks, "Constitutions of the Northwest States," 78.

101. Hicks, "Constitutions of the Northwest States," 84, 87–88, 88 n. 27; S.Dak. Const. Article VIII, §§4–6, 11.

102. William Cronon, *Nature's Metropolis: Chicago and the Great West* (New York: W. W. Norton, 1992), xv, 110.

103. Cronon, *Nature's Metropolis*, 121, 145, 214.

104. Hicks, *Populist Revolt,* 4. On Garland's invention of the term "Middle Border," see Newlin, *Hamlin Garland,* 7.

105. L. E. Q., "New Empires in the Northwest"; Briggs, *Frontiers of the Northwest,* 412–13, 415–18.

106. Hamburg, *Influence of Railroads,* 105. On the impact of the railroad on Dakota Territory, see John E. Miller, "Town Building in Eastern South Dakota during the Great Dakota Boom," unpublished manuscript, 1. One study found that "South Dakota is notable among the four new [Omnibus] States and indeed among most of the western States as having no railroads running entirely across the State east and west." Because the transcontinental railroads preferred to locate in other states, South Dakota had "the advantage and disadvantage of having all the railroads that have been extended into it built for itself alone. It is indeed a magnificent tribute to the worth of South Dakota in and of itself, that so many miles of excellent road have been constructed within its borders, for every mile of railroad in South Dakota exists there for the reason that South Dakota east of the Missouri River can furnish profitable traffic and business for the line." *North Dakota, South Dakota, Montana & Washington,* 39–40.

107. Hamburg, *Influence of Railroads,* 132.

108. Hicks, *Populist Revolt*, 12, 13.

109. James W. Ely, Jr., *Railroads and American Law* (Lawrence: University Press of Kansas, 2001), 58.

110. Hamburg, *Influence of Railroads,* 59.

111. Bruce Nelson, *Land of the Dacotahs* (Minneapolis: University of Minnesota Press, 1946), 133.

112. Ely, *Railroads and American Law*, 58, 62.

113. McNall, *Road to Rebellion,* 81 (20 percent of land); Michael P. Malone, *James J. Hill: Empire Builder of the Northwest* (Norman: University of Oklahoma Press, 1996), 111 (24 percent of land).

114. Hicks, *Populist Revolt,* 72.

115. Miller, "The State of South Dakota," 1107.

116. Hicks, *Populist Revolt,* 60; Benton H. Wilcox, "An Historical Definition of Northwestern Radicalism," *Mississippi Valley Historical Review,* vol. 26, no. 3 (December 1939), 385.

117. Hicks, *Populist Revolt,* 61, 64.

118. Nelson, *Land of the Dacotahs,* 252; Hicks, *Populist Revolt,* 69;

119. Robinson, *History of North Dakota,* 202; Hyatt, "A Legal Legacy for Statehood" 438. See also Albro Martin, *James J. Hill and the Opening of the Northwest* (New York: Oxford University Press, 1976). The activities of Dakota railroads were closely scrutinized as the antitrust movement gained political traction in the late nineteenth century. In the 1890s a de facto merger united the Northern Pacific and Great Northern, setting in motion the famous *Northern Securities* antitrust litigation. The *Northern Securities* case was one of the first decisions to interpret the Sherman Antitrust Act, passed in 1890 in response to concerns about anti-competitive behavior by corporations. *Northern Securities Co. v. United States,* 193 U.S. 197 (1904); Irene D. Neu, "Empire Builder, American Style," *Reviews in American History,* vol. 5, no. 4 (December 1977), 533. In 1955, the Northern Pacific and the Great Northern again attempted a merger, which, this time, the Supreme Court approved. As a result, the Great Northern; Northern Pacific; Chicago, Burlington, & Quincy; and Spokane, Portland & Seattle merged on March 2, 1970, to form the Burlington Northern Railroad. The effect of this merger "was to undo the 1904 decision of the Supreme Court in the *Northern Securities* case, which had blocked the same combination as a violation of the antitrust laws." Ely, *Railroads and American Law,* 276.

120. Hicks, *Populist Revolt,* 147.

121. Ely, *Railroads and American Law,* 89; Bakken, *Rocky Mountain Constitution Making,* 76–78.

122. Charles W. McCurdy, "Justice Field and the Jurisprudence of Government-Business Relations: Some Parameters of Laissez Faire Constitutionalism, 1863–1897," in Lawrence M. Friedman and Harry N. Scheiber (eds.), *American Law and the Constitutional Order: Historical Perspectives* (Cambridge, Mass.: Harvard University Press, 1978), 246.

123. Miller, *Railroads and the Granger Laws,* 75–76, 81. On the trend toward including traditionally legislative matters such as economic regulation in state constitutions, see Albert L. Strum, "The Development of American State Constitutions," *Publius: The Journal of Federalism,* vol. 12, no. 1 (Winter 1982), 67–68; Hall, "Mostly Anchor and Little Sail," 389–90, 403.

124. Ely, *Railroads and American Law,* 86.

125. Ely, *Railroads and American Law,* 86–87; Miller, *Railroads and the Granger Laws,* 58; Gerald Berk, *Alternative Tracks: The Constitution of American Industrial Order, 1865–1917* (Baltimore: Johns Hopkins University Press, 1994), 77.

126. Miller, *Railroads and the Granger Laws,* 173; Berk, *Alternative Tracks,* 81.

127. Miller, *Railroads and the Granger Laws,* 187–88; Robert G. McCloskey, *The American Supreme Court,* 3rd edition, revised by Sanford Levinson (Chicago: University of Chicago Press, 2000), 85–88. The *Munn* decision also noted the tradition of regulating ferries, bakers, millers, and other commercial interests and traced the practice back to regulations adopted in England. See also Harry

N. Scheiber, "Government and the Economy: Studies of the 'Commonwealth' Policy in Nineteenth Century America," *Journal of Interdisciplinary History,* vol. 3 (1972), 135–51.

128. "The Nebraska Constitution of 1875 and the Texas Constitution of 1876, for instance, declared railroads to be public highways and authorized the legislature to set 'reasonable maximum rates of charges.'" Similar efforts were made in the Georgia constitutional convention of 1877 and the California constitution of 1878–79. "These railroad clauses were part of a trend toward prolix state constitutions in the late nineteenth century; they also reflected deep concern over the economic power of railroads." Ely, *Railroads and American Law,* 89 (source of quote) (citing Bakken, *Rocky Mountain Constitution Making,* 76–78).

129. Miller, *Railroads and the Granger Laws,* 40–41.

130. McCloskey, *The American Supreme Court,* 82–84.

131. Berk, *Alternative Tracks,* 80. See also Johnston, *Radical Middle Class,* 74–75.

132. Berk, *Alternative Tracks,* 14, 76, 100–101, 163.

133. Hicks, "Constitutions of the Northwest States," 93–94; S.Dak. Const., Article XVII, §9.

134. Hicks, "Constitutions of the Northwest States," 123–24; S.Dak. Const., Article XIII, §1.

135. Lotze, "How South Dakota Became a State," 480; Hicks, "Constitutions of the Northwest States," 98; S.Dak. Const., Article XVIII, §§2–3.

136. "The Constitutional Convention Pushing Its Labors with Commendable Vim"; Charles Lowell Green, "The Administration of the Public Domain in South Dakota," *South Dakota Historical Collections,* vol. 20 (1940), 140–41.

137. Hicks, "Constitutions of the Northwest States," 90; Ely, *Railroads and American Law,* 99.

138. Hicks, "Constitutions of the Northwest States," 91 n. 2.

139. Ibid., 90; *Dakota Constitutional Convention, 1885,* 307.

140. "Sioux Falls Convention," *St. Paul Pioneer Press,* September 4, 1883; *Dakota Constitutional Convention, 1885,* 6.

141. "Sioux Falls Convention"; Lamar, *Dakota Territory,* 201.

142. "Sioux Falls Convention"; Dollard, *Recollections of the Civil War,* 266.

143. "Sioux Falls Convention"; "Address to the People: Call for a Gathering to Create a Constitution, March 12, 1883," FF H75.30, DB 3537A, SDSHS.

144. Dollard, *Recollections of the Civil War,* 269.

145. *Dakota Constitutional Convention, 1885,* 6.

146. Dollard, *Recollections of the Civil War,* 233–34, 41–42.

147. "Sioux Falls Convention."

148. Dollard, *Recollections of the Civil War,* 267.

149. "The State of Dakota," *Sioux Falls Daily Leader,* September 3, 1883; "Proceedings from the Convention in Sioux Falls."

150. "A Probability That the Convention Will Adjourn Tomorrow Night," *Yankton Press and Dakotaian,* September 14, 1883.

151. The *Sioux Falls Daily Leader* proudly noted that Lauren Dunlap, manager of the *Chicago Inter Ocean's* Dakota Bureau, was in town to cover the event and that "of all the great papers" the *Inter Ocean* was "the staunchest and most helpful friend to Dakota." "The State of Dakota." Dunlap signed his reports with his name in reverse "Palnud." He also served as the Dakota commissioner of immigration. Lamar, *Dakota Territory*, 50, 225–26; Lois Melvina Drake, "The Influence of the Newspapers of Dakota Territory upon the Administration of Nehemiah G. Ordway, Governor from 1880 to 1884" (master's thesis, University of Missouri, Columbia, 1941), 50. The official debates of the 1883 constitutional convention, alas, "were not preserved." *South Dakota Constitutional Convention, 1889,* 1.

152. "Dakota Statehood," *St. Paul Pioneer Press*, September 5, 1883.

153. "Bartlett Tripp Elected Permanent President of the Convention," *Yankton Press and Dakotaian*, September 5, 1883 (bombshell quote); "Organic Law for Dakota," *St. Paul Pioneer Press*, September 6, 1883.

154. *Sioux Falls Daily Leader,* September 5, 1883.

155. "Bartlett Tripp Elected Permanent President of the Convention."

156. "South Dakota Convention," *Bismarck Tribune*, September 21, 1883.

157. "The Sioux Falls Convention," *Bismarck Tribune*, September 7, 1883.

158. Dollard, *Recollections of the Civil War*, 257.

159. "Organic Law for Dakota"; "Taking a Constitutional."

160. "Dakota Deliberations," *St. Paul Pioneer Press*, September 9, 1883.

161. "Devising a Constitution," *St. Paul Pioneer Press*, September 12, 1883.

162. "The Doings of the Constitutional Convention at Its Recent Session at the City of Sioux Falls," *Bismarck Tribune*, September 7, 1883.

163. *Chicago Inter Ocean Correspondence*, September 20, 1883.

164. "Dakota Deliberations."

165. "Devising Organic Law," *St. Paul Pioneer Press*, September 11, 1883.

166. "Devising a Constitution," *St. Paul Pioneer Press*, September 12, 1883.

167. "South Dakota: The Constitutional Convention," *St. Paul Pioneer Press*, September 13, 1883.

168. "The Dakota Law-Makers," *St. Paul Pioneer Press*, September 18, 1883; "Progress of the Constitutional Convention Work," *Press and Dakotaian*, September 18, 1883.

169. "Interesting Resume of the Work of the Constitution Makers," *Yankton Press and Dakotaian*, September 20, 1883.

170. Ibid.; "Journal of the Constitutional Convention," *South Dakota Historical Collections,* vol. 21 (1942), 440.

171. "Constitution Complete," *St. Paul Pioneer Press*, September 19, 1883.

172. "Devising a Constitution," *St. Paul Pioneer Press*, September 12, 1883.

173. "Devising Organic Law," *St. Paul Pioneer Press*, September 11, 1883.

174. "Devising a Constitution," *St. Paul Pioneer Press*, September 12, 1883. The period 1865–75 saw a local-government borrowing binge, and the subsequent depression of 1873–77 "ruined state credit ratings and fueled measures,

even more far-reaching than those following the Panic of 1837, that clamped strict controls on public borrowing." Hall, "Mostly Anchor and Little Sail," 405.

175. "The Constitutional Convention," *St. Paul Pioneer Press*, September 14, 1883.

176. "Continuation of the Proceedings of the Constitutional Convention," *Yankton Press and Dakotaian*, September 15, 1883.

177. "Devising a Constitution."

178. "The Sioux Falls Convention," *Bismarck Tribune*, September 14, 1883; "Constitution Complete."

179. Bakken, *Rocky Mountain Constitution Making*, 23–24. According to Kermit Hall, "by about 1800, formal bills of rights, which limited state interference with individuals (and which had not been part of many of the first state constitution), became common." Hall, "Mostly Anchor and Little Sail," 396.

180. "Continuation of the Proceedings of the Constitutional Convention."

181. "Journal of the Constitutional Convention," 402.

182. "Tenth Day's Proceedings of the Constitutional Convention," *Yankton Press and Dakotaian*, September 17, 1883; "Journal of the Constitutional Convention," 402.

183. "Journal of the Constitutional Convention," 339.

184. "Tenth Day's Proceedings of the Constitutional Convention." The convention also adopted a Mellette amendment to allow a trial by a judge in criminal cases if both parties agreed.

185. "Dakota Deliberations."

186. "Dakota Statehood."

187. "Getting Ready for Important Business."

188. "South Dakota: The Constitutional Convention."

189. "Devising Organic Law."

190. "Concocting a Constitution," *St. Paul Pioneer Press*, September 15, 1883.

191. "Discussion on the Prohibition Subject," *Yankton Press and Dakotaian*, September 18, 1883.

192. "Interesting Resume of the Work of the Constitution Makers," September 19, 1883.

193. "Concocting a Constitution," *St. Paul Pioneer Press*, September 15, 1883.

194. "Discussion on the Prohibition Subject," *Yankton Press and Dakotaian*, September 18, 1883.

195. "The Dakota Law-Makers," *St. Paul Pioneer Press*, September 18, 1883.

196. "Constitutional Creation," *St. Paul Pioneer Press*, September 16, 1883; "Interesting Resume of the Work of the Constitution Makers," September 19, 1883. On the unpopularity of electing state officers before statehood had been granted by Congress, see Berwanger, *Rise of the Centennial State*, 42.

197. "Interesting Resume of the Work of the Constitution Makers," September 20, 1883.

198. "A Lively Discussion over the Election of Officers Clause," *Yankton Press and Dakotaian*, September 15, 1883; "Concluding Labors of the Constitutional Convention," *Yankton Press and Dakotaian*, September 21, 1883.

199. "The Dakota Law-Makers"; "Progress of the Constitutional Convention Work."

200. "Constitution Complete."

201. James Ely notes that a "number of states in the nineteenth century levied taxes based on the gross receipts of rail companies" and that these taxes were "repeatedly sustained" by the courts. Ely, *Railroads and American Law*, 208 (citing *State Tax on Railway Gross Receipts*, 82 U.S. 284 [1873]). See also *McHenry v. Alford*, 168 U.S. 651 (1898) (addressing Dakota Territory's gross earnings tax on railroads).

202. Hicks, "Constitutions of the Northwest States," 129; *Dakota Constitutional Convention, 1885*, 545–46. The Supreme Court of Dakota Territory held that territorial taxing authorities must recognize a tax exemption provided in a railroad land grant. *Winona & St. Paul Railroad Company v. County of Deuel*, 12 N.W. 561, 562 (Dak. Terr., 1882). See also *Northern Pacific Railroad Company v. Rockne*, 115 U.S. 600 (1885) (holding that railroads did not have to pay taxes on land grant property); Hyatt, "A Legal Legacy for Statehood," 502. In 1886, the Northern Pacific's gross earnings were calculated to be $2.7 million, $400,000 of which was earned in Dakota Territory. The Supreme Court of the territory held that the gross earnings tax could apply only to the $400,000 of "local business" conducted by the NP. Any tax on nonterritorial earnings constituted an "intermeddling with, and an effort to tax, the earnings or proceeds arising from interstate commerce, and the attempted usurpation of a power which, under the constitution, is to be solely and exclusively exercised by congress." *Northern Pacific Railroad Company v. Raymond*, 40 N.W. 538, 542 (Dak. Terr., 1888).

203. One of the People, "The Sioux Falls Railroad Constitution," *Dakota Herald*, October 6, 1883.

204. "To the People: An Address from the State Executive Committee Touching upon Various Constitutional Points Now under Discussion: Ample Evidence That Dakota's Constitution Is the Best Ever Framed," *Yankton Press and Dakotaian*, October 25, 1883.

205. Ibid. Much of the criticism of the tax provision was carried by the *Dakota Herald*, a Democratic organ known to oppose statehood. Lamar, *Dakota Territory*, 200, 255. Given the tax exemptions of the Northern Pacific and the constant litigation over the payment of railroad taxes, a reasonable solution was elusive. The issue would persist into the twentieth century.

206. "The South Dakota Constitution," *St. Paul Pioneer Press*, September 20, 1883.

207. "Concluding Labors of the Constitutional Convention."

208. "Dakota's Constitution," *St. Paul Pioneer Press*, September 20, 1883.

209. "Constitution Complete"; "Dakota's Constitution," September 20, 1883.

210. "Constitution Complete." In 1885, the convention adopted a resolution providing for the printing of 100,000 copies of the constitution in English, 10,000 in German and 10,000 in Norwegian. "Continuation of the Work at Sioux Falls—The End of the Convention Approaches," *Yankton Press and Dakotaian*, September 25, 1885.

211. "Constitution Complete."

212. "Dakota's Constitution," *Press and Dakotaian*, November 15, 1883.

213. *Dakota Constitutional Convention, 1885*, 44.

214. "Dakota's Constitution," November 15, 1883. Iowa: 1845, constitution lost 7,235–7,656; Iowa: 1846, constitution passed 9,492–9,036; Nebraska: 1866, constitution passed 3,938–3,838; Wisconsin: 1846, constitution rejected 20,233–14,119; Wisconsin: 1848, constitution passed 16,442–6,149; Missouri: 1865, constitution passed 43,670–41,808.

215. *Yankton Press and Dakotaian*, September 2, 1885.

216. *Dakota Constitutional Convention, 1885*, 45.

217. Dollard, *Recollections of the Civil War*, 274; *North Dakota, South Dakota, Montana & Washington*, 30.

218. "The Constitution," *Yankton Press and Dakotaian*, September 12, 1885.

219. Kingsbury, *History of Dakota Territory*, 1737; "The Work at Sioux Falls," *St. Paul Pioneer Press*, September 12, 1885.

220. "The Constitutional Convention," *Bismarck Tribune*, September 10, 1885.

221. Lotze, "How South Dakota Became a State," 474. Lotze notes that the "sources of the constitution, that can be discovered, are very incomplete, because of the fact that most of the work was done in committees which left no record of their proceedings." It is therefore necessary to rely heavily on contemporary newspaper accounts.

222. "An Address to the People of South Dakota," *Yankton Press and Dakotaian*, September 30, 1885.

223. "The Work at Sioux Falls," *St. Paul Pioneer Press*, September 12, 1885.

224. "The Constitution," *Yankton Press and Dakotaian*, September 14, 1885.

225. "Dakota's Organic Law," *St. Paul Pioneer Press*, September 28, 1885.

226. "Harmony at Sioux Falls," *St. Paul Pioneer Press*, September 22, 1885.

227. Ibid. The corporations committee emphasized that it did "not seek to be original at all" and that it "studied the best constitutions and selected from them the Constitution on Corporations," highlighting the Pennsylvania constitution in particular. *Dakota Constitutional Convention, 1885*, 439–40.

228. Larry Remele, "'God Helps Those Who Help Themselves': The Farmers Alliance and Dakota Statehood," *Montana The Magazine of Western History*, vol. 37, no. 4 (Autumn 1987), 30–31.

229. "Dakota's Organic Law." In fall 1885, voters adopted the prohibition measure by a margin of 15,570–15,337. *Dakota Constitutional Convention, 1885*, 47.

230. *Dakota Constitutional Convention, 1885*, 340.

231. Kingsbury, *History of Dakota Territory*, 1739; *Dakota Constitutional Convention, 1885*, 341–42.

232. Kingsbury, *History of Dakota Territory*, 1742; *Dakota Constitutional Convention, 1885*, 364.

233. Hicks, "Constitutions of the Northwest States," 150.

234. Dollard, *Recollections of the Civil War*, 279–80. Delegates argued that a larger legislature would be less susceptible to corruption. *Dakota Constitutional Convention, 1885*, 179.

235. Kingsbury, *History of Dakota Territory*, 1744.

236. "A Constitution Made," *St. Paul Pioneer Press*, September 26, 1885.

237. Affidavit, Arthur C. Phillips, December 9, 1929, FF 29.7.2, A. C. Phillips Collection, Siouxland Heritage Museum.

238. Hicks, "Constitutions of the Northwest States," 12.

239. *Dakota Constitutional Convention, 1885*, 47.

240. *Aberdeen Daily News*, November 7, 1888.

241. Kingsbury, *History of Dakota Territory*, 1542.

242. Robert Edwin Albright, "Politics and Public Opinion in the Western Statehood Movement of the 1880s," *Pacific Historical Review*, vol. 3, no. 3 (September 1934), 302.

243. *Dakota Constitutional Convention, 1885,* 47–48.

244. Hicks, "Constitutions of the Northwest States," 23. For discussion of the North Dakota constitution written in Bismarck in 1889, see Robert Vogel, "Sources of the 1889 North Dakota Constitution," *North Dakota Law Review,* vol. 65 (1989), 331. Vogel, a former justice of the North Dakota Supreme Court, concluded that the influence on the North Dakota constitution of the Northern Pacific Railroad, the bête noire of the southern Dakota statehooders, has been underestimated. Vogel, "Sources of the 1889 North Dakota Constitution," 342. See also Herbert L. Meschke and Lawrence A. Spears, "Digging for Roots: The North Dakota Constitution and the Thayer Correspondence," *North Dakota Law Review,* vol. 65 (1989), 343.

245. "To Overstep Limitations," *Daily Argus-Leader*, July 11, 1889, 1; "South Dakota," *St. Paul Pioneer Press*, July 20, 1889; "South Dakota Convention," *Bismarck Tribune*, July 11, 1889; "The Two Dakotas," *St. Paul Pioneer Press*, July 4, 1889.

246. "Four New Constitutions," *St. Paul Pioneer Press*, July 6, 1889.

247. In 1889, the separately submitted prohibition measure also passed 40,234–34,510. *Dakota Constitutional Convention, 1885*, 48.

248. Lamar, *Dakota Territory*, 230–31, 266–67, 230, 244, 251–52.

249. Kleppner, *Cross of Culture,* 37 n. 2.

250. See chapter 5.

251. Gordon Morris Bakken notes that it was common for charismatic leaders to play a large role in Western constitution writing. Bakken, *Rocky Mountain Constitution Making*, 13.

252. Baker, *Affairs of Party,* 7.

253. Boyd Schaffer, "The American Heritage of Hope," *Mississippi Valley Historical Review,* vol. 37, no. 3 (December 1950), 433.

254. Dollard, *Constitutional Debates,* 1:646. The *Yankton Press and Dakotaian* called the Pennsylvania constitution of 1873 a "popular granger constitution, of which the Dakota constitution is largely a copy." "Dakota's Constitution."

255. "Dakota's Organic Law." Positive commentary from the *St. Paul Pioneer Press* is especially noteworthy since it was considered "devoted to the interests of the Northern political gang." *Yankton Press and Dakotaian,* September 8, 9, 10, 1885 (gang quote from September 10). Lamar and Drake also noted that the *St. Paul Pioneer Press* supported the interests of Bismarck, Ordway, and the Northern Pacific. Lamar, *Dakota Territory,* 219; Drake, "The Influence of the Newspapers of Dakota Territory," 46. It should also be noted that Lamar's critical interpretation of the statehood movement relies heavily on the *Dakota Herald,* a Democratic newspaper strongly opposed to statehood, in keeping with the sentiments of the national Democratic Party. Lamar, *Dakota Territory,* 200; Bergman, "Printing in South Dakota during the Territorial Period," 29. For a complete review of the battles between the pro-northern and pro-statehood newspapers, see Drake, "The Influence of Newspapers of Dakota Territory."

256. "Sioux Falls," *Bismarck Tribune,* September 15, 1885.

257. "Harmony at Sioux Falls."

258. Consistent with the territory's political culture, the Dakota Farmers' Alliance operated within the republican tradition and promoted community involvement and social activities, including church services, lodge meetings, conventions, speeches, chautauquas, educational sessions on cropping techniques, circulating libraries, newspaper and pamphlet circulation, "picnics, dances, card parties, literary societies, clubs, and lodge activities." Unruh, "South Dakota in 1889," 171; Hicks, *The Populist Revolt,* 128–31. The Alliance was active in the political sphere, encouraging its members to run for political office within the existing party system and supporting their campaigns. Kenneth Hendrickson, Jr., "Some Aspects of the Populist Movement in South Dakota," *North Dakota History,* vol. 34, no. 1 (1967), 91. The Alliance also "invoked the Declaration of Independence, the 'Great Commoner' Abraham Lincoln, and a pantheon of popular symbols" and, until it supported the creation of a third party in 1890, emphasized its political independence and focused on "good government and the preservation of democratic ideals." Remele, "'God Helps Those Who Help Themselves,'" 30.

259. Elwyn B. Robinson, *History of North Dakota* (Lincoln: University of Nebraska Press, 1966), 204. The Alliance began to organize chapters in the territory as early as 1881. Delegates met in 1884 to form the territorial Alliance. The influence of the Alliance is noted in *North Dakota, South Dakota, Montana & Washington,* 50.

260. Hicks, "Constitutions of the Northwest States," 32; Hendrickson, "Some Political Aspects of the Populist Movement in South Dakota," 80.

261. With the support and leadership of farmers, the territorial assembly had already passed laws creating a railroad commission in 1885 and regulating grain

elevators and warehouses in 1887. Hendrickson, "Some Political Aspects of the Populist Movement in South Dakota," 78.

262. Remele, "'God Helps Those Who Help Themselves,'" 30 ("farmers'" quote). Herbert Schell noted that "the *Dakota Ruralist*, the official Alliance paper for Dakota Territory, repeatedly during 1889 endorsed the 1885 document as a 'farmers constitution,' as did club after club at Alliance meetings." Herbert Schell, review of Lamar, *Dakota Territory*, in *Mississippi Valley Historical Review*, vol. 43, no. 4 (March 1957), 691. In his comprehensive history of South Dakota, Schell also found that the "Alliance wholeheartedly advocated the re-adoption of the Constitution written at Sioux Falls in 1885, which they called a farmers' constitution." Schell, *History of South Dakota*, 226.

263. "South Dakota Too," *St. Paul Pioneer Press*, July 3, 1889. This is not to argue that members of the Alliance did not wrestle with non-Alliance members for positions of power within the Republican Party, especially toward the end of the 1880s. It is rather to emphasize that the Alliance did not object to the Dakota constitution. The political battles waged by the Alliance reinforce the argument that the organization could have undermined the referendum on the constitution had it wanted to.

264. "The Constitution Makers," *Yankton Press and Dakotaian*, October 4, 1883, citing *Chicago Inter Ocean Correspondence*, September 20, 1883; Lotze, "How South Dakota Became a State," 473.

265. "An Address to the People of South Dakota."

266. "Devising Organic Law" (deal fairly quote); "The Constitution Makers," citing *Chicago Inter Ocean Correspondence*, September 20, 1883 (delegates from Germany and Norway). In a goodwill gesture toward foreign-born immigrants, Dakota lawmakers reduced the residency requirement for voting and for being elected to office from three years to six months if the citizen declared his interest in becoming a citizen. "Devising Organic Law," *St. Paul Pioneer Press*, September 11, 1883.

267. *St. Paul Pioneer Press*, June 29, 1889.

268. Daniel Rylance (ed.), *Guide to the Microfilm Edition of the Dakota Territorial Records* (Grand Forks: University of North Dakota, 1969), 19. On the openness of the frontier political process, see Stanley Elkins and Erik McKitrick, "A Meaning for Turner's Frontier Thesis," *Political Science Quarterly*, vol. 69 (July 1954), 330, 334.

269. Lamar, *Dakota Territory*, 226, 229, 250.

270. *Dakota Herald*, September 1, 1883.

271. *Press and Dakotaian*, September 3, 1883. As late as 1889, wheat was still the "king" crop in Dakota, although more corn was being grown and fed to hogs. Unruh, "South Dakota in 1889," 82. The wheat crop was usually ready to cut by early August. Briggs, "Development of Agriculture in Territorial Dakota," 23; South Dakota Crop and Livestock Reporting Service, "South Dakota Field Crops from Planting to Harvest," (U.S. Department of Agriculture, June 1980), 9.

272. *Dakota Constitutional Convention, 1885*, 50.

273. Fred to Brother George, August 26, 1885, FF H92-125, DB 3327B, SDSHS. In 1890 the North Dakota Farmers' Alliance scheduled a convention for September 25, which further indicates farmer acceptance of September meetings. D. Jerome Tweton, "Considering Why Populism Succeeded in South Dakota and Failed in North Dakota," *South Dakota History*, vol. 22 (Winter 1992), 331.

274. A. A. Cheney to Sister, August 18, 1886, FF H92-125, DB 3327B, SDSHS. Lamar also wrote, citing a speech by Robert Dollard during the constitutional debates, that Dollard claimed that the conventions were timed to conflict with the harvesting season. Lamar, *Dakota Territory*, 226, 229, 250; *Dakota Constitutional Convention, 1885*, 644–47. In this passage, Dollard objects to the election of a slate of officers to serve the new state and criticizes the notion that without the immediate declaration of statehood the "people" would revolt. He apparently believed that those arguing that the territory was on the brink of revolution were attempting to justify the immediate declaration of statehood so that they might win election to one of the new state's offices. He rejected the view that the territory was on the brink of revolution by noting that few Dakotans participated in the election for constitutional delegates. Dollard does not say, however, that the convention was timed to conflict with the harvest season. Herbert Schell also rejected the argument that the September constitutional conventions coincided with the harvest. Schell, review, 691. Although he commended parts of Lamar's book, Schell viewed it as "dogmatic" and found some of its conclusions "far-fetched" and others "mere hypotheses." Ibid.

275. Campbell thought this would place the "burden of proof" upon Congress. "Taking a Constitutional," *St. Paul Pioneer Press*, September 8, 1883.

276. "South Dakota Statehood."

277. "Dakota's Organic Law."

278. *Dakota Constitutional Convention, 1885*, 51; "Dakota's Organic Law"; "An Address to the People of South Dakota."

279. Lamar, *Dakota Territory*, 244.

280. When discussing a Catholic priest that he viewed as "radical," for example, Lamar claims that he "advocated socialism." Lamar also criticizes the "class" of business interests that opposed reform, indicating a socialistic, or class-based, critique. Lamar, *Dakota Territory*, 245, 259.

281. The Dakota Alliance, in fact, was known for its business ventures. Hicks, *Populist Revolt*, 128, 132–34; Robert C. McMath, *American Populism: A Social History, 1877–1898* (New York: Hill & Wang, 1993), 101. Gilbert Fite also emphasized the "sanctity of property ownership" among farmers. Fite, *Farmers' Frontier*, 22. On the frontier, as Ray Allen Billington once wrote, "everyone was a real or potential capitalist." Billington, *America's Frontier Heritage*, 148.

282. Lamar, *Dakota Territory*, 230.

283. *Dakota Constitutional Convention, 1885*, 328.

284. Elizabeth Sanders, *Roots of Reform: Farmers, Workers, and the American State, 1877–1917* (Chicago: University of Chicago Press, 1999), 4.

285. Sanders, *Roots of Reform*, 268 (ideology quote); Cayton and Onuf, *The Midwest and the Nation*, 99.

286. Worth Robert Miller, "A Centennial Historiography of American Populism," *Kansas History,* vol. 16, no. 1 (Spring 1993), 54–69; Berthoff, "Writing a History of Things Left Out," 3; William F. Holmes, "Populism: In Search of Context," *Agricultural History,* vol. 64, no. 4 (1990), 45; Stanley B. Parsons, *The Populist Context: Rural versus Urban Power on a Great Plains Frontier* (Westport, Conn.: Greenwood Press, 1973), 147; Degler, "Remaking American History," 17–18; John Dibbern, "Who Were the Populists? A Study of Grass-Roots Alliancemen in Dakota," *Agricultural History,* vol. 54, no. 4 (October 1982), 681; Jeffrey Ostler, *Prairie Populism: The Fate of Agrarian Radicalism in Kansas, Nebraska, and Iowa, 1880–1892* (Lawrence: University Press of Kansas, 1993), 2; Cayton and Gray, "The Story of the Midwest," 19; McNall, *Road to Rebellion,* xiv, 145; Cherny, *American Politics in the Gilded Age*, 30–31. After statehood, agrarian activists in South Dakota did form a state Populist party, but their efforts were not as successful politically as they hoped because the majority Republican Party also addressed many farmers' concerns. After 1892, when the Populist Party began to include some socialists, it alienated prominent supporters and its reputation suffered for attracting "cranks." Tweton, "Considering Why Populism Succeeded in South Dakota and Failed in North Dakota," 340; Hendrickson, "Some Aspects of the Populist Movement in South Dakota," 91–92; Dibbern, "Who Were the Populists? 691; Woodward, *The Burden of Southern History,* 159; Morgan, *From Hayes to McKinley*, 371. Despite the inclusion of some socialists in South Dakota's Populist Party, Dibbern emphasizes that Populism in South Dakota "was not a class movement." Dibbern, "Who Were the Populists?" 682. Scott McNall also notes that the Populists were "petty capitalists" who embraced the "republicanism of petty producers," which did not challenge the "dominant economic system" and simply sought "fair play" from monopolists. McNall, *Road to Rebellion*, xiv. See also Holmes, "Populism: In Search of Context," 44–45.

5. THE INTELLECTUAL ORIGINS OF DAKOTA TERRITORY

Epigraph: Bogue, "Frederick Jackson Turner Reconsidered," 215.

1. *Dakota Territory* has been designated the "most definitive history of the political development of Dakota Territory." Rylance, *Guide to the Microfilm Edition of the Dakota Territorial Records,* 25. Elwyn B. Robinson relied heavily on Lamar in his history of North Dakota and calls *Dakota Territory* the "best account" of the Dakota statehood movement. Robinson, *History of North Dakota,* 577. Richard White also relies upon Lamar in his New Western History book *"It's Your Misfortune and None of My Own": A New History of the American West* (Norman: University of Oklahoma Press, 1991), 176. Clyde A. Milner II concluded that Lamar "redefined the study of the territorial era of the American West with his two books, *Dakota Territory* (1956) and *The Far Southwest* (1966)." Clyde A. Milner II, "A Note on the Author," in Howard R. Lamar, *The*

Theater in Mormon Life and Culture (Logan: Utah State University Press, 1999), v. Lamar's *Dakota Territory* is also praised in Lewis L. Gould, review of Cronon, Miles, and Gitlin, *Under an Open Sky, Western Historical Quarterly,* vol. 23, no. 4 (November 1992), 499; Paul Sharp, review of *Dakota Territory, American Historical Review,* vol. 63, no. 1 (October 1957), 145; and David J. Weber, "A Southerner at Yale Views the West: A Roundtable on the Work of Howard Lamar," *Western Historical Quarterly,* vol. 36 (Summer 2005), 134.

2. Weber, "A Southerner at Yale Views the West," 134.

3. Allan G. Bogue, "Social Theory and the Pioneer," *Agricultural History,* vol. 34, no. 1 (January 1960), 21.

4. Steiner, "From Frontier to Region," 480.

5. Lamar has noted that territorial history is no longer "a major area of research." Howard R. Lamar, "Earl Pomeroy, Historian's Historian," *Pacific Historical Review,* vol. 56 (November 1987), 559 n. 45. Peter S. Onuf, however, has published studies on the workings of the Northwest Ordinance. See Onuf, *Statehood and Union,* and *The Origins of the Federal Union* (Philadelphia: University of Pennsylvania Press, 1983).

6. Lamar, "Much to Celebrate," 397.

7. Lamar, interview with the author, June 5, 2006.

8. Lamar noted that, when he wrote *Dakota Territory,* western history was not considered a "mainline" field in American history. Lamar, "Much to Celebrate," 397.

9. Lamar's southern roots made his choice to study the West instead of the South that much more significant. The president of the short-lived Republic of Texas, Mirabeau Buonaparte Lamar, is Lamar's grandfather's uncle. David J. Weber, Preface to Cronon, Miles, and Gitlin, *Under an Open Sky,* xi (information on Texas presidency). Lamar's relative Lucius Quintus Cincinnatus Lamar, who served as a U.S. representative and senator from Mississippi, Secretary of the Interior, and a Supreme Court justice, was famously chronicled in John Kennedy's *Profiles in Courage,* published in 1956, the same year as Lamar's *Dakota Territory.* L. Q. C. Lamar was also credited by one scholar with making an important contribution to Turner's frontier theory. Wirt Armistead Cate, "Lamar and the Frontier Hypothesis," *Journal of Southern History,* vol. 1, no. 4 (November 1935), 497–501. Also see Cate's longer book on L. Q. C. Lamar entitled *Lucius Q. C. Lamar: Secession and Reunion* (Chapel Hill: University of North Carolina Press, 1935). When he was Secretary of the Interior in the 1880s, L. Q. C. Lamar famously complained about the constant demands of job seekers and the operation of the spoils system. Cherny, *American Politics in the Gilded Age,* 14. Richard Hofstadter viewed L. Q. C. Lamar as an "ingratiating Southern statesman." Hofstadter, *The Progressive Historians,* 54.

10. Lamar interview, June 5, 2006.

11. Ibid. Charles Beard, who was from Indiana, similarly noted that easterners thought that those beyond the Hudson River were "uncouth savages." Hofstadter, *Progressive Historians,* 54. A Wisconsin historian who was a visiting

professor at Harvard in 1937 said, "Most people here are quite unaware of the rest of the country." Novick, *That Noble Dream,* 181. John Higham also noted that midwesterners "complained that the typical eastern historian could scarcely see west of the Hudson River and that American history was being written as an extension of New England." John Higham, *History: Professional Scholarship in America* (Baltimore: Johns Hopkins University Press, 1965), 174.

12. Billington, *Genesis of the Frontier Thesis,* 87, 93.

13. Hofstadter, *The Progressive Historians,* 47–48; Burns, *Kinship with the Land,* xi, 8, 19–22.

14. Walter Prescott Webb, *The Great Frontier* (Reno: University of Nevada Press, 2003 [1952]), 6.

15. Fox, *Sources of Culture in the Middle West,* 3.

16. Billington, *America's Frontier Heritage,* 14–15, vi.

17. Billington, *Genesis of the Frontier Thesis,* 4; Higham, *History,* 202.

18. Lamar, "Frederick Jackson Turner," 99. According to Richard Hofstadter, Beard thought the "frontier idea" was "overlaid with a kind of conservatism and even of nationalist complacency." Hofstadter viewed Turner as "unsuited to the activist mood demanded by any radical attempt to cope with the Depression. The vogue of Marxism among intellectuals turned attention to class conflict and made historians more skeptical of an emphasis on geographic conflict and sectionalism." Hofstadter, *Progressive Historians,* xiii, 93. "In the thirties," according to Lewis S. Feuer, economic "determinism was part of the vogue of materialistic Marxism," and "the influence of Marxism had ramified through every department of intellectual life. . . . By the end of the thirties one might have said among the intellectuals and ideologists: 'We are all Marxists now.'" Feuer, *Ideology and the Ideologists* (New York: Harper Torchbooks, 1975), 52–53. Turner also noted the political inclinations of his critics, explaining to his daughter that Beard was "an ex-Columbia professor, radical in tendency," who attempted to read "the struggle of capital and labor" back into earlier periods of American history. Beard quoted in Bogue, "Frederick Jackson Turner Reconsidered," 200.

19. Warren I. Susman, *Culture as History: The Transformation of American Society in the Twentieth Century* (Washington, D.C.: Smithsonian Institution Press, 2003), 18 (the chapter cited here was first published as "The Useless Past: American Intellectuals and the Frontier Thesis, 1910–1930," *Bucknell Review,* vol. 11 [March 1963]). Peter Novick notes the "increasing acknowledgment by historians that the writing and teaching of history, when not narrowly antiquarian, inevitably had political implications of one sort or another" and the "marked increase in the extent to which explicit and avowed political purposes appeared in historians' books and classroom lectures." Novick, *That Noble Dream,* 239–40.

20. Susman, *Culture as History,* 21. A political activist, Beard "was in the wing of the [Progressive] movement that shaded off into reformist socialism." Novick, *That Noble Dream,* 96, 255.

21. Thomas Bender, "The New History—Then and Now," *Reviews in American History,* vol. 12, no. 4 (December 1984), 615. According to Richard

Hofstadter, Beard's book was "at the zenith of its appeal" during the 1930s, when the "economic interpretation of history [was] congenial to the day of popular-front Marxism and sociological literary criticism." Hofstadter, "Beard and the Constitution: The History of an Idea," *American Quarterly,* vol. 2, no. 3 (Autumn 1950), 209.

22. Forrest McDonald, "A New Introduction," in Charles A. Beard, *An Economic Interpretation of the Constitution of the United States* (New York: Free Press, 1986 [1913]), xv.

23. McDonald, "A New Introduction," xxii–xxiii. "Within the intellectual community [during the 1930s], Beard was *the* American historian," according to Peter Novick. "A study of college textbooks in 1936 showed that his *Economic Interpretation of the Constitution* had become virtual orthodoxy." Novick, *That Noble Dream,* 240.

24. Susman, *Culture as History,* 31, 33–36; Bogue, "Frederick Jackson Turner Reconsidered," 201–203. Ray Allen Billington argued that the exaggerated claims of some Turner "disciples," along with the "changed intellectual atmosphere of the Great Depression years, triggered a torrent of attack" on the Turner thesis. Billington, "The Frontier and I," *Western Historical Quarterly,* vol. 1, no. 1 (January 1970), 12.

25. Susman, *Culture as History,* 36.

26. John Lauritz Larson, "Grasping for the Significance of the Turner Legacy: An Afterward," *Journal of the Early Republic,* vol. 13, no. 2 (Summer 1993), 244. J. H. Hexter finds, by the 1930s, the "addiction of some 'advanced' historians in the United States to a sort of Marxism." Hexter, *On Historians: Reappraisals of Some of the Makers of Modern History* (Cambridge, Mass.: Harvard University Press, 1979), 16.

27. Ibid., 245.

28. Hofstadter, *The Progressive Historians,* 93.

29. Richard Hofstadter, introduction to Hofstadter and Seymour Martin Lipset (eds.), *Turner and the Sociology of the Frontier* (New York: Basic Books, 1968), 5.

30. Lamar interview, June 5, 2006; Jon Lauck, "The Making of *Dakota Territory*: How Serendipity Yielded a Famous Book about South Dakota," *South Dakota Magazine* (September–October 2006), 22–28.

31. Gabriel, *Course of American Democratic Thought,* 318, 323, 322.

32. Lamar is fond of citing Clarence E. Carter's comment that territorial history constituted the "Dark Age of American historiography." Lamar, *Far Southwest,* 1; Lamar, "Earl Pomeroy," 548. Lamar called Pomeroy's book on territorial policy an "excellent study" and deemed his work "indispensable." *Dakota Territory,* 18 n. 18, 290. He also praises Pomeroy's work in "Earl Pomeroy," 547–60. Pomeroy's book was the "first serious analysis of the territorial system and its administration in the American empire." Nash, *Creating the West,* 117. Pomeroy stressed the "institutional continuities" present on the frontier that made the West less distinctive than Turner imagined. Bogue, "Frederick Jackson Turner

Reconsidered," 204. Lamar notes that Pomeroy embraced Frederic Logan Paxson's emphasis on using a "political framework" in writing history. "Earl Pomeroy," 551. Pomeroy said, "Paxson found the political framework, among other conventional frameworks, indispensable in telling a general story." Pomeroy, "Frederic L. Paxson and His Approach to History," *Mississippi Valley Historical Review,* vol. 39, no. 4 (March 1953), 688. Efforts to organize the territorial papers in the 1920s and 1930s and the work of Clarence Carter are described in Ian Tyrrell, *Historians in Public: The Practice of American History, 1890–1970* (Chicago: University of Chicago Press, 2005), 178–79.

33. Lamar's *Dakota Territory* "utilized the theme of the West as a colonial region shaped by the political institutions of the United States Territorial system." Nash, *Creating the West,* 121.

34. Rodman W. Paul and Michael P. Malone, "Tradition and Challenge in Western Historiography," *Western Historical Quarterly,* vol. 16, no. 1 (January 1985), 45. Pomeroy also emphasized the "frontiersman's tendency to borrow from eastern precedents rather than innovate," a theme embraced by Lamar. Ibid., 32. See generally Pomeroy, "Toward a Reorientation of Western History, 579–83.

35. William Rowley, foreword to Webb, *Great Frontier,* ix. Gregory Tobin notes Webb's assumption in *The Great Plains* of "a direct link between environment and institutional development." Tobin, *The Making of a History: Walter Prescott Webb and "The Great Plains"* (Austin: University of Texas Press, 1976), 50. Rodman W. Paul and Michael P. Malone took particular notice of "Fred Shannon's pitiless exposure of the weaknesses" of Webb's *The Great Plains.* Paul and Malone, "Tradition and Challenge in Western Historiography," 34. See Fred Shannon, *An Appraisal of Walter Prescott Webb's "The Great Plains": A Study in Institutions and Environment* (New York: Committee on Appraisal of Research, Social Science Research Council, 1939). Peter Novick reviews Shannon's attack on Webb and the historical profession's reaction. Novick, *That Noble Dream,* 201–202. See also Susan Rhodes Neel, "A Place of Extremes: Nature, History, and the American West," Milner, *A New Significance,* 106–107.

36. Webb contended that "he had worked out his own ideas independently of Turner and that he should not be regarded as a product of the Turner school." Tobin, *Making of a History,* xv, 51. According to David J. Weber, however, "it is clear . . . that Webb had read Turner's essay before writing his book." Weber, "Turner, the Boltonians, and the Borderlands," 73.

37. Lamar interview, June 5, 2006.

38. Ibid.

39. Alfred Whitney Griswold, *Farming and Democracy* (New Haven, Conn.: Yale University Press, 1948).

40. Pomeroy, *The Territories and the United States,* v; Hicks, *Populist Revolt.* Lamar found Hicks's work on Populism "excellent." Lamar, *Dakota Territory,* 290. Given that several state studies of Populism appeared at the time of his writing, Hicks, while teaching at the University of Nebraska, concluded, "It seemed evident that the thing for me to do was to aim at an all-over treatment of the subject." Hicks

said the agricultural depression of the 1920s contributed to his "sympathy" for Populist farmers in *The Populist Revolt*. John D. Hicks, *My Life with History: An Autobiography* (Lincoln: University of Nebraska Press, 1968), 139, 146.

41. Robert W. Larson, *Populism in the Mountain West* (Albuquerque: University of New Mexico Press, 1986), 7 (lingering spirit quote); James Turner, "Understanding the Populists," *Journal of American History,* vol. 67, no. 2 (September 1980), 354 (dean quote). Hicks wrote in 1968, "When I wrote *The Populist Revolt* I was still uncritical, as were most American historians, of Turner's theories, and found greater significance in the passing of the frontier than I would now think reasonable." Hicks, *My Life with History,* 145–46. Paxson wanted Hicks to become "an authority on the constitutional history of the western states." According to Hicks, Paxson "brushed aside my suggestion that I should like to write on some aspect of Populism, and plunged me instead into the morass of state-making." Although Hicks reduced the scope of the project, he ultimately completed a thesis on the six states admitted to the Union in 1889, including the Dakotas. He said he "was never very proud of my thesis, and later came to regret that it achieved publication." Hicks, *My Life with History,* 86–88. Hicks's study of state making was published as "The Constitutions of the Northwest States," *University of Nebraska Studies,* vol. 23 (January–April, 1923).

42. Hicks, *My Life with History,* 37, 81, 134.

43. C. Vann Woodward, *The Burden of Southern History,* 142. "One of Paxson's students, John D. Hicks, developed the most successful American History texts ever written. His *The Federal Union* (1937) and *The American Nation* (1941), which are still used in revised editions, did much to popularize and disseminate the frontier interpretation." Paul and Malone, "Tradition and Challenge in Western Historiography," 33.

44. Lamar, "Frederick Jackson Turner," 100.

45. George Wilson Pierson, "The Frontier and American Institutions: A Criticism of the Turner Theory," *New England Quarterly,* vol. 15, no. 2 (June 1942), 224. Richard Hofstadter called Pierson's essay "one of the most influential early essays in Turner criticism." Hofstadter, *The Progressive Historians,* 92.

46. Pierson, "The Frontier and American Institutions," 225, 245, 246, 251, 237, 243.

47. Ibid., 237, 243.

48. In 1931 Yale launched the course American Thought and Civilization, which was cotaught by Ralph Henry Gabriel. Two years later the university established a new department—History, the Arts, and Letters—which awarded its first Ph.D. to A. Whitney Griswold, whose degree "has been claimed as the first American Studies, or American Studies–like, Ph.D. ever granted." Gene Wise, "'Paradigm Dramas' in American Studies: A Cultural and Institutional History of the Movement," in Lucy Maddox (ed.), *Locating American Studies: The Evolution of a Discipline* (Baltimore: Johns Hopkins University Press, 1999), 177.

49. The Yale American Studies Program "was first announced for academic year 1948–49, with Gabriel as Chairman" and Griswold as director of Graduate

Studies. Sydney E. Ahlstrom, "Studying America and American Studies at Yale," *American Quarterly,* vol. 22, no. 2, part 2 (Summer 1970), 512. "And in 1950, Yale was to receive a substantial endowment from the wealthy benefactor William Robertson Coe, and that year announced a $4.75 million drive to expand its American Studies enterprise." Wise, "'Paradigm Dramas' in American Studies," 182. The former chair of the Yale American Studies program, Sydney Ahlstrom, believed that the Coe endowment was the "most decisive for its scope and budgetary stability." Ahlstrom, "Studying America and American Studies at Yale," 512.

50. Lamar, *Dakota Territory*, 290; Smith, *Virgin Land.* Leo Marx calls Smith's book the "first substantial work of American studies scholarship." Leo Marx, "Believing in America: An Intellectual Project and a National Ideal," *Boston Review* (December 2003), http://bostonreview.net/BR28.6/marx.html. Smith has also been deemed the first American Studies Ph.D. (Harvard, 1940). Lawrence Buell, "Commentary," in Maddox, *Locating American Studies,* 13.

51. Neil Jumonville, *Henry Steel Commager: Midcentury Liberalism and the History of the Present* (Chapel Hill: University of North Carolina Press, 1999), 210–11.

52. Ibid., 217.

53. Kerwin Lee Klein, "Reclaiming the 'F' Word, or Being and Becoming Postwestern," *Pacific Historical Review,* vol. 65, no. 2 (May 1996), 209.

54. Marx, "Believing in America." As Jumonville also notes, "Nearly all the figures in the classic cohort of American studies believed that political activism was an important part of their intellectual role," which fulfilled Van Wyck Brooks's ideal of scholars finding a "usable past" and then using it. Jumonville, *Henry Steel Commager*, 209.

55. Henry Nash Smith, "Symbol and Idea in *Virgin Land*," in Sacvan Bercovitch and Myra Jehlen (eds.), *Ideology and Classic American Literature* (Cambridge: Cambridge University Press, 1986), 31.

56. Lamar, *Dakota Territory*, 244.

57. Ibid., 271. One reviewer commented that Lamar's account "dwelt on human skullduggery." Muriel E. Hidy, review of Lamar, *Dakota Territory, Agricultural History,* vol. 32, no. 2 (April 1958), 144.

58. Peter Novick notes that Beard's *An Economic Interpretation of the Constitution* was "central to the Progressive view of American history as the enduring struggle between 'the people' and 'the interests.'" Novick, *That Noble Dream*, 334–35. Despite his Beardian overtones, Lamar does not cite Beard's work, which might be explained by Beard's controversial legacy. Beard, for example, had instructed Arthur M. Schlesinger, Sr., not to mention his name in his dissertation: "It is the red flag to the historical bull." Ibid., 97. By the 1940s, Beard's reputation also suffered greatly due to his opposition to American participation in World War II.

59. Lamar, *Dakota Territory*, 245, 246, 15.

60. Lamar interview, June 5, 2006.

61. Lamar, "Frederick Jackson Turner," 107, 106.

62. W. Turrentine Jackson, review, *English Historical Review,* vol. 73, no. 286 (January 1958), 175.

63. Lamar, *Dakota Territory,* 283. In *The Far Southwest,* Lamar also argued that the Turner thesis did not apply to Arizona, New Mexico, Utah, or Colorado. Lamar, *The Far Southwest,* 4–5.

64. Lamar, "Frederick Jackson Turner," 107 (quoting Pomeroy, "Toward a Reorientation of Western History," 581–83).

65. Lamar, "Frederick Jackson Turner," 107. The "creativity" of the frontier was the "supposed burden of the Turner thesis," although Mary Young argued that this overstated Turner's thesis. Mary Young, "The West and American Cultural Identity: Old Themes and New Variations," *Western Historical Quarterly,* vol. 1, no. 2 (April 1970), 144.

66. Lamar, *Dakota Territory,* 217, 242.

67. Lamar, "Frederick Jackson Turner," 105.

68. Lamar, *The Far Southwest,* 14. Lamar's students also note that newer histories of the West emphasize how much was borrowed from the East and Europe. Cronon, Miles, and Gitlin, "Becoming West," 4.

69. Lamar, *Dakota Territory,* 266, 212, 282, 268, 273.

70. Ibid., 282–83, xiii.

71. Lamar, "Frederick Jackson Turner," 107. Mary Young interpreted Lamar's book in a similar way: "Widespread popular participation in politics became the norm at the end of the frontier period, when a new, larger population with problems the oligarchy refused to solve proceeded to unseat the clique." Young, "The West and American Cultural Identity," 148.

72. John D. Hicks noted the currency of Beard's ideas about the formation of the Constitution at the time Lamar was writing his book: "Beardian revisionism, based as it was on the temporarily popular idea of economic determinism, and reinforced by the experiences of the Great Depression, got a long play." John D. Hicks, "Changing Concepts of History," *Western Historical Quarterly,* vol. 2, no. 1 (January 1971), 30.

73. Lamar, *Dakota Territory,* 229–30. John D. Hicks also notes that Dakotans "copied the ideas of the older states." Hicks, "Constitutions of the Northwest States," 33.

74. Lamar, *Dakota Territory,* 251, 252.

75. Lamar, *Dakota Territory,* 266. Others have similarly concluded that Lamar "views the old guard statehood men as leaders of a conspiracy against the farmers of the Territory." Rylance, *Guide to the Microfilm Edition of The Dakota Territorial Records,* 25.

76. John P. Diggins, *The Bard of Savagery: Thorstein Veblen and Modern Social Theory* (New York: Seabury Press, 1978), 214–16; Hine, *Community on the American Frontier,* 128–29. "In 1938 when the editors of the *New Republic* conducted a symposium on 'Books That Changed Our Minds' and asked a number of American liberal intellectuals to suggest titles that ought to be discussed, the two most frequently mentioned titles were Beard's *An Economic Interpretation*

of the Constitution and Veblen's *Theory of the Leisure Class*." Hofstadter, "Beard and the Constitution," 209.

77. C. Wright Mills, *The Power Elite* (New York: Oxford University Press, 1956).

78. Singal, "Beyond Consensus," 980–81, 988 n. 29.

79. David Brooks, "Cracking the Shells," *New York Times*, August 20, 2006. Brooks notes that *Peyton Place* chronicles the "scandals, betrayals and lusts that lurk beneath the placid surface of a New England small town. 'Peyton Place' became the best-selling novel in American history up to that time. It inspired a movie, a TV show and, as Leonard Cassuto notes in *The Chronicle of Higher Education*, the modern soap opera as we know it."

80. John L. Thomas, *A Country in the Mind: Wallace Stegner, Bernard DeVoto, History, and the American Land* (New York: Routledge, 2000), 18, 51.

81. Michael Kammen, *In the Past Lane: Historical Perspectives on American Culture* (New York: Oxford University Press, 1997), 28. Potter became an assistant professor of history at Yale in 1942, and in 1947 was selected to serve a term as Harmsworth Professor of American History at Oxford. Yale won Potter back from Oxford and made him head of the new American Studies program. To avoid losing him to Northwestern University, Yale named Potter a full professor in 1949. In 1950 he was named to the Coe professorship. Kammen, *In the Past Lane*, 54–55.

82. Robert M. Collins, "David Potter's *People of Plenty* and the Recycling of Consensus History," *Reviews in American History,* vol. 16, no. 2 (June 1988), 324; David Potter, *People of Plenty: Economic Abundance and American Character* (Chicago: University of Chicago Press, 1954).

83. Lamar, "Frederick Jackson Turner," 100.

84. Collins, "David Potter's *People of Plenty*," 325.

85. According to Peter Novick, "From 1948 onward, among historians as among other academics and intellectuals, there was an accelerating abandonment of dissidence, a rapid accommodation to the new postwar political culture." Novick, *That Noble Dream*, 323.

86. Ibid., 332. Novick concludes, "No project was more central to historians from the late 1940s onward than the revision and refutation of the alleged deficiencies of the Progressive Historians who had preceded them."

87. Limerick, "What on Earth is the New Western History?" in Milner, Limerick, and Rankin, *Trails,* 62. Allan Bogue says that "neo-Turnerianism was born" in the 1950s and 1960s. Bogue, "Frederick Jackson Turner Reconsidered," 204.

88. Novick, *That Noble Dream*, 325.

89. Stephen Skowronek, *Building a New American State: The Expansion of National Administrative Capacities, 1877–1920* (Cambridge: Cambridge University Press, 1982); Peter B. Evans, Dietrich Rueschemeyer, and Theda Skocpol (eds.), *Bringing the State Back In* (Cambridge: Cambridge University Press, 1985); Karen R. Merrill, "In Search of the 'Federal Presence' in the American West," *Western Historical Quarterly,* vol. 30, no. 4 (Winter 1999), 449–73.

90. Lamar, "Frederick Jackson Turner," 109.

91. Lamar interview, June 5, 2006.

92. Although many historians at the time Lamar wrote *Dakota Territory* considered "ideas" as mere "smokescreens" for one's ideological interests, in subsequent decades the study of ideas, symbols, and the various components of "political culture" gained legitimacy. Joyce Oldham Appleby, Lynn Hunt, and Margaret Jacob, *Telling the Truth about History* (New York: W. W. Norton, 1995), 139–40.

93. See the works cited in note 286 in chapter 4.

94. Lamar, "Much to Celebrate," 411–12; Lamar, "Persistent Frontier," 7.

95. Lamar interview, June 5, 2006.

96. Limerick, *Legacy of Conquest*, 22.

97. Worster, "Beyond the Agrarian Myth," 8, 10. Susan Rhodes Neel has noted, "Worster and Limerick have been explicit in calling for an activist or reformist western history." Neel, "A Place of Extremes," 122 n 13.

98. Worster, "Beyond the Agrarian Myth," 13, 21, 15,16. Worster concluded that "we need a new past." Worster, "A Country without Secrets," in *Under Western Skies: Nature and History in the American West* (New York: Oxford University Press, 1992), 253. Jeffrey Ostler also notes that the New Western historians were searching for a "usable past." Ostler, "Empire and Liberty," 202. Robert Johnston believes that the New Western historians have not done enough to highlight past alternatives to capitalism, which has the effect of constraining contemporary politics. Citing Roberto Unger, Johnston argues that "if our history suppresses past challenges to the ultimately dominant institutions of modern capitalism, then our ability to envision alternatives to the present order is substantially harmed." Johnston, "Beyond 'The West,'" 262.

99. Klein, "Reclaiming the 'F' Word," 180.

100. Thompson, "The New Western History: A Critical Analysis," 58.

101. John Mack Faragher, "The Frontier Trail: Rethinking Turner and Reimagining the American West," *American Historical Review,* vol. 97 (February 1993), 111. Allan G. Bogue notes that "some of the new issues or approaches [in western history] seem to trace back well beyond the 1980s" and that the "break between the new and the old western history is . . . difficult to identify." Bogue, "Frederick Jackson Turner Reconsidered," 212.

102. Donald J. Pisani, "Is There Life after Turner? The Continuing Search for a Grand Synthesis and an Autonomous West: A Review Essay," *New Mexico Historical Review,* vol. 67, no. 3 (1992), 292–93.

103. Nash, "The Global Context of the New Western History," in Gressley, *Old West/New West,* 149–50.

104. Nash, *Creating the West,* 276.

105. Worster, "Beyond the Agrarian Myth," 23.

106. Degler, "Remaking American History," 19.

107. Novick, *That Noble Dream,* 241.

108. White, "A Southerner at Yale Views the West," 138.

109. Lamar interview, June 5, 2006.

110. Lamar's students note that "Turner's critics ultimately went too far in their attacks on his work." Cronon, Miles, and Gitlin, "Becoming West," 6; Cronon, "Revisiting the Vanishing Frontier," 160.

111. Robert V. Hine and John Mack Faragher, *Frontiers: A Short History of the American West* (New Haven, Conn.: Yale University Press, 2007).

112. Patricia Nelson Limerick, "Turnerians All: The Dream of a Helpful History in an Intelligible World," *American Historical Review*, vol. 100, no. 3 (June 1995), 708.

113. Johnson notes that her study began with a suggestion from Lamar. Susan Lee Johnson, *Roaring Camp: The Social World of the California Gold Rush* (New York: W. W. Norton, 2000), 16.

114. Karl Jacoby, *Crimes against Nature: Squatters, Poachers, Thieves, and the Hidden History of American Conservation* (Berkeley: University of California Press, 2001); Karl Jacoby to Jon Lauck, January 11, 2008. In his most recent book, Jacoby closely analyzes four different points of view on an event in western history. *Shadows at Dawn: A Borderlands Massacre and the Violence of History* (New York: Penguin Press, 2008).

115. Louis Warren, *The Hunter's Game: Poachers and Conservationists in Twentieth-Century America* (New Haven, Conn.: Yale University Press, 1999); Louis Warren to Jon Lauck, January 18, 2008.

116. Howard Lamar, "From Bondage to Contract: Ethnic Labor in the American West, 1600–1890," in Hahn and Prude, *The Countryside in the Age of Capitalist Transformation*, 293–324; Gunther Peck, *Reinventing Free Labor: Padrones and Immigrant Workers in the North American West, 1880–1930* (New York: Cambridge University Press, 2000).

117. Philip J. Deloria, *Playing Indian* (New Haven, Conn.: Yale University Press, 1998) (this is the book that grew out of Deloria's Yale dissertation), and *Indians in Unexpected Places* (Lawrence: University Press of Kansas, 2004). On the general revival of Native American history as discussed by a student of Lamar, see Miles, "To Hear an Old Voice." See also Lewis, "Native Americans in the Nineteenth-Century American West."

118. Karl Jacoby notes that *The Far Southwest* "proved foundational to much of the Chicano history that came later." Karl Jacoby to Jon Lauck, January 11, 2008. In the 1980s Richard White described the "current flowering of Chicano history which began with Howard Lamar's *The Far Southwest*." White, "Race Relations in the American West," 397.

119. Truett believes that *The Far Southwest* "remains influential because no other book has ever come close to replacing it. It is a classic." He also notes that Lamar "led me into the borderlands through his interest in the U.S. Southwest and its Mexican legacy and sent me south beyond the Americanist pale with characteristic encouragement, curiosity, and wisdom. This work builds on his legendary zeal for crossing frontiers and borders." Truett, *Fugitive Landscapes: The Forgotten History of the U.S.-Mexico Borderlands* (New Haven, Conn.: Yale University Press, 2006), ix. William Cronon served as co-director of Truett's dissertation.

120. David Milch is a 1966 graduate of Yale and the producer of *Hill Street Blues, NYPD Blue,* and *Deadwood.* Peter Hawes, "Lights! Camera! Yale!" *Yale Alumni Magazine* (April 2001); Nancy Franklin, "Dead On: David Milch Explores the Dakota Territory," *New Yorker,* June 12, 2006; Mark Singer, "The Misfit: How David Milch got from 'NYPD Blue' to 'Deadwood' by way of an Epistle of St. Paul," *New Yorker,* February 14, 2005; David Milch, panel discussion, "Got Yourself a Gun: Frontier Violence in American History," co-sponsored by the Autry National Center and the Howard Lamar Center, September 29, 2006, Yale University. Hampton Sides is a 1984 graduate of Yale. Clyde Milner, interview with Jon Lauck, January 8, 2008; Hampton Sides, *Blood and Thunder: The Epic Story of Kit Carson and the Conquest of the American West* (New York: Doubleday, 2006).

121. Lamar, introduction to *Dakota Territory* (1966 edition), xx.

122. Richard Bernstein, "Unsettling the Old West," *New York Times Magazine,* March 18, 1990.

CONCLUSION

Epigraph: "Minnie Hanneman Schultz," FF GFWC, Lake County A–, DB 6830, SDSHS.

1. Briggs, *Frontiers of the Northwest,* 421–22, 424–26.

2. H. C. Halvorson, *The First Fifty Years in Lake Sinai Township* (Brookings, S.Dak.: privately printed, 1956). Halvorson recorded his recollections of the settlement period in the 1930s, but they were not printed by the Sinai Lutheran Church until 1956.

3. Kerwin Lee Klein notes that late-nineteenth-century terms such as "people," "race," "blood," and "stock," which imply thinking in racial categories, would currently be understood to mean "culture." Klein, "Reclaiming the 'F' Word," 186. Frederick G. Detweiler concluded that what "Americans really mean when they talk about Anglo-Saxon origins is the entire body of political, legal, and intellectual tradition brought here by our colonists in the seventeenth and eighteenth centuries." Detweiler, "The Anglo-Saxon Myth in the United States," *American Sociological Review,* vol. 3, no. 2 (April 1938), 185. On the belief in Anglo-Saxon institutions as a model for liberty, see Bailyn, *Ideological Origins of the American Revolution,* 66–67, 79–83; Colbourn, *Lamp of Experience,* 7–8, 26–36; McDonald, *Novus Ordo Seclorum,* 76–77.

4. Matthew Frye Jacobson, a prominent analyst and critic of the racial categories that republicans at times employed, even concedes that within the logic of republicanism lay the seeds of abolitionism and, it should be added, the later movements for civil rights and racial equality. Jacobson, *Whiteness of a Different Color,* 27.

5. Stephen M. Berk, *Year of Crisis, Year of Hope: Russian Jewry and the Pogroms of 1881–1882* (Westport, Conn.: Greenwood Press, 1985), 54–55; I. Michael Aronson, "The Anti-Jewish Pogroms in Russia in 1881," in John Doyle Klier and Shlomo Lambroza (eds.), *Pogroms: Anti-Jewish Violence in Modern*

Russian History (New York: Cambridge University Press, 2004), 44–61; Ronald J. Ross, *The Failure of Bismarck's Kulturkampf: Catholicism and State Power in Imperial Germany, 1871–1887* (Washington, D.C.: Catholic University of America Press, 1998); Adam Hochschild, *King Leopold's Ghost: A Story of Greed, Terror, and Heroism in Colonial Africa* (Boston: Mariner Books, 1999).

6. Degler, "Remaking American History," 20. Degler noted, for example, that blacks in the antebellum South also held slaves. Some historians have correctly recognized that the interpretation of the American West "follows no one master narrative and no single factor or plot." Clyde A. Milner II, "Introduction: America Only More So," in Milner, O'Connor, and Sandweiss, *The Oxford History of the American West*, 2. Eric H. Monkkonen also promotes the "appreciation of historical complexity" in "The Dangers of Synthesis," *American Historical Review*, vol. 91, no. 5 (December 1986), 1155.

7. Limerick, *Something in the Soil*, 23. Although she has described her more critical interpretation of western history as part of a new "orthodoxy" in western historiography, Limerick also stresses that her actual goal is complexity: "The deeply frustrating lesson of history in the American West and elsewhere is this: human beings can be a mess—contentious, conflict loving, petty, vindictive, and cruel—*and* human beings can manifest grace, dignity, compassion, and understanding in ways that leave us breathless." Ibid., 21. Limerick's latter conclusion, however, has received less attention from historians than the former.

8. David S. Brown, *Richard Hofstadter: An Intellectual Biography* (Chicago: University of Chicago Press, 2006), 451.

9. Lears, *No Place of Grace*, xx. On using history to demonstrate human agency and its potential to shape historical events, see Michael D. Bess, "E. P. Thompson: The Historian as Activist," *American Historical Review*, vol. 98, no. 1 (February 1993), 18–38.

10. Lasch, *True and Only Heaven*.

11. Hicks, "Development of Civilization in the Middle West," 97–98. More recently, other historians have urged greater attention to the democratic energies of people in the West who have not received their due. Robert D. Johnston, *The Radical Middle Class: Populist Democracy and the Question of Capitalism in Progressive Era Portland, Oregon* (Princeton: Princeton University Press, 2005).

12. McClay, *The Masterless*, 13.

13. When discussing the unifying effects of patriotism in frontier Wisconsin, Merle Curti emphasized the importance of "general and voluntary participation . . . on terms of relative equality," a description that matches the Dakota experience. In general, Curti found that the frontier county he studied in Wisconsin was a "story of progress toward democracy." Curti, *The Making of an American Community*, 131, 448.

14. Lasch, *True and Only Heaven*, 24.

15. Royce, *California*, 313; Turner, "The Significance of History" (1891), 57; Miyakawa, *Protestants and Pioneers*, 17. On conservatism and social order, see William R. Harbour, *The Foundations of Conservative Thought: An*

Anglo-American Tradition in Perspective (Notre Dame, Ind.: University of Notre Dame Press, 1982), 113–26; Billington, *America's Frontier Heritage,* 148.

16. Bogue, "Social Theory and the Pioneer," 25–26; Cayton and Onuf, *The Midwest and the Nation,* 30.

17. Cayton and Onuf, *The Midwest and the Nation,* 31 (source of quotation); Don Harrison Doyle, *The Social Order of a Frontier Community: Jacksonville, Illinois* (Urbana: University of Illinois Press, 1978), 5; Faragher, *Sugar Creek,* 237; Hicks, "Development of Civilization in the Middle West," 79; Steiner, "From Frontier to Region," 489, citing Wallace Stegner, *Where the Bluebird Sings to the Lemonade Springs: Living and Writing in the West* (New York: Modern Library, 1992), 116, 199–206; Billington, *America's Frontier Heritage,* 144; Barron, *Mixed Harvest,* 12–13; Wright, *Culture on the Moving Frontier,* 12. Leo Ribuffo has chided contemporary historians of American conservatism for not recognizing "how deeply this persuasion is rooted in American life." Leo P. Ribuffo, "Rediscovering American Conservatism Again," *History News Network,* May 21, 2007, http://hnn.us/articles/38415.html.

18. Ronald G. Walters, "Signs of the Times: Clifford Geertz and Historians," *Social Research,* vol. 47, no. 3 (Autumn 1980), 551.

19. William Deverell, "Fighting Words: The Significance of the American West in the History of the United States," *Western Historical Quarterly,* vol. 25, no. 2 (Summer 1994), 189, 192.

EPILOGUE

1. Dewey quoted in Robert Westbrook, *John Dewey and American Democracy* (Ithaca, N.Y.: Cornell University Press, 1991), 314.

2. Robert D. Putnam, *Bowling Alone: The Collapse and Revival of American Community* (New York: Touchstone, 2000), 345.

3. See Rodgers, "Republicanism."

4. Wood, *Creation of the American Republic,* 53.

5. Ibid., 51, 53.

6. Frederic C. Lane, "At the Roots of Republicanism," *American Historical Review,* vol. 71, no. 2 (January 1966), 419.

7. Sean Wilentz, *Chants Democratic: New York City and the Rise of American Working Class,1788–1850* (New York: Oxford University Press, 1984), 61, 95.

8. Oscar S. Person, *In the Green Valley Township, Miner County, South Dakota: Sixty Years of History and Other Historical Writings* (n.p.: privately printed, 1944), 38.

9. Wood, *Creation of the American Republic,* 52.

10. Leif I. Fjellestad, *Early History of Miner County* (Sioux Falls, S.Dak.: CWS, 1981), 16, 18, 29–30, 31–32.

11. Ibid., 31–32; Stuart McConnell, *Glorious Contentment: The Grand Army of the Republic: 1865–1900* (Chapel Hill: University of North Carolina Press, 1992), 86.

12. Garry Wills, *Lincoln at Gettysburg: The Words That Remade America* (New York: Simon & Schuster, 1992), 42; Fjellestad, *Early History of Miner County,* 33.

13. Fjellestad, *Early History of Miner County,* 33.

14. Lauck, Miller, and Hogan, "Contours of South Dakota Political Culture," 158.

15. McConnell, *Glorious Contentment,* xiii–xiv.

16. Eric Foner, *Free Soil, Free Labor, Free Men: The Ideology of the Republican Party before the Civil War* (New York: Oxford University Press, 1995).

17. Fjellestad, *Early History of Miner County,* 2.

18. Ibid., 47.

19. Berthoff, "Peasants and Artisans, Puritans and Republicans," 591, 594.

20. Merle Curti and Kendall Birr, "The Immigrant and the American Image of Europe, 1860–1914," *Mississippi Valley Historical Review,* vol. 37, no. 2 (September 1950), 220.

21. Ibid., 27–28. On churches in rural Miner County, see Leroy Iseminger, "Rising to the Challenge: Thriving Rural South Dakota Congregations Ministering to Cultures at Risk," (Ph.D. dissertation, Luther Seminary, St. Paul, Minn., 2007), 45–51.

22. Ibid., 32–33.

23. Person, *In the Green Valley Township,* 38–39.

24. *South Dakota: A State to Behold* (n.p.: SD Extension Homemakers, 1975), 102.

25. Fjellestad, *Early History of Miner County,* 7.

26. Untitled, undated manuscript, FF Miner, Nelson, DB 1, Beede Family Papers, Richardson Library Archives, University of South Dakota.

27. McConnell, *Glorious Contentment,* 85.

28. Howard Community Club, *Howard, South Dakota: On the Move* (Howard: East River Electric Cooperative, 1965).

29. Wendy Rahn, "A Survey-Based Assessment of Community Life in Miner County: A Report to the Northwest Area Foundation" (October 1, 2001; unpublished ms. in author's possession), 7.

30. Ibid., 9, 16, 18–19.

31. Ibid., 30, 33, 34–35.

32. Christopher Lasch, *The Revolt of the Elites and the Betrayal of Democracy* (New York: W. W. Norton, 1995), 85–89, 97. See also R. R. Reno, "We Need Roots," *First Things: The Journal of Religion, Culture, and Public Life,* November 24, 2008, http://www.firstthings.com/onthesquare/2008/11/we-need-roots.

33. On efforts to promote economic development in Miner County, see Jonathan Eig, "In Bid to Hang On, Miner County, SD Downsizes Dreams," *Wall Street Journal,* March 25, 2005; and Peter Harriman, "Rural Revival Gets $8M Home," *Sioux Falls Argus Leader,* September 3, 2009.

NOTE ON SOURCES AND FUTURE RESEARCH

When Howard Lamar traveled to Pierre in 1948 to gather materials for his book *Dakota Territory*, he conducted his research at the Soldiers' and Sailors' Memorial Building. Will Robinson, director of the State Historical Society, gave Lamar the keys to the building so he could work through the night and during weekends. (For more on Lamar's research trip, see Jon Lauck, "The Making of *Dakota Territory*: How Serendipity Yielded a Famous Book about South Dakota," *South Dakota Magazine* [September–October 2006], 22–28.) Since those pioneering days for researchers, historical spadework on South Dakota has become much more formal and the materials better organized. In 1989, in honor of the state's centennial, the Cultural Heritage Center in Pierre was opened, and now it houses the state's historical research materials. The center is a natural place to begin research on Dakota history. Territorial records located in Bismarck were microfilmed in the 1960s, and a guide to these materials was produced by Dan Rylance entitled *Guide to the Microfilm Edition of the Dakota Territorial Records* (Grand Forks: University of North Dakota, 1969). In 1963 the National Archives microfilmed many of the papers in its possession related to Dakota Territory, but not the appointment papers. The National Archives has also recently produced a new and helpful guide to the territorial records in its possession, edited by Robert M. Kvasnicka and titled *The Trans-Mississippi West, 1804–1912: A Guide to Federal Records of the Department of the Interior for the Territorial Period* (2008).

While I am a strong proponent of more historical research on the Dakotas and wish more had been written about their history during the western history boom of the past several decades, a number of important contributions have been made to the field. The journal *South Dakota History* remains a strong source of new scholarship and is known for its exacting reviews of manuscripts, although many of its recent articles focus on Western South Dakota, which is not analyzed in this study. Older printed volumes produced by the State Historical Society entitled *South Dakota Historical Collections* are also a valuable complement to the more recent issues of *South Dakota History*. The South Dakota State Historical Society has also launched a new book publishing program in recent years that has and will result in important contributions to state history.

The Center for Western Studies at Augustana College in Sioux Falls, which holds a number of valuable manuscript collections, released a volume of useful essays in 2005, *A New South Dakota History*. The center hosts the annual Dakota History Conference, which brings together many people of varied backgrounds who are dedicated to Dakota history. Other valuable repositories for those interested in researching early Dakota history include the Siouxland Heritage Museums in Sioux Falls and the South Dakota Agricultural Heritage Museum in Brookings.

Since one of the purposes of this book is to generate interest in future historical research on Dakota Territory, a few lines of future inquiry are worth noting.

A more precise and exhaustive examination of the role of social status and the "whiteness" hierarchy that has interested historians in recent years would be useful. Life in Dakota was undoubtedly simpler for a white, Yankee farmer from Wisconsin than for a Norwegian immigrant fresh from the fjord who could speak no English. While immigrant Norwegians and Germans to Dakota Territory seem generally to have fared well, much more remains to be said about the integration process. Examining the less numerous populations of Irish and Czech Catholics, especially given the existence of Protestant-Catholic frictions, would also be a worthy pursuit.[2] (Existing, preliminary works include Bill McDonald, *The Nunda Irish* [Stillwater, Minn.: Farmstead, 1990]; David Kemp, *The Irish in Dakota* [Sioux Falls, S.Dak.: Rushmore House, 1992]; Michael F. Funchion, "South Dakota," in Michael Glazier, *The Encyclopedia of the Irish in America* [Notre Dame, Ind.: University of Notre Dame Press, 1999]; Joseph A. Dvorak, *History of the Czechs in the State of South Dakota* [1920; repr., Tabor, S.Dak.: Czech Heritage Preservation Society, 1980]). These studies could be fashioned in a manner comparable to works by Frederick Luebke on Nebraska or Jon Gjerde on the upper Midwest and build on the work of Kathleen Neils Conzen, John Hudson, and Robert Ostergren. Immigration history has long been an interest of historians, but Dakota Territory has still yet to find its definitive historian in this area.

The people in Dakota Territory who were not farmers or merchants could also be studied, along with those who were outside the general republican and Republican mainstream. This group might include southerners, Democrats, Catholics, the saloon element, wage workers, seasonal farmworkers (sometimes called "tramps" and "hoboes"), and others. While this book focuses on the main currents of political and social life in Dakota, certainly other smaller and less visible groups and their characteristics deserve study.

Although their numbers pale in comparison to other regions, instances of lynching in Dakota would make an interesting study. The growing number of historians of lynching could turn next to Dakota Territory and analyze how differing social and ethnic conditions resulted in differing conceptions of law and order. Michael Pfeifer's scholarship in this arena has paved the way for such a study.

The notion of social capital offers a useful organizing principle for future study, especially given the Dakotas' high ranking in measures of that asset. Dakota was replete with fraternal societies such as the Elks, Odd Fellows, Masons, Modern Woodmen, Knights of Pythias, and Knights Templar and a range of garden clubs, study groups, and other social organizations. A related aspect of this study might include the popularity of sports activities and hunting and shooting clubs.

The growing number of environmental historians should also be encouraged to examine Dakota Territory. Life on the edge of the prairie and Great Plains entailed many environmental challenges in the form of wind storms, dry spells, blizzards, and insect infestations. The intersection of settlement and nature in Dakota Territory provides an important angle of vision on the western past. The environmental histories of Walter Prescott Webb, William Cronon, Richard White, Donald Worster, Dan Flores, John Hudson, and Brian Donahue serve as useful models for such a study.

While Dakota settlers were generally market oriented, this aspect of life is open to a more detailed examination. The number of land offices, land sales, mortgages, and banks, and the land and grain markets in general, along with town-country relationships and the limits of the settlers' market orientation are deserving subjects. Past studies by Allan Bogue, Malcolm Rohrbaugh, Robert Swierenga, and Paul Wallace Gates would provide important background. A future historian could also focus on the Yankee merchants of Dakota's small towns—their relationship to their farmer customers, their civic participation—and could generally place them in the context of Deirdre McCloskey's studies of bourgeois culture, John Miller's analyses of midwestern small towns, or John Hudson's work on the development of towns on the northern plains.

All of these potential lines of inquiry could also be advanced through micro studies of South Dakota's forty-four East River counties, similar to the famous social-history works of Merle Curti and John Mack Faragher. County-based studies could provide a template for future examination of settlement patterns, ethnic combinations, the prevalence of institutions of social capital, topographic divisions, and political currents. A number of locally sponsored county histories, although dated, could provide a place to begin.

All of these potential areas of research are suggestive and future historians will surely develop and refine their own angles of vision. But the field is open, and I hope others will find research on the Dakotas as rewarding as I have.

INDEX

References to illustrations appear in italic type.

Abolitionists, 68, 259n4

Adams, Herbert Baxter, 16

African Americans, 18; in Dakota, 192–93n88; racist attacks against, 170

Agrarianism, 90, 155. *See also* Farmers; Farmers' Alliance; Granger laws

Ahlstrom, Sydney, 254n49

Alabama, 77

Albion's Seed (Fischer), 63

Alcohol and drunkenness, 53–54, 61, 213n225. *See also* Prohibition

Allen, William V., 198n38

American Flag Association, 45

American historiography, 15–22; Beard's influence on, 150, 250–51n21, 251n23, 254n58, 255nn71–72, 255–56n76; consensus school of history, 159, 160; debate in over primacy of ideology, 161, 217n28, 257n92; economic determinism in, 128–29, 250n18, 255n72; emphasis on economic interests and class conflict in, 17, 20–21, 133, 134–35, 150–51, 155, 156, 160, 162, 165, 166; frontier heritage debate in, 16–17, 27, 55, 149, 150, 153, 173, 250n18, 252n34, 253n43; ignores interdenominational frictions, 82; Lamar and, 19, 146, 147–48, 160, 163, 165, 248–49n1; limitations on scholarship in 1930s and '40s, 147, 161; marginalization of religion in, 21, 59, 194n101; and Marxism, 154–55, 250n18, 251n26; New Western historians, 5, 21, 160, 162–64, 165, 194nn101–102, 257n98; political nature of, 149, 250n19, 254n54; on Populism, 134, 152–53, 157, 161; post–New Deal, 160, 256nn85–86; post–New Western History, 163–64; progressive history school, 5, 20–21, 59, 153, 160, 163, 171; on republicanism, 17, 20, 21, 22, 89, 100–101, 175–76, 194n101; territorial system not studied by, 147, 249n5; Turner and, 17, 19, 147, 149, 150–51. *See also* Beard, Charles; Lamar, Howard; Turner, Frederick Jackson

American Lutheran Church, 220n75

American Nation, The (Hicks), 253n43

American Political Tradition, The (Hofstadter), 160

American Protective Association, 69, 222n101, 223–24n124

Anglo-Saxon traditions, 28, 30, 38, 46, 95; "Anglo-Saxon doctrine," 46, 207n170; meaning of citations to, 169, 259n3

Anti-Catholicism: and Bible reading in schools, 76–78; and Catholic-run schools for Indians, 79–82; during Civil War, 68; and Dakotans'